Oh My God! We're Parenting Our Parents

How To Transform This Remarkable Challenge Into A Journey Of Love

by

JANE WOLF WATERMAN, M.S.W., J.D.

- POP PUBLICATIONS/NYC, LA -

First softbound edition: March, 2013

ISBN: 1479104884

ISBN 13: 9781479104888

Library of Congress Control Number: 2012914827
CreateSpace Independent Publishing Platform
North Charleston, South Carolina

POPARENTING BEGAN WITH THE WOLF FAMILY (BELOW) AND THE GEIST FAMILY (NEXT PAGE):

(From top left) Al Wolf and wife Betty, George Wolf and wife Miriam, Lillian and Jack Wolf,
Frieda Wolf Jaffe and husband Sam, cousin Diane with Henry and little Louie.
(Bottom from left) Cousin Rick Moss, Molla Wolf Moss with Jane on her lap and cousin Dick Wolf.

(From top left) Abe and Charlotte Geist, Farberman, Lillian, Phil Geist and Jack.
(Bottom) Cousin Jacob, Jane and cousin Kalman Geist.

Oh My God!
We're Parenting Our Parents

How To Transform This Remarkable Challenge Into A Journey Of Love

by

JANE WOLF WATERMAN, M.S.W., J.D.

- POP PUBLICATIONS/NYC, LA -

TABLE OF CONTENTS

Prologue

That Christmas vacation when I first caught sight of my folks who'd aged unrecognizably since my recent visit and then saw the dirt and disorder that had taken over their immaculate home, I knew two things. The first was that my parents needed assistance. But almost as clearly, I saw that I too would need help and lots of it!

Although I had no idea then how much help I'd need nor where that help would come from, I did sense that something very different was happening and that major changes were ahead. As events unfolded, that prediction proved disarmingly accurate. It was a life changing moment and neither I nor my Mom and Dad would ever be quite the same again.

My parents, Lillian and Jack Wolf, were then 85 years old and living as they always had – in their home "independently." But I was no longer their teenage daughter doing my homework down the hall. I'd grown up and moved a continent away many years before. Recently in mid-life, I'd returned to graduate school in order to begin a second career. Earlier that winter I was very busy, building my new practice as a psychotherapist working with seniors and their families. I'd been excited to share all of that with my parents.

You might imagine that someone with my background would have been better at predicting that my parents and I would have "some accommodating" to do as we all aged. Somehow, I'd managed to plan ahead for very little of that and instead lived with what, in hindsight, was a surprising level of denial. The bald truth was that I was an only child and my folks were octogenarians who lived thousands of miles away from me. What could possibly go wrong?!

Although it seems unimaginable that my parents would conceal their health, home and how they'd been living from me, it's not at all uncommon for older parents to do so. Like Jack and Lillian, many of your parents may have feared the unknown consequences of "inviting" their family in to help them and, instead, resorted to hiding things from you. Once I saw for myself what was really happening with my folks, I had to play "catch-up" for not having planned better as well as deal with my grave concerns for their ill health.

When I was able to deal with the shock, slow down, respond rather than react and look more deeply, I discovered that my parents' needs were vast and pressing. It became apparent I would not only need to make sense of what was happening medically but step in to repair a whole laundry list of non-medical items for them. Before long I was wishing I could have taken care of things earlier but recognized I was now trying to solve problems that, even a day before, I hadn't considered mine.

When I found a few moments to come up for air, I instinctively turned to books and the Internet, my usual sources for comprehensive information and perspective. I was searching for some author, some "expert" to tell me how to become a more caring and involved daughter at this stage of the Circle of Life.

As a specialist myself in the field of geriatric psychotherapy, I was familiar with the literature on aging, death and loss. I'd always regretted that there wasn't a really good book – not even a helpful magazine article on "raising" older parents, nothing useful on television or the web – to recommend to my middle-aged or older patients as they traversed the journey my parents and I now apparently had begun. In the past I'd wanted those resources to offer "biblio-therapy[1]" – intelligent, empathic wisdom – to help my clients steer their courses during this part of life. Now it was I who was feeling confused, lonely and bereft: I needed guidance of my own!

I was beginning to understand that I would need to take on a different role ahead with Jack and Lillian, one requiring skills and qualities I generally associated with good parenting. I was desperately seeking some smart professor's book or reputable organization's research study to help me make sense of what this new role and my new job would entail. But nothing was out there. I considered that perhaps this new relationship with my parents was in fact all about parenting. This was new parenting however, parenting which appeared in a radically different context. It was "parenting" by adult children who had turned around now to care for elderly parents who, so long ago, had cared for them.

I could even see ahead to the day when this role reversal would be fully realized: many of us would quite naturally be "Parenting Our Parents™"[2] (or doing POP™ for short). It was then that I first came to recognize the book I was so longing for: one to guide me and maybe mentor generations through the phase of a hitherto-unnamed 21st century developmental stage of life I called the POPcycle™[3].

---

[1] That is healing work done by reading books, articles, and magazines.

[2] See Glossary.

[3] See Glossary.

The term "POPcycle" describes with eerie precision what happened over time in my family and what occurs in most other families. The POPcycle starts when the older generation begins to cede some decision-making and control to those in the younger generation; the younger generation, "adult children," simultaneously find themselves taking on more and more responsibility for many aspects of their aging parents' (and other beloved relatives') lives.

Dr. Benjamin Spock's "Baby and Child Care"[4] was legendary because his book comforted generations of young parents starting with my own by educating them to the predictable stages of their children's developmental cycle. Similarly the authors of the popular series called "What to Expect When You're Expecting[5]" were heralded by decades of soon-to-be parents for guiding them through the developmental stages of the life cycle that comprises pregnancy.

What people Parenting Our Parents needed was such a book for our generation's new "assignment!" I saw that what I'd so pined to find was a handbook to show me how to successfully manage the hardest parenting challenge of all: "POParenting" or parenting those people who'd raised me.

I'd have been overjoyed to have found a single magazine about Parenting Our Parents like the dozens I'd seen for parenting kids, let alone to have located a whole book on it! I'd have been ecstatic to have discovered a way to "chat" online with others who, like me, who were wide awake at 3 AM as we tried to figure how to install grab bars before our parents returned from their post-surgical rehabilitation the next day.

I still vividly recall my aloneness and yearning for connection, community and for some words of wisdom from others who were doing for their parents what I'd begun doing for mine. And if I, with all my geriatric training and experience, were feeling so lonely and "clueless," how would someone without all my background and expertise be able to cope?

I'd watched POParents struggle with the same feelings and issues I'd had. Even when they'd been working with me, my clients often expressed a desire for something additional to read, a book to help them travel their POP journey with more competency and meaning, maybe even more fun and healing.

---

[4] The latest edition, entitled "Dr. Spock's Baby and Child Care, 8th Edition," as authored by Benjamin Spock, M. D. and updated by Robert Needlman, M. D., Pocket Books, New York, 2004.

[5] Heidi Murkoff and Sharon Mazel, published by Workman Publishing in 1984, currently in 4th edition and consistently on the bestseller list.

It was interesting that some of those most interested in reading a comprehensive book were the elder parents themselves. Appreciating that their bodies, minds and their relationships with their adult children were changing, savvy seniors wanted to educate themselves as well as their children on how to best navigate the POPcycle they were sharing. They've asked to pre-order four books, keeping one for themselves but wanting three more to send their grown offspring.

I'd longed for a book that included and then went beyond a simple "how to" book approach. My patients and I wanted and deserved something that helped us beyond the activities of caregiving, picking up prescriptions or creating viable health care proxies. We needed a book that would help us find the meaning, healing and joy of doing POP.

Originally I'd hoped to find a memoir that might illustrate a micro-view, something up close and personal I could learn from. I'd thought that maybe by reading another person's story, I could more easily create the vision of how to do POP in my own family? I'd wanted to locate a treatise on "How to Care for Your Mom and Dad While Still Having Your Own Life" to address my concerns about how to balance all my new POP responsibilities on top of everything else already "on my plate." How would this work for me, adding Jack and Lillian's concerns to my existing stress, to everyone else who was "competing" for my time and attention?

I'd also wanted to be shown a macro-view, as if I were standing up high on a movie director's crane or perched up on a tall tree branch. From there I could better "oversee" POP for the phenomenon it had become, something being replicated in millions of homes across this nation and beyond, but especially in the States with our seemingly shrinking "safety net" beneath America's aging families.

Eventually I knew that it was I who'd have to sit down and write the book I'd so desperately wanted but never found. My goal in doing so was to make the Parenting Our Parents (POP) experience for you and so many others easier, more comprehensible and, yes, more enjoyable than it had been for me.

Since that catastrophic Christmas in 1997 when my family's POPcycle began, of course an awful lot has occurred. You and I now have the Internet and the electronic world replacing books for many as their primary source of information. The web's capability to instantaneously and continuously connect us to each other and to vast quantities of information has created extraordinary opportunities, ones that exceed almost everyone's expectations. The web is especially impressive with regard to the its potential to bring together and invigorate communities online. Hmmm...

At the same time I was working on this book, my concern was growing for the fragmented and fragile social net under our nation's most susceptible demographic, our seniors. I began to see an expanded vision, one far bigger than any single family's journey. I came to realize that those of us doing POP needed more than even a good book.

What we also require is a POP community, a movement "behind" all of us, something that will provide us momentum and successfully equip us to fulfill the enormous responsibilities and accomplish the tasks in POParenting our own parents.

I began to imagine: what if those of us who choose to complete the Circle of Life this way, by Parenting Our Parents, create our own POP community? Everyone would benefit from having something in addition to a book to guide us. A POP community would help us "prop up" ourselves and our fellow POParents as well. It could offer us all information, advice, inspiration and online invitations to events, could show us how to "do POP" by giving us examples, provide us models of good (or not-so-good) POParenting to learn from. Maybe the government wouldn't need to set up new institutions or provide additional benefits if we created a POP community that worked well enough to yield our own safety net?

When you're next awake at 3 AM worrying about your parents and how you'll best cope, no one from the government will be by your side helping to solve your latest POP problem. Now however, you'll possess two other very useful things close by. You'll have your copy of this book, "OH MY GOD! WE'RE PARENTING OUR PARENTS: How to Transform this Remarkable Challenge into a Journey of Love" and you'll have your POP community at www.ParentingOurParents.org.

At the website, you'll have access to extraordinary POParents 24/7. POParents are people from families like yours. We are all alike in working to make this a time of safety, healing, order and joy for everyone involved. The POP community consists of geriatric "experts" and compassionate POParents, people like you and me who are interested in healing the wounds of our past and creating loving family experiences in our present. Www.ParentingOurParents.org is based on the premise that all of us doing POP have much to teach and much to learn from each other and we all do some of each – teaching and learning – in the POP community.

Writing this book presented "impediments" that were unknown to me when I began, much like parenting my parents had been. One of my biggest challenges was publicly sharing the intimacies of my family's POP journey. My Mom and Dad had always guarded their privacy zealously, like so many of their generation. Writing "My Story" almost felt like a betrayal, even though my parents had passed long before the book was published. Over time however, I came to realize that my folks would applaud my literary efforts, knowing that our family's experiences was being made available to help others.

Moreover, the customary practice of my psychotherapy profession involves the patient revealing his or her life story, not the therapist. Eventually I came to accept that I needed to step outside that comfortable "anonymous zone" and allow you to authentically know my family and me. Only then would my words gain real credibility.

So why did I write this book and start this POP community? I did so because I wanted to support you and others like you to manifest your vision of POP love and loyalty. By being part of this new POP community, you and I may be "taking baby steps" to positively alter the face and character of our nation. Should this book and the POP community help you transform your family relationships into ones you've always wanted, you will have made a significant contribution to there being more joy in your life, the lives of your loved ones and even throughout our planet.

Chapter 1

Finding Out Our Parents Need Someone To Help Them

My Story

During the previous few years, it hadn't simply been my desire to spend time with my parents that led me to make more trips cross-country. Instead, a protracted illness plaguing Mom for "just too long" or an unexpected angiogram that my Dad needed were the specific factors that motivated me to leave home in southern California for New York City, especially during the bracing winter months. Even then, my visits to see my Mom and Dad were neither as habitual nor as frequent as they'd soon become.

When I came to town that life-changing December, it had only been a matter of months since I'd seen them last. Since I'd left home for college, my parents had always been so excited to see their only child that they'd come and pick me up from whatever airport I flew into rather than wait for a taxi to deliver me to their apartment. But this visit, in the freezing night air, no one was at the airport for me.

Not only was there no warm welcome, but when I called them on the phone from the hotel where soon I would become a "regular," my Dad was curt, monosyllabic and distant. That was so unlike him. Also sounding extraordinarily exhausted, he tried putting off getting together for dinner until the last possible moment. It seemed as if Dad wished I would cancel the evening entirely.

When I finally met up with Lillian and Jack Wolf at a cozy neighborhood restaurant that unnerving evening, I didn't recognize the old, worn-down couple in front of me. Having always known her to be a perfectionist, my Mom's appearance was shocking. She looked like someone had pulled some old dress from the back of her closet and stuffed her into it. Mom's customary hairstyle – immaculately combed and carefully organized into a white-haired bun – appeared to have had a comb half-heartedly dragged through it. My hitherto elegant Mother would never have let herself out of the house looking like that.

In other ways too, she was a shadow of her former self. My Mom's breathing was clearly labored as she dragged herself to our table at a glacial pace. When I kissed her cheek, my Mom's skin was eerily cold to the touch. My sense was that she was icy from the inside all the way to the surface, not merely chilled by the cold temperatures outside.

Earlier in the week, when we'd spoken on the phone, I detected nothing unusual, but the woman in front of me could hardly formulate whole sentences. She had difficulty following our conversation and couldn't focus on the ordinary restaurant tasks of reading a menu and ordering. When she allowed Dad to order her meal and then speak for her, I knew something was seriously amiss. My "real" mother would never have heard of such a thing.

Dad was acting nothing like his normal self either. He radiated fatigue of such a deep nature that no amount of sleep looked like it would restore him. When I was still back in L. A. talking to him long distance, his voice had been able to deceive me. He had successfully concealed this complete exhaustion – physically, emotionally and mentally – but now in person, I could see the true nature of his condition. One of my Dad's signature characteristics was his fascination with life's details and his daughter; in my dating years I'd often had to pry my boyfriends away from talking to him. But that night Jack showed little interest in anything.

As I lay tossing and turning in bed later that night, I couldn't deny that there was something very troubling going on. I'd wanted to chalk up my parents' disturbing ways to "a bad evening." Certainly we all have them, I told myself. But I just kept thinking: Who stole my parents? Who were these doddering people?

I tried playing detective by thinking back to their histories. Generally, my Mom had been as healthy and energetic as women years younger. However a few years before she'd contracted a case of pneumonia serious enough to require hospitalization. During that stay, some attending doctor while conducting rounds informed me by long-distance telephone that my Mom had dementia of the Alzheimer's type. It was a diagnosis I'd questioned at the time due to the tests he'd used and other factors, like her being disoriented in an unfamiliar hospital setting. But lying in bed, I wondered if what I was seeing now could be Alzheimer's?

In 1974 I moved to California from the East Coast, where I'd been raised and schooled. By the time I made this holiday visit in 1997, I'd lived out west for nearly 25 years. I was approaching middle age and my parents were each 85. Although I'd seen aspects of my Mom's memory dimming during earlier visits, I was shocked when that doctor broke the "news" to me of his medical opinion. Watching her work her beloved crossword puzzles for many years following this "diagnosis" supported my suspicion that it had never been properly determined.

However this sleepless night in my search for a reasonable explanation of her bizarre behavior, I feared that my Mom was finally "showing her Alzheimer's." Understanding the slow and progressive course of the disease as I did from years of working as a geriatric therapist, I soon ruled out that dementia had suddenly "descended" on my poor Mother. It wasn't possible that she had declined so rapidly as to need institutionalization, between the time on Monday when she'd talked lucidly on the telephone and Friday when I saw her in the restaurant. There must be something else going on... As for my Dad, I thought that perhaps he too had gotten sick while caring for and worrying about Mom. I was troubled by his appearance and lack of spirit as well.

My most pressing problem was to discover what was causing them to seem so unlike themselves - so very old and needy. The next morning, bleary-eyed from lack of sleep, I called to arrange to have breakfast with them. Dad put me off, postponing our getting together that day completely. "Mom's still under the weather," he said casually. "Go enjoy your friends and the wonderful show at the Met." The following morning, I called again and got more excuses. In fact, Dad seemed more determined than ever that I stay away.

A part of me wanted to obey him and let them rest alone. But another part just couldn't do the "Good Daughter" thing and comply because something wasn't right.

Once I'd made up my mind I needed to see for myself what was going on, the taxi-ride across town seemed to take forever. The look on my Father's face when he opened the door to their apartment, and his cold stare were both foreign to me: "I told you not to come. What are you doing here?" Once inside, the sight left me in shock, stone cold. It wasn't long before sad and even mad joined the emotion of shock.

My Mom, always so attentive to the appearance of her home, herself and her things, had allowed their apartment to become caked with dust. I quickly calculated that much dust must have taken a while to accumulate. I learned as I walked in but couldn't believe it that my folks had gotten rid of their longtime housekeeper at a time when they particularly needed someone to clean and cook for them. Nostalgically, I remembered how Dad used to joke that my Mom was so neat "she'd make the bed in the middle of the night, even before I returned from the bathroom." That seemed like a lifetime ago.

Heading into their bedroom, I witnessed my venerable parents were sleeping in sheets that had turned a deep gray from their original white. Neither of them had taken a bath in several weeks, as it turned out. Mom had been too weak to navigate the tub and Dad was afraid to leave her alone long enough to bathe himself. Predictably, their moods were equally low. My Mom was confused, alternately passive and then aggressive, even lashing out violently if she felt she was being "challenged."

My Dad seemed deeply disturbed, not only by his own fatigue, but perhaps more pressingly by his inability to care for his sick wife and whatever meaning he was attaching to that. It all seemed to be dangerously depressing him. I finally understood why my Dad hadn't wanted me to come over. They both had been hiding from me the extent of their medical conditions, their home and their need for help! In that moment, I "feared" for all of us, for myself as well as for them. Things had gotten totally out of control and someone needed to straighten them out.

There was no one but me. I had no siblings nor even close friends who lived near enough to enlist for the type of help I was now envisioning my parents were going to need. I previously had no plans to stop working; quite the opposite as I had just started my "second" career thousands of miles away. Although surrounded by my clearly dependent parents, I suddenly felt alone. And in spite of my years of seemingly relevant education and experience, I was lost and panicky.

I saw that I'd been pretty much ignoring the fact that someday my parents would need help. I had been reluctant to ask them important questions until this crisis forced me to. Up until that visit, I had avoided looking ahead and had made no plans for my parents' future. Now I needed to do a lot of back pedaling, thinking fast and catching up. My New York "vacation" had been scheduled to end in three more days when I was slated to return to my life in California.

What life? My life - as I'd known it up until then -- seemed like it was about to be altered forever. Slowly I saw there were significant choices I would need to make. Would my attention, time and resources become increasingly trained on my parents? It seemed I might be choosing to honor and preserve the threesome my life had begun with or that "'til death do us part" might refer to my "new" relationship with my parents! I might even have to contemplate parenting my own parents as my commitment grew over time.

Was I ready and willing to parent my own parents? They seemed to need something different from me than I'd ever considered before. If I decided to care for Lillian and Jack, I might have to give up many of my previous pictures of how my life was supposed to be. I would need to make important decisions, maybe different ones than I'd previously expected.

I didn't yet know that I would find myself maneuvering through complicated role reversals, balancing my need for my parents' safety with their "independence" and discovering how to honor both their wishes as well as my own. I couldn't even imagine how long caring for my parents might last or what kinds of changes I would need to face. Nor did I realize at that moment that I'd remain "on call" and never leave a phone unanswered for the next ten years lest my parents or their doctors might need me.

But I'm getting ahead of myself. That freezing December morning at my folks' home that marked the birth of our family's POPcycle, there were no tree ornaments or other symbols to suggest any festivities at the Wolf home. Instead, that morning marked a time of intense nostalgia as the girl in me longed for the old days, when things were fine. It felt like I was going through the rigors of birthing a new phase of my life. Maybe more importantly in that moment, it felt like death - the end of another era.

If I were to take on this challenge of parenting my own parents, things would have to become different. Unlike when I was the child, I would be caring for them this time around. Over the course of the years ahead, Lillian, Jack and I would need to reverse our roles. That Christmas, we were beginning our last journey together, down a cycle that would be one-directional and irreversible. I could see ahead enough to imagine the way it would go: my parents would inevitably become increasingly unable to care for themselves and the details of their lives. They would become more and more dependent on me. Simultaneously, I would become more and more responsible for them, making more and more of their decisions and acting increasingly parental.

Their Story – Dad

Since Lillian had started coughing and wheezing, maybe two weeks earlier, she had become weaker and was acting more bizarrely each day. I too had come down with something physically unpleasant, a tickle in my throat and some sneezing, but I avoided taking my temperature. Instead, I just kept popping aspirin. I saw it as my responsibility to look after Lillian, after all I always had.

When we'd first met, taking care of Lillian had been all I'd wanted. Our "fit" seemed a natural. Not only was she a strikingly beautiful and smart woman, she was also the youngest in a family of six, vulnerable from having lost her Dad as a mere girl of five. I was the eldest son and I had always "protected" my younger brothers – organizing the boys, making sure everyone had enough food and pocket money and that their homework was done. My Dad didn't pay that much attention to us kids. That was the way at the time. My Mom was absent a lot, having been a political activist and a newspaper columnist. So I learned to do a lot of "family caregiving" from the time I was fairly young. Probably it was also in my nature.

I had thought that looking after Lillian now, with her coughing and weakness, would be fairly simple. I'd bring her what she needed – some aspirin, something to help her breathe better, some chicken soup – but nothing I did was helping her much. My wife seemed to be getting worse rather than better. I didn't really know what to do.

As Lillian's physical condition worsened, her behavior also became increasingly irrational. She had been insistent that I not tell Jane how ill she had become. When I suggested we invite Jane over to help us since she was in town, Lillian's response had been immediate: "Absolutely not! She'll just want to come in here and tell me what to do," Lillian had cried. I didn't know what to do but decided to keep my wife calm by agreeing with her. Usually that worked.

The night we met Jane for dinner at the restaurant was our first venture out of our apartment in some weeks. It took a lot out of both of us. For days we hadn't really bathed or changed our clothes very often. I didn't have enough strength to lift Lillian high enough to get her into or out of our bathtub although we both did need to wash, after a while. When I reached the point I knew I needed to bathe, I was afraid to leave her alone long enough to run my own tub and soak there. So I just kept waiting, thinking eventually it would all pass and things would return to normal. I was so exhausted I often couldn't sleep. My body and mind were beyond any fatigue I'd ever known, or at least as I can recall at this point.

In order to go out to meet Jane for dinner, I'd been forced to get some clean clothes on Lillian and myself and to straighten her hair out as well. She would barely let me put a comb through her beautiful white hair, generally perfectly organized but that night it looked all ratted up and silly. I have hardly any hair of my own so tending hers was not something I did well.

Dressing her was another matter. I found a dress in her closet that she used to like wearing but she wasn't very cooperative. When I was done, she looked amazingly disheveled as if someone had poured her into someone else's dress. I thought to change her but didn't have the energy to start all over again.

I know Jane was taken aback that first night when she saw us both, especially Lillian." My approach was just to get us through the evening – order for Lillian, eat and make some conversation I can't even remember. I was so stressed, trying to keep everything seem "normal." I was still hoping that pacifying Lillian would get us beyond this particular crisis and then we'd be able to get back home without Jane's becoming too "suspicious.

Putting Jane off for a day or two after that dinner seemed to work. But then she showed up unexpectedly at our front door, after I'd told her specifically not to come. Finding Jane there was a shock. Her Mother and I had always encouraged her to have "a mind of her own" and I'd been proud to see her develop as a bright and independent thinker. But Jane was also an obedient girl, having given us no real trouble and doing what we'd asked of her most of the time, as far as I knew. That morning was the first time I remember her ever defying me directly. While we were on the phone I'd said clearly to my daughter: "Do not come here" but before it was even out of my mouth, she was at our door.

I wouldn't have tried to keep the state of Lillian's ill health or our home from Jane, if it were totally up to me. I thought Lillian's dissembling was ill conceived, especially since Jane was coming to town and, most certainly, would observe the condition of our apartment and our health. But Lillian had always been concerned to "be her own person" and had some fearfulness that Jane would take that away: she had also become increasingly paranoid as this illness wore on. I had been torn, wanting Jane to know but not wanting to upset Lillian.

And then all of a sudden, Jane was there at our door. I felt like we'd been caught red-handed!! After my shock and short-lived anger retreated, I recognized I was enormously relieved! I didn't have to hide anything anymore. The "truth" Jane saw was not pretty. Lillian had always been a perfectionist about her home and her appearance and a really clean person. But she had begun to let everything go. She didn't open the mail or clean a dish. Things were just used and then left everywhere. The dust was caked on our beautiful antiques she and I had so carefully chosen years before. I understood how badly my wife must have been feeling to let everything go like this. To Jane's eyes, the current scene was the exact opposite of her childhood home: it must have been frightening.

We hadn't changed the sheets or done a laundry in a while either, so Lillian and I were sleeping on pretty badly graying sheets. Everything was becoming harder and harder to take care of. Things were piling up around us. I had taken to calling in for our meals from our favorite delis and coffee shops in the neighborhood, so we did stay fed. As or me, I was desperate to see Lillian's special smile reappear and I would have done anything to bring it back.

Now that Jane had seen fit to defy me and show up, I knew that she would help me.

Your story

If you are fortunate enough to still have "older" living parents or other close loved ones who are seniors, you must have seen them change over time. Whether your attention was drawn to this slowly and imperceptibly through the years or dramatically one day, you must have seen that, after a while, even the most robust of our elders starts to "slow down."

Not everyone has as dramatic or traumatic a Christmas "revelation story" as I did, thankfully. Your discovery that your parents need help will come in its own way. Maybe you first "noticed" when your parents uncharacteristically began asking you for advice and then actually took it. Or maybe your folks simply started expecting you to help them with many more things, far more often than they used to.   Perhaps it was your Mother-in-law's continued refusal to accept your help when she clearly needed it that caught your eye.

Maybe your Mom took a fall a few months ago and even though she tries, she can't really get "back on her feet." Now maybe she's having trouble going back to work and even getting to the market. Cooking, which she'd always loved, is becoming a chore. She's feeling badly that she can't take care of your kids on Saturdays, as she used to.   According to recent report, eighty (80%) percent of patients in skilled nursing[6] homes took such a fall. Sixty-five (65%)[7] percent of those will never return to living in their own homes.

Or perhaps your "wake-up" call came in the form of your Dad's calling you, incensed about some man repeatedly phoning him about some unpaid hospital bill who is getting increasingly hostile. Although he doesn't remember being hospitalized, your Dad would like this bill paid just to stop the disturbing phone calls. Maybe he did pay the bill, he tells you. He's not really sure if he's been in a hospital recently or not, so he's asked you: "Honey, would you please speak to this man for me? It would really help me out."

Maybe your parents have recently stopped coming to Sunday night dinners at your house. At first they offered weak excuses, but one day your Mom finally revealed: "Your Dad doesn't like to drive at night any more." On a hunch, on your next visit to your parents' home, you take a look at his vintage car and notice the passenger door is dented and the car has a flat tire. You reason that it's more than "night driving" your Father is no longer doing.   You wonder if

---

[6] See Glossary.

[7] CBS-Radio News.

he's been afraid to drive or if he even should. Did your Dad have an accident? Was anyone hurt? Is there a lawsuit pending? Is he confused on the road? Is he afraid to tell you that he dented the car? Maybe he really wants you to know. You ask a few more questions and find out: "I had a small accident. I didn't think you needed to know."

These examples may provide you "telltale" signs that your parents are beginning to need some help. The people who raised you may now need you and/or your siblings or even an occasional caregiver[8] to do a few tasks so everything can "get back to normal." But your parents, like mine, will continue to slow down, progressively age and eventually, if they live long enough, your parents may resemble childlike, even infantile, versions of their earlier selves. You are witnessing the final chapter in the Circle of Life, the POPcycle.

As you look to pay further attention to these "initial" signs of aging and stop to evaluate your parents' level of frailty, fragility or even "senility," you may also be catching a glimpse of yourself. You may be choosing to enter a unique part of your own life cycle that begins with your noticing your parents need help. If you also choose to parent your own parents, you will be joining a special cadre consisting of tens of millions of loving people who are taking on more and more responsibility for our aging parents' wellbeing.

Soon you may be taking your parents to their doctor appointments where you often act as their historians, truth-tellers and translators. Then you're probably finding yourself interceding for your parents with Medicare[9] and Social Security[10]. Next, you're getting their "all too numerous" prescriptions filled and re-filled and picking up some adult diapers –- since you're already at the pharmacist. And before long, you're paying their delinquent, "misplaced" bills, shopping for healthier food for your Mom and Dad. And one bizarre day soon, you may be telling the very people from whom you used to borrow the family car that they need to stop driving.

Many of you have begun attending to your aging parents, some full-time and some part-time. Your involvement is likely to soon become critical to your parents' everyday living. The truth is that you and I are developing new relationships with our senior parents, ones we probably never expected we would have. Over the course of time, you are likely to become substantially involved in your parents' lives emotionally, financially and even spiritually. Some of you may leave your jobs, give up your homes and move across states to POParent your folks. Given the longevity of today's seniors and the current offering of new medical treatments and pharmaceuticals, no matter how many years you "raised" your children, you may end up parenting your parents for even longer.

---

[8] See Glossary.

[9] See Glossary.

[10] See Glossary.

If you choose to parent your parents, you will be joining me and countless others who've made the similar choice – to Parent Our Parents, to do POP. You will be part of the millions of loving adult children who are deciding we wish to devote ourselves to caring for our aging relatives and making this POP time a special one for all concerned. Your realization of your parents' aging and neediness and the requirement that you face this decision may be as shocking as mine was. Ultimately, you may join us in saying: OH MY GOD! WE'RE PARENTING OUR PARENTS! We're doing POP!! And "doing Mom" too, as it usually turns out.

Choosing to do POP at this important juncture can provide unexpected opportunities for completion and closure for you, your family and certainly for your parents. How you choose to use this special time is limited only by your imagination. Some of you will make up for "missed time" from the past. Others of you will establish more intimate connections with your parents than you've ever had before. Still others of you will undo decades-long estrangements with your parents and siblings.

How will you know if your time for doing POP may have begun? How might your parents display their "changes" to you? How can you learn to read the signs soon enough so that, hopefully, you will have figured this out before you face the kind of crisis I encountered. Will you be able to demonstrate the necessary confidence, "guts" and/or determination to discover whether, how much and when your parents need POParenting?

You will need a method to evaluate your parents' needs at this point and then again later. Likely you will have to do so repeatedly over your years of doing POP. To help you better conceptualize what is happening developmentally between you and your parents, their growing dependency and your increased responsibility and decision-making, I offer you "the POPcycle" (not necessarily pronounced "Popsicle").

You can "chart" the relevant factors in your senior parents' functional dependence/ independence to see when, where and how you will want or need to increase the support and protection for your aging loved ones. It is useful to have the POPcycle as a measurement of where your parents are since the chronological model that pediatricians use to assess your child's development is of little value to the geriatrician or the POP family seeking to evaluate your aging parents' development. The POPlan (POPlan) below will help you become better informed about many elements of your parents' needs.

Once you've done your initial assessment of your parents' current circumstances, you will need to discover many other important things. You will either choose to "jump in" or else discover if there is or can be someone else to take on the POP job. But for that, you will want to move on to chapter 2.

POPlan #1: Assessing Where Your Aging Parents Are On The POPcycle

This POPlan like the others in each subsequent chapter is aimed at concentrating your attention on what you'll need to do to successfully complete this stage in your family's POPcycle.

Your goal is to produce the most accurate evaluation possible of your aging loved ones, who are the first part of the POPcycle equation. Although there are two parts to the equation, first you must assess your parents to discover the extent of their needs, now and in the predictable future. Then, in the upcoming chapter you will look at the second part, you, the POP generation. What is it you're willing and able to give your aging parents? What resources, time, money, energy, skills and motivations do you have to POParent your loved ones?

Part of the task in understanding your parents' needs is trying to predict and plan for the unknown future. How do your parents' current needs, dependencies and disabilities inform you about their future ones? No one can see into the future but you can best plan ahead when you know what shape your parents are in physically, cognitively, financially, dentally, legally, emotionally and even spiritually today.

Begin your inquiry with these three organizing principals.

- *Who are the best people to help you* evaluate your parents' current and predictable POP needs?

- *What specific steps can you take* to evaluate your parents' existing conditions accurately so you know how to create a workable and well-thought-out POPlan?

- *When should you start* to evaluate your parents to make your first POPlan – how will you know it's time?

The first thing to do is to determine *who are the best people to help you* assess your aging parents? Obviously that will vary from family to family but it's likely you will want to create a "POP core group," consisting of those most active in making these POP decisions and then seeing them through. You may wish to include in your "POP core group" your siblings (hopefully, all of them), your life partner, children, grandchildren, perhaps your business partner and, if it seems appropriate, your parents themselves.

You may also wish to put together a larger and changing "TEAM POP" including any or all of the following: your parents' minister, accountant, physicians, psychotherapist and physical therapist. At this juncture, these professionals may offer much help in your initial assessment. You may also meet periodically to hear other information they will provide you to update your assessment. Others, such as your parents' caregivers, those providing them domestic help and even your parents' neighbors may all have relevant data and become part of your TEAM POP. During this assessment phase, you will find it helpful to have as much information from as many people as possible. You can learn a lot from a kindly neighbor who regularly sees your Mom taking a walk every morning or doesn't see her. People on TEAM POP can be added or removed at different stages of the POPcycle as they are needed.

I am a big fan of the team approach to support your aging parents and your family as you go through your POPcycle. Teams can offer POP families much support, emotional and practical, to undermine things that seem much more frightening if and when we're POParenting alone. Your being able to talk with others who are part of TEAM POP, committed like you are to your parents' wellbeing, will ease your individual burden and often improve how you're doing your POP task.

Although amassing the people on your team in one location at one time may be difficult, you can use technological advances to your family's advantage rather than delaying these meetings or missing the attendance of important members, Today's world provides you tools not available as recently as the late 1990's when I began POParenting my folks. To maximize the involvement of desired participants at meetings, I use videoconferencing/ Skype and teleconferencing for all kinds of multi-person conversations.

This technology is especially useful when I'm doing POP Family Coaching,[11] a program I designed to help families navigate through the POPcycle or I'm convening other TEAM POP meetings: everyone on the call can speak and be heard and, depending on your technology, sometimes you can even see each other on your computer screens.

If your family is one where communications have become loud or very upsetting when certain matters appear on the agenda, you might consider asking a professional – a family or spiritual counselor or someone trained specifically in POP Family Coaching – to "moderate" or translate during difficult family meetings. This counselor or POP Family

---

[11] POP Family Coaching™ is a customized program in which your family is coached to navigate the stages of your POPcycle on an as needed basis. For more information about finding or becoming a POP family coach, go to www.ParentingOurParents. org.

Coach can facilitate hearing each other's points of view and "good intentions" during group meetings, ultimately helping your family to craft workable solutions.

Should you include your aging parents in your initial assessment process and if so, at what point? Again, the answer will vary from family to family. Since you know your parents, ask yourself this: if they aren't a part of these initial meetings, how might that impact their participating later one? Are your parents willing and able to talk about their conditions, fears and their need for help? If they are capable of participating and offering valuable insights, will they comply with a POPlan if they aren't part of its creation? Or in your family, will there never be a POPlan if your Mom and Dad are "in" on the initial meetings since no one else will feel free to speak honestly?

We know that timing is frequently critical to the successful resolution of most interpersonal matters. Be aware that seniors are usually better able to focus earlier in the day, less so after the sun goes down.[12] Their moods may also vary with the time of day and, like most of us, your parents are more difficult to deal with when they are hungry, angry, lonely or tired.

Use your intuition and years of experience with your parents to gain the most desired POP results. For example, if your big brother Bobby still has "a way" with your Mama and makes her smile wider than anyone else, make sure he's present when you're having more "difficult" talks with your Mom. You may also find that your parents give different responses to the same question depending upon who's asking or who's present at the time.

Since you've ascertained the best people to help you in your POP evaluation, those you'll question to learn the answers and you've decided whether or not to include your parents in the early conversations, your next step is discovering *what specific steps should you take to accurately and fully evaluate your parents' current conditions?*

Prepare and then go down your list of POP-related questions and ask everyone involved to contribute anything relevant into a "pool" of information.

Learn everything you can about any of your parents' recent changes in their abilities/disabilities as this will ultimately help your assessment and planning.

When someone offers an opinion, inquire as to how the person reached that conclusion so your family can best understand the basis for everyone's point of view rather than just accepting their opinions or conclusions as fact.

If possible, always seek specifics and examples when someone "concludes" something about your aging loved ones.

---

[12] Hence the clinical term "sun-downing" to describe this diminished cognitive state.

Your assessment is not complete if you only find out about your parents' bodies. At the minimum, you'll also need to know a fair amount about their minds, their spirits and their money. Realistically, there may come a time when you need to know about every aspect of their lives – just as you did if you ever raised a child.

If your aging relatives are able to supply information, someone or several people in the family will need to ask them many questions and also to "evaluate" their answers. You'll recall that my parents weren't very straightforward with me in the beginning; you too may need to "read between the lines" on occasion.

This assessment may also require TEAM POP members to act as detectives, looking around your parents' bathrooms, checking into their refrigerators, eying unopened bills on your parents' desk. Remember that you're not there to judge your parents nor their choices, just to evaluate their abilities – to live alone, care for themselves, write their own checks. Does it seem to you that your parents can live safely where they're now living? Do they make good decisions on their own? How would they respond to an emergency without others around to help them?

Asking the right questions should reveal what solutions are appropriate. For example, if you receive these types of answers when you question yourself about your parents, consider it a red flag. There's POParenting ahead.

Q: How "reliable" are my parents to be their own medical or legal "historians" if they go alone to meet with such professionals? Do I believe I'm really hearing what happened there? A: NO.

Q: Have I been able to verify all the information given me by my parents? A: I SURE TRIED, BUT IT'S NOT EASY GETTING A STRAIGHT ANSWER FROM MY FOLKS AND THE DOCTORS DON'T WANT TO TALK BECAUSE OF THEIR CONCERNS ABOUT CONFIDENTIALITY AND HIPAA.

Q: Is my parents' version of what happened yesterday accurate? A: NOT REALLY AND RARELY IS IT COMPLETE.

You may need to designate a family member, one best suited, to become your parents' "POP doc accompanier" and advocate. Perhaps the designee, local to your parents and their physicians, could go to doctor visits with your parents and may be the best one to receive your parents' hitherto confidential information. Interestingly, my senior patients tell me that they get "better" medical attention, longer visits and more answers to their queries when their adult children accompany them to doctors. Does your family have someone who's well informed about Medicare or willing to learn, maybe not intimidated by doctors or insurance companies?

Finally, you will need to ask yourself this: *when should I start to evaluate my parents to make our first POPlan – how will I know it's time?* Frankly, there is little danger in erring on the side of evaluating your parents "too soon," aside from the possibility that you may annoy or anger them. If you see a "telltale" sign or someone who knows your parents sends you a message of their concerns, it would be okay to start your assessment then. If your parents have been hiding their limitations from you, you have a better chance of helping them if you uncover their disabilities sooner rather than later. On the other hand, if your evaluation turns out to reveal they are functioning well on their own and doing POP is "a bit premature," your parents will likely be grateful that you care enough and that they're "fine."

A word of caution: even if you've done a recent assessment, that doesn't preclude that things might have changed quickly. They often do with your senior parents. I would say that when anyone – your parents' caregiver, dentist or even a neighbor –tells you of any notable change in your parents, you will want to pay attention and perhaps contact TEAM POP for a quick conference call and a bit more investigation. It may be that getting answers to a few more questions may make a huge difference in your parents' wellbeing.

Your parents may well move down the POPcycle quickly or inexplicably. It may be just a cold or flu that "got them down" but now your aging folks might need a great deal more help. Or it may be a temporary setback that requires your immediate POParental attention.

ASK YOURSELF THESE QUESTIONS TO DEVELOP YOUR INITIAL POP EVALUATION OF YOUR AGING PARENTS:

When did your parents' doctors, dentists, lawyers, mental health professionals, etc. last "examine" each of your parents? What did those people observe, predict and recommend? How do you know that? How "reliable" are your parents to be their own medical or legal "historians" when they go alone to professional visits or tell you what happened there? Have your parents followed up on the recommendations made? Are matters improving, staying the same or worsening? Have you gotten the necessary consents to be allowed to communicate with your parents' doctors? Have you verified any information given you by your parents? Is it accurate?

Do you observe that your parents have a limited ability to learn new things? How does that impact their everyday lives? What is the state of your parents' short-term memories? Does that seem to pose a problem for their everyday living? How so? Could your parents be hiding the full extent of their limitations? How can you learn if that's so?

Are your parents set up with the wills or trusts or other documents they want or will need? Would your helping them do so put their minds at greater rest? How well prepared are your parents financially for living into their future years, especially considering the ever-escalating medical and care expenses? Do they still work or are they already retired? Do your folks feel the need to do something productive and can they volunteer, mentor or foster others?

Do your parents need help to manage their money, pay their bills on time, make budgets, discover how to save and when to spend? Do they own their own home? Have your parents recently obtained a reverse mortgage? Would you be informed if they forgot to make a payment? Do your parents already have estate documents such as wills and trusts signed, executed and safely stored? Do they have a Power of Attorney[13] and a Durable Health Proxy[14] that legally designate others to make their decisions? Would that be supportive? Are they capable of executing such paperwork now?

How do your parents feel about themselves emotionally or spiritually? How do you know that? Are they at peace with their life experiences emotionally? Are your beloved seniors anxious about the unknown? Can you comfort them? Do your folks have a religious or spiritual counselor who could help them with their concerns?

Whew!! Take another breath yourself. Now, please stop and congratulate yourself! By knowing good questions to ask, locating the right people to help you and having the courage to begin, you're on the road to getting what and whom you'll need to begin doing POP. Soon you will have designed your first POPlan, your family's initial plan. If it's anything like mine, it will change repeatedly.

But now take a couple of moments to acknowledge your efforts and yourself. Try every day to consider and hold on to this uplifting thought: *No matter the past, by POParenting today you're bringing an irreplaceable gift to your parents and to yourself.* By repeating that sentiment over *and* again, like a mantra of hope and peacefulness, you will be helping yourself become a more loving parent to your parents and supporting yourself to do a better POP job.

---

[13] See Glossary.

[14] See Glossary.

Now that you've assessed your parents' needs, that side of the POPcycle equation, you're going to have another candid assessment to conduct. This time it will be about you. We will talk more about this in chapter 2, but for now you may want to consider:

- *How willing and able are you to be there for your parents?*

- *Are you okay with performing some limited POP tasks but not necessarily willing to "be responsible" and really POParent them?*

- *Are you already feeling overburdened from previously existing commitments?*

- *Do you have siblings who are committed to your parents' wellbeing who live closer or may otherwise be better equipped to POParent them?*

- *What are your options if, and when, your parents' needs increase?   (And likely as not, they will.)*

Chapter 2

Choosing POP – Or Not

My Story

After accepting the irrefutable fact that my parents needed serious help and that it should have started yesterday, I attempted to process the additional information that they'd been actively concealing the state of their affairs from me. Me, of all people! I found myself flooded with all sorts of feelings, memories, thoughts and questions. I decided to allow my mental meanderings to emerge and see where they would lead me. But I knew enough not to necessarily use them as the basis for my decision of whether I'd choose to do POP.

When I was 17 years old I moved out of my parents' apartment in New York City and went off to dorm life at Wellesley College. It was located in the suburbs of Boston, about a four-hour drive from my parents' home. In high school they'd warned us that we would be "little fish in a big pond" at college. So when I got there, I studied long, hard and often. I became a history major because I was fascinated to understand how people managed their lives at other times and in other places. I also widened my window on the world, by living "on my own," away from my folks and their daily influence. At Wellesley, I was surrounded by the new friends I met there, women with whom I was beginning life-long relationships, people who would impact me more than the studies I'd come there for—people I still cherish and rely on for their advice and love, long after my parents have gone.

Following my undergraduate years, I spent three more years continuing my education at the Boston University School of Law. There I specialized in the emerging field of "poverty law" since I wished to be a part of making our world and our country a fairer place to live in. My becoming a lawyer and fighting for the rights of the poor, a disadvantaged group, gave me a bird's eye view on how tough life can be for "the underdog" in the United States. Later on in life, when I focused my concerns on the what was happening with the elderly, I came to see the parallel: our older parents, especially those with disabilities and chronic illness had, in many ways in our country, joined the ranks of the "underdogs."

During the 1960's and 70's, when many Baby Boomers were completing schooling and starting careers, California was regarded as a Mecca. It represented the cutting-edge of what was evolving in our country – politically, musically, culturally and socially. Some were lured out to California by the promise of a climactic paradise, others by the freethinking and free living, many went for careers or any number of reasons. I'd long dreamed of living in the sunny and inviting state, even of driving a convertible where I could "rock and bop" to the radio on the highways they called "freeways."

When the pull of work led me to California, I made those dreams into my reality. After three years of practicing law in Boston I joined those who placed even larger distances between ourselves and our parents, moving all the way to the West Coast. Beyond the attraction of the geography, many were also expressing an alienation that stemmed from disagreeing with our parents' generation over a variety of choices they'd made. My generation held on to both a sense of hope – that we could create a different world, a better world than those who'd tried before us – and a sense of despair, having seen our leaders assassinated and our peers killed in a war we watched on TV during dinner.

My parents' cultural values – love and marriage and being able to rely on a caring family – was something they held in common with each other and shared with me. I don't imagine any of us expected how those principles would play out or affect us in the way they did, so many years after I'd left their home.

It was largely because of those values, because of who my parents were and how they'd raised me that I was now choosing to parent them, the ones who'd parented me. It would not be a smooth road for any of us, as you will soon read, but the worth of our life experiences isn't necessarily a function of its ease.

My parents met back in 1940 when my Mother brought a dirty dress into my Dad's cleaning store. Although their siblings had known each other in their small town, my folks had been unaware of each other's existences until that day. Their families had come from the same place in Europe and then, oddly, settled in the same "New World" city of Paterson, New Jersey. It always struck me that there was a good fit with my Dad, Jack being the oldest boy, the protective one in his family and my Mom, Lillian the "baby" and the most vulnerable child in hers.

Despite some similarities, my parents' childhoods were very different from each other. Jack's family did well and quickly moved away to a nicer part of town. His memories of his youth were largely filled having fun with his brothers, playing tennis and laughing happily. Early on my Dad acquired an optimism that supported his belief in himself – he could accomplish almost anything if he set his mind to it. He spent the rest of his life pretty much proving himself right.

By contrast, my Mom's siblings weren't playmates, but older family who, from her perspective, soon abandoned young Lil to a busy, widowed mother and a sense of loneliness and envy. She would tell me that the kids in school laughed at her for smelling of garlic, called her "an orphan" after her Dad died and that she never fit in. Young Lillian experienced a lot of shame that seemed to play a devastating part in my Mom's lifelong view of herself. Unlike Jack, Lillian so often felt uncomfortable. Years later when my Mother "dragged" her young daughter to endless classes, she explained that she wanted me to be able to be comfortable in any setting.

Both my parents grew up watching their Moms work outside the home, which was very unusual for that day. My Dad's Mom was a passionate and engaged political activist with a newspaper column. The young Jack became a witness to having a woman's opinions be respected at home and out in the world; it's likely that seeded his notion of how critically important a good education would be for his daughter.

My Mom's middle-aged mother was forced to go out and work when her husband died and her youngest child, Lil, was barely five. In order to make a living for the family, she took over her husband's candy store. Never having been taught to read or write, my grandmother had to invent a language and number system of her own to keep track of inventory and make change. That helped to explain my Mother's oft-repeated advice that sounded "revolutionary" back in the 1950's: "Always have something to fall back on that you can do for yourself. Never rely totally on a man – not for your wellbeing or for your money."

The year was 1929, when Lillian and Jack were graduated from high school. The Great Depression was sweeping our nation and impacting the choices of that generation. My Dad bought a cleaning business from his brother-in-law despite having no prior background in the field. In part he did so to employ himself and his three younger brothers during troubling times and in part, to rescue his brother-in-law's family from economic exhaustion.

When World War II came, my Dad was excluded from the military because of a medical condition and he performed alternate service in a nearby airplane factory. Never one to "sit around," during the six-minute break he had before the next valve would come down the assembly line, Jack started putting words to the music that the factory piped in. After World War II, Jack became a professional songwriter. I always loved that my Dad wrote songs for a living. I loved that my father could be creative at work, since so many other parents seemed to have mundane jobs that they really didn't enjoy.

I was proud he'd chosen to do work he loved and that the product of that work, his songs, brought so much joy to himself, to others and to me, too. I also liked that, since he worked for himself and therefore had a great boss, he could design his own schedule. That afforded me lots of his attention and flexibility when it was needed. I was also thrilled that on occasion I could "help" Dad with his work. When I was in high school, endlessly practicing Beethoven's "Fur Elise," Jack used my piano playing to inspire him to compose words to the piece, creating a popular song. At other times Dad requested my "teenage ears" to evaluate the "currency" of his lyrics. Years later I was struggling to decide whether I could change careers to become a psychotherapist and do work I hoped to love with no promises of future income. I recalled my Dad's "fearlessness" in choosing to support his family with only royalties and no regular salary and used him as my inspiration.

My Dad was my mentor in creating the workable philosophy that people should figure out what they want in life and "go for it." I would watch him discover a direction he wanted to go towards and then see him hone in on making it happen. When the situation presented itself for my parents to have their version of the American Dream, a home of their own, Jack refused to let anything stand in the way. When the Board of Directors of the building turned down his application because Dad's livelihood writing songs would bring unwanted "entertainment business traffic," Jack brought in photos of my Mom and me, his quiet family and convinced the naysayers they'd never regret admitting our family.

My Mom's career path also began in 1929 but with some regret. She'd dreamed of becoming an English teacher but confessed she'd chosen to go to work over college as a reaction to her poor upbringing and the many financial challenges of the day. With a good job in New York as Lillian would soon get and make much of, my 17-year-old Mom had the funds to "do as she pleased" and to finally dress elegantly. As a result, she abandoned her dream and commuted daily to an office job in New York City.

Her persistence, another trait Mom shared with my Dad, paid off. Lillian worked her way up the corporate ladder into an executive position in a large insurance company, a place few women had ever gone before. Later on in our POPcycle, when I had to delve into my parents' storage boxes, I unearthed my Mom's high school yearbook where I saw her sweetly innocent face and her nickname: "Giggles!" And although I could hardly recall her ever laughing with complete abandon, I had one of those moments most of us have from time to time when we realize: how little I really know about my own folks!!

I missed not meeting Giggles and Mme. the Executive. The Lillian I knew worried a lot, was frequently temperamental and challenging with her perfectionism. Sadly my Mom often had difficulty feeling as much happiness as I'd have liked her to feel but, by the time we'd been doing POP for a while, she seemed to get that she'd never be abandoned and finally allowed herself to become more peaceful.

Who knows what attracts us to our mates? Jack had seen a sophisticated well-dressed beauty walk into one of his cleaning stores bearing a stained dress. "Who's the babe?" he'd asked his brothers. Lillian went home and told her nieces of the "perhaps too young man" who'd caught her notice, however briefly, with his attentiveness and caring ways.

Within several months, Jack had wooed her, monopolized her and happily married Lillian. Together they left Paterson, their ten siblings, their parents and "emigrated" to their chosen home in the Big Apple, New York City. There my folks rented an apartment on their own and started their life together, doing it "their way."

The years went by quickly as Jack wrote songs, Lillian attended to me, Dad and the house and I grew up. While I'd been on the move from New York to Boston to L. A., my parents had remained in the same location, the apartment that Jack had fought to buy. They gradually transitioned my former bedroom into the headquarters for my Dad's international background music library business. As tapes and later CD's piled up where I'd formerly slept, it became less and less hospitable to sleep over. So after I went off to college, I rarely went back to their home for very long.

My sights, like those of most young people, were pointed towards my future: the direction I was heading and not behind me, to the past or the places I'd come from. Perhaps like others I didn't look back to notice that to some in our parents' generation, our choices seemed to be an abandonment or even a rejection of them. My parents had never expressed that thought to me directly but until that Christmas visit, I'd never thought to ask. As I looked at them now with the new eyes that allowed me to see my parents' vulnerability differently, I wondered about Jack and Lillian's feelings when their only child had moved so far away from them.

Whatever the rationales for leaving our first families, the result was that emotional distances frequently accompanied the physical distances between generations as well. Many very "nice" people in my generation would go for months, sometimes years, without seeing our parents during our 20s, 30s, 40s and 50s. Sometimes people got married, bought homes, joined the Peace Corps and even had children that their parents had not yet met. Looking at Lillian and Jack in the apartment I'd grown up in, now so "upside down," disarranged and dusty, I considered that I had actually gone sometimes for years without seeing my folks after I'd moved across country. During that time, we had stayed in touch with regular phone calls and that had seemed to suffice.

All that had been so long ago, I thought as I willed myself back into the present moment. I knew that, given all I was faced with, I would need to focus my attention on how we were going to navigate our interconnected futures, not ruminate too long on the past. Nonetheless, focusing was a challenge. Images and memories of years gone by kept appearing: the great times Mom and I had, staying with her family "in the country" when I was recovering from pneumonia at seven; Dad happily playing his latest song for his eager fan club president, me; the birthday my beloved Aunt Miriam gave me my first pet, a wonderful kitten we'd named after a hit musical Dad's writing partner had on Broadway then.

I kept returning to the question: how would choosing to "be there" for Jack and Lillian in this new POP way change us and the relationships we'd had with each other up until now? I wondered how doing POP might alter the "balance" we'd been able to create in the dynamic of our family relationship but could find no template nor any model to supply the answer. I was particularly concerned because my parents' needing help was showing up at the same time I'd already committed to many other "priorities" as well. There were my patients, family, friends and all the other things at home I'd said: "yes!" to. How could I include Mom and Dad on top of an already over-filled plate? And then again, how could I not include them?

I saw little, if anything, I could cross off my existing list of obligations. Whatever care or help I would be able to offer my parents would have to be "added-on" to my current responsibilities. I didn't know yet where I would find the time or energy. I also had difficulty visualizing how caring for my Mom and Dad would work on a practical basis. One question led to the next and the next.

Would I move back to New York and live with them? No. I knew immediately that wasn't going to be feasible for me. Could they live in some senior home in New York? Could my parents come out to California to visit me as an interim solution? Would I find caregivers - one or more - for them in New York and then just "jet home" and leave them? How would I be able to "supervise" people working for my parents from such a long distance? Did they really need an official "caregiver" or would a domestic who could clean up the apartment and cook a meal now and then suffice? If my Mom and Dad really needed to be looked after by a professional caregiver, how long could we expect that to last? And what might be the cost?

My head began to swim but the questions kept coming at me. How many hours a day of care would they need? And how many days a week? Would I set up a plan to visit Mom and Dad in New York, say once a month? Every month? Would visiting once a month be sufficient to accomplish all I might need to do for them? Or would visiting my parents monthly be too frequent, even feel oppressive to them? Would I need to have my aging folks move closer to me - now or in the future? The questions my mind came up with were endless. The answers were far less available.

Even when I thought I'd finished "badgering myself" with the as-yet unknown, I found I had still more unanswered questions. But this time, my questions were pointing to something more uplifting and less confusing. I found that, after a while, my mind was leading me to figure out the benefits that might accrue from taking on these new responsibilities.

Maybe I was being offered an unexpected invitation to show my generous and caring parents how much I appreciated all their sacrifices for me. Couldn't this be a chance to repay them for parenting me? Perhaps having this unique parenting experience with Jack and Lillian would help me be a better parent to my adult step-kids or their kids, my grandchildren. Wouldn't they all benefit from seeing me model caring for my Mom and Dad? Wouldn't my doing POP improve my skills as a psychotherapist as I helped others deal with their aging parents? I even wondered if

24

caring for my parents would teach me how to be a more loving parent to the "inner child" in me?

As I started generating these answers, I felt more calmness come over me. I recognized that eventually I would get my inquiries asked and answered – or maybe I wouldn't. I had long counseled others that when the time comes to make important decisions, we always have to operate with "limited information" or somewhat less than we'd like to know. Since it's impossible to know everything we'd like to know before deciding, at some point we must simply jump into choosing.

Choosing to do POP for my own Mom and Dad became one of those "leaps of faith" for me. Put another way, the "invitation" to parent my parents evoked in me a humorous reference to The Godfather:[15] for me, parenting Jack and Lillian was "an offer I could not refuse."

As I let the truth of that thought sink in, I noticed feeling an internal sense of peacefulness. My breathing became deeper, longer and more energizing. I sensed a proper fit – there was "rightness" to my decision. I experienced a sense of wholeness in choosing to parent the people who'd parented me, even though I wasn't at all sure what that would look like. The Circle of Life was indeed completing itself.

I observed that I could choose to do POP in spite of having thoughts and feelings that were not always so loving or "nice." There were times I was angry, concerned and confused at my Mom and Dad for having hidden their problems from me. In a flash, I had a recollection of when I'd been young and my parents had dissembled about various medical conditions they'd been diagnosed with, for fear I'd become insecure knowing how old they were. As "late in life" parents, they had even lied to me about their ages until one night when they left me "alone" with my babysitter. I pulled down a book from their bookshelves that referenced Dad's musical compositions and age and learned the truth.

Accessing those memories of their concealing certain things allowed me to recall a long-forgotten family pattern that had persisted for years. However disturbing it was that they'd been hiding their conditions from me, remembering this behavior to be consistent with an old pattern actually comforted me. Back then, my parents had concealed things to protect me from what I didn't need to know or might have difficulty handling due to my childhood immaturity.

Although I didn't like what they were doing now, at least they were acting like the parents I'd known. As time evolved in our POPcycle, I often got sad, feeling that my

---

[15] Mario Puzo, The Godfather © 1969 G. B. Putnam & Sons, N. Y.

parents were "disappearing." I would look for things that reminded me of how they used to be. Gazing at the people sitting in wheelchairs or lying in bed most of the day, sometimes I would search for the parents I used to know. Especially as they became frailer and weaker, I wanted to retain my memories of Jack and Lillian as vibrant, the way they'd been when I was young and the way they'd looked in photos before there'd even been a "me."

I was fortunate that my Dad's personality stayed pretty much intact right through to the end of his life. He had a definite sweetness about him and an appreciative way that made it easy for anyone who attended to him. "Thank you, thank you, thank you," he'd say with a cute grin. Mom's progressive dementia made it harder to watch. I tried to make my way through the cloud that increasingly surrounded her. She would often be living in her past, hopelessly looking for her own Mom to come visit her. Nonetheless, there were moments when I could still find Lillian, even at 95, and I particularly cherished the times when I could find her "still in there."

As a youngster when I had discovered they were concealing information, not only had I had disagreed with their model, but I also had disliked the feelings it evoked in me. I felt excluded, condescended to and resentful that others held valuable information I'd like to know. I even determined that I would have been better served by seeing how my parents resolved the challenges. I could have learned from their problem-solving skills rather than being left blind-sided or falsely holding on to illusions, believing that the problems didn't exist. Now years later, although I could detect remnants of "protecting Jane" by having hidden their need for my help, I saw it more clearly as my parents "protecting themselves" mistakenly from all that would happen – and did happen – once their true situation was revealed to me.

As a POParent, I would eventually concede some wisdom to my parents' point of view. There are moments when it's appropriate POParenting to determine what is or isn't "useful" for an aging parent to know and, if they should be told, when. As Jack and Lillian got older, they became less coherent and more cognitively challenged. And as is often the case, my parents worried more as they aged than they had before, especially about little things. They also developed increased difficulty in processing information and especially my Mom had increased difficulty in hearing me altogether. This combination of factors led me to re-think some of my knee-jerk childhood conclusions that "complete truth-telling" is always helpful.

To make this point even clearer, there were times late on in our POPcycle when I would find myself not telling Mom or Dad certain things. If I suspected something would greatly upset them, ironically maybe now a medical condition of my own, I might not bring it up. At other times, if I could see that a topic was going be too complicated for them to comprehend, I might skip talking about it or censor something that previously I would have wanted to share with them.

In order to "protect" my aging parents, on rare occasions I would even lie to them. When they didn't wish me to supplement what their insurance company paid for their beloved caregiver, Florence, saying: " Don't pay any more for us," I failed to tell them that I did. Supplementing the caregiver was the best POParental choice. Occasionally I'd say their insurance was paying for a treatment I felt was necessary when it was I actually paying. I don't recommend dissembling as an everyday practice but as we continued along our POP journey together, I found myself gaining an unexpected appreciation for some of my parents' earlier-in-life parenting decisions. But, I'm getting ahead of myself again.

I discovered I could choose to do POP despite having reactions and thoughts I was ashamed of – like the denial I'd been living with. How could I have imagined my parents would remain strong and living home alone forever? I knew the statistical likelihood that one of two Americans over 85 would have some form of dementia and my parents were each 85. What had I been thinking or not thinking? Had I been my own patient, I would have counseled me, gently but definitely to wake up from my delusions, since they held danger for all concerned. My denial had been "effective" in only one way – it left us all unprepared and in the middle of a crisis that could have been predicted. Maybe even prevented, too.

Sitting with my thoughts that day, I also uncovered a new feeling, an odd sense of power and influence I was pretty sure I didn't like. Maybe my Mom and Dad were simply fearful of how much control I'd end up having over their lives and that was why they'd concealed recent events from me? That thought brought me no joy, I noticed. Having power over my parents' lives - or worse yet, responsibility for them - was still intimidating and overwhelming for me. I had difficulty owning it but knew that the truth was: increasingly over time, I would have to exercise my responsibilities – making decisions on their behalf and wielding my influence to get things accomplished for them, these new familial "charges" of mine.

It wasn't power that I wanted. Rather than being buoyed by my sway, I felt small and stressed by the pressures I was taking on – to organize a better or, at least healthier, life for two adult people. Planning a day for a 10-year old child home from school on vacation is one thing, but planning a new life for my 85-year old parents took on awesome dimensions in my mind. What I really longed for was a magic wand so that my Mom and Dad wouldn't be ill, in pain, disabled or die. But that was a momentary fantasy that came and went.

Knowing my parents, I knew they wouldn't be happy with the result or me, if I immediately started changing a lot in their lives or their home. I wasn't sure that my parents and I would agree on what a "better life" for them would look like. Nor was I certain what that was or how I could help create it for them. What I did know was that some things would need to change whether my parents liked it or not. My inner voice was already sounding more POParental.

Time pressures were compounding my stress. Lillian and Jack were ill. I would need to return to California soon and they'd barely been diagnosed – with what turned out to be pneumonias – let alone recovered from these diseases. Was it irresponsible for me to leave them and go home? Was it irresponsible for me to stay with my parents, leaving things undone at home? It seemed like the POP version of the working mother conundrum: do I leave stuff undone at home or at work?

I didn't know how much I could accomplish for Mom and Dad before getting back to "competing obligations" at my home base. I didn't know when I could next afford to return to New York or how long I'd need to stay the next time. By "affording" to return, I wasn't simply referring to money for plane tickets or a hotel in New York City. I knew that each trip I made to attend to my folks meant leaving my practice, my family and a host of responsibilities. How much time away could I afford and how would my extensive travel schedule affect me?

I also wondered how much help I could be to my parents from a distance? Once I left New York, back in the pre-Skype/ Face Time days, I couldn't electronically or personally interview any geriatric care managers[16], caregivers or domestic help. Once back in L. A., I couldn't go to my parents' doctors with them nor could I ensure they follow the recommended treatments. I wondered if my parents would revert to their pattern of hiding things from me after I returned home? How much could I rely on paid people to follow through and report to me about Lillian and Jack's progress or compliance with doctor's orders?

Earlier when I'd felt guilty that I didn't want to "give up my life" to do POP, I'd found myself focusing on all I might lose. My concentration had been on what sorts of "sacrifices" choosing POP might create for me. Fortunately my education proved helpful again, this time reminding me of something I knew but had forgotten. One definition of the word "sacrifice" is "something we make sacred," like an offering. Remembering this, I was able to re-visit the notion of loss by asking myself: was this

---

[16] See Glossary.

reversal of our customary roles something I could choose to make sacred rather than fill it with struggle and loss?

All of a sudden, I saw an opening in my thinking. I'd found a way to look at this choice that moved me from potential losses to possible gains. I saw myself surfacing some different thoughts. What sorts of joy might doing POP generate? How much healing might all three of us find together now? How could doing POP expand my life? I didn't yet have the vision to see that, as with parenting children, the "sacrifices" of doing POP would ultimately pale in contrast to how much I would grow. I anticipated that the losses would be inevitable but at this early point, I had no appreciation for how extensive my rewards would be.

In the quiet of where I decide important things and "take the leap," what it came down to was this: POParenting Jack and Lillian was the "right thing" for me to do. I have no distinct memory of making a one-time, life-altering choice to parent my parents. It felt more like a gradual acceptance, making one choice at a time. I had no idea of precisely how but I got that it would all work itself out somehow.

What I did choose that December day were our first POP steps in a journey of uncertain specificity or duration. However these unknowns turned out, parenting my parents was the right decision for me. It seemed that everything that had come before also now brought me to here.

I would face many more POP decisions in the days ahead, almost too many. I intuitively recognized that taking those first POP steps represented a larger commitment to never leaving them alone – the people who'd raised me. With the choices I started making that December day, I knew I would remain aboard the POP ship with my parents, captaining it, in spite of rough seas and unforeseen weather, until it safely reached its final destination. That destination would culminate in their final breaths when Jack and, in turn, Lillian would no longer need me.

Their Story – Mom

After all the hours I spent in psychotherapist offices and all the money Jack spent on the mission of my greater understanding and happiness, I should have noticed my denial more easily.

But who amongst us wants to admit that at a certain age neither you nor your spouse can really "make it" without additional help from someone? Certainly I, who always prided myself on my ability to take excellent care of my family, my surroundings and myself never expected to see such a day dawn. But it did more than dawn that Christmas Jane visited us from California – it kind of exploded.

She walked in on us unannounced after Jack had told her twice not to come. The place was pretty bad, so much dust and disorder. It had piled up and was just too much for me to handle on top of my exhaustion and coughing. I just couldn't function and that itself had completely thrown me for a loop.   Ordinarily I never get sick. And poor Jack could hardly keep up, trying to cook for us or order in and then clean up after. He just looked wiped out. I felt bad for him but I was also scared: if he fell apart, who would take care of me?

As I look at it now, I think there had been some mutual denial going on between both Jane and us. Jane's been gone a long time. She moved away at 17 to go to Wellesley and then stayed away, only returning home one summer to work in the City. We had to get used to her not being around and not coming back but I'd long ago made my peace with that – with a little help from my first psychiatrist.

Jack and I managed well over the years, in spite of missing our only daughter. We were lucky enough to afford domestic help but after a while, Jack gave up his office and we liked it nice and quiet at home. So after a while we let our cleaning lady Louise go and just took care of the marketing, laundry and dusting ourselves. It had worked fine until I got sick, I think. Maybe Jane would disagree with me about that.

She's a great arguer and an articulate advocate, Jane. A natural lawyer, my girl.   But sometimes she gets a bit scary when she makes her mind up to do something or challenge you. And I don't want her to think she can come in here and tell us what to do and, frankly, I see a bit of a slippery slope here.

When my Mom had her Parkinson's and couldn't care for herself at home, I remember how much my siblings and I fought over what to do with our Mom. We all argued.   There was no one in the family who could really nurse her at home and I had Jane who was just a baby. I felt terrible, never wanting her to go to a nursing home. My big brothers won out and she died there. I vowed that would never happen to me.

I do agree with this much: Jack and I need some help. But if we let her help with some things, how far will that go? I worry if Jane starts caring for us, where would that end? Not only that but she's very busy back home in L. A. and neither of us wants to interfere with that.

But I worry about how we'll manage everything if my sweet husband and I get sick again? Jane's getting people in to help right away but in the long run, what will happen to us? Will we have to move? Will I end up like my Mom?

Damn, this is overwhelming me. I wish I could keep this all a little better organized in my mind. I used to have such a remarkable memory.   I think I need to lie down for a while.

Your Story

Some of you feel you have no choice when it comes to parenting your parents. You are the only child or, simply, you love them. Others of you may feel you have few POP choices because of the mandates of the culture you grew up in. You may have heard since you were a child: "You must bring your aging parents into your home and care for them. This is what we do." Or you may have become the "designated" POParent by your sibling because you live close by and everyone else lives at a distance or, in some traditions, because you are the only daughter among sons.

I would like you to interrupt that type of reacting, believing that you have no choices, which could be called a form of "automatic" thinking. Anytime you feel you have only one choice in life you may be operating "on automatic" as contrasted with being and thinking "in the moment." One of the most important things you will need as someone beginning to POParent is the willingness to think for yourself, based upon what is happening "in the now."

Being your own thinker is often challenging, especially since so many "thoughts" are little more than automatic reactions to how you've been acculturated or trained to consider events. You have a wide range of choices in many circumstances and, in most instances, you have more options and solutions than you'd first considered.

Even if you can't imagine "thinking the thought" that you wouldn't invite your aging parents to live with you, you still have a host of choices to make about what and how you will help them. If you've already noticed your parents need some help, you will also need to consider: what kind of help do you think they will accept? What kind of help do you think they need? Knowing your parents, do you believe they will accept help from you? From whom else would your parents accept help? Who in your family is best suited to provide what your parents need – now and in the foreseeable future?

You have read how many different types of questions I asked myself during those initial days as I tried to surface answers about choosing POP and how I could reasonably "afford" to be there for them. When you need to make difficult or complicated decisions, ones that interlock with other decisions, asking yourself the right questions and then listening without censoring your answers is critical. Because of sharing the questions that came up for me to grapple with, you have the benefit of my questions as well as all those you'll surface for yourself.

Certainly one of the critical inquiries is this: should you be the one who gives your parents POP help? What I mean is: are your parents' requirements weightier than your ability to help or your actual willingness to do so? Simply because your parents are getting older and need some attention or care, doesn't automatically mean you must be the one to POParent them. If you have siblings who live closer to your parents, more energetic adult grandchildren, or if one of your parents is much younger or healthier than the other, you may not need to take on the "lead role" in their POP. Maybe your role in POParenting will be better played out as a supporting one?

Did I think POP was a choice worth making? Of course I did, but it was a wise one and the best one for the three of us, given our circumstances and choices. Should everyone parent his or her own parents? No! Not in all cases.

Before any of you begins a POP journey, one caveat: POP is not for everyone!! If your view of your family history is that your parent or parents abandoned you, abused you, neglected or betrayed you and you are still carrying emotional or physical scars to show it, perhaps you should stop right here. At the least, I recommend you seek further advice from a professional – a religious or mental health counselor or a certified POP Family Coach – before you undertake to do POP.

In certain circumstances, both you and your parents would be better off were the POP job turned over to others – siblings, professionals, neighbors, others. If your instinct tells you there are dangerous waters ahead in doing POP, get some sage advice and consider it carefully. You need to listen carefully to yourself as well as contemplate the advice you receive from those you've sought to counsel you. Parenting isn't for the "faint-hearted" and POParenting is hardly an exception to that rule. If you're feeling guilt or confusion associated with parenting your parents – or not doing POP – you and they are likely to benefit from your getting some professional counseling beforehand. If you reflect on how "casual" some of us were about choosing parenthood when we were young, you'll see some of the benefits of carefully considering the POParental choice before you commit to it.

Some of you already have decided you're going to choose POP. And although you think you "should" act in a loving and kind way, you may discover you are still filled with unspoken, even unconscious anger or unresolved bitterness towards your family. Doing this job and being around your parents more often may "kick up" long-forgotten memories and feelings, some of which may not be desirable. Again, this would be a good time to seek a little help from an expert, someone wise and equipped to help you heal unwanted feelings – before you get too deeply involved with POP. As you will soon discover, doing POP while you're still harboring those types of feelings is not optimal.

Why is POParenting out of obligation or with resentment a tough go? Caring for your elderly loved ones requires a lot of consistency and follow-through, just like parenting your children did. If you're "stewing" inside while you're "trying" to act caringly, that might emerge in ways that further damage your aging parents or the new relationship you're aiming to build with them.

Have you started down an irretrievable path to becoming your parent's parent just because you agreed to make a few phone calls for your Mom or volunteered to balance her bank statements? No. Can't you just do a few odd jobs for your aging folks when you're available without having to start a whole POP relationship? Yes, you can.

If you make those calls or do some odd jobs are you then obligated to go to all your parents' doctor appointments or move them into your home? No, you're not. You'll only be making one POP choice at a time. You should make only the commitments that you're willing to follow through to their completion. And your follow through involves checking in: how is your recent POP decision actually working out? Are the results as you'd intended? Is that commitment working well for your parents and for you?

Sometimes it's hard while doing POP to "keep good boundaries," a term therapists use to talk about healthy emotional distances we place between others and us. Often doing POP intrudes on your comfortable or traditional boundaries with your parents. These shifts in your long-held roles may end up challenging you in ways you can't expect. You have a new kind of "power" over your parents. They may be leaning on you, even literally, as you used to need to lean on them. You're making important choices for them, like they used to do for you when you were a child. You may now be deciding where they'll live, who'll care for them or when they'll go to senior day care.

How do you keep good boundaries when you're feeling so many emotions – literally looking down on your parents in their wheelchairs, shouting at them so they can hear you or helping them transfer into your car's backseat like you did with your infants? You will need to take good care of yourself through this process. Take some time to find out what's okay with you and what doesn't "feel right" and then learn to articulate these boundaries with kindness.

Fortunately, you don't do POP all at once and that makes having all these feelings far more manageable. You only can do one POP thing at a time. You take one POP step before you take another. One POP decision will lead you to the next step. Things may feel "out of our control" when you're doing POP. POPlan#2, later in this chapter, will provide you an example of how you can work with the spiraling sequences of POP.

You will want to ask yourself: will you be there, if your POP journey lasts for a decade or longer? The average number of years people parent parents is increasing as we are all living longer. Many gerontologists believe that people who are now 50 may spend at least eighteen years caring for their aging parents, given the increasing longevity of seniors and other factors. Your POP years may even exceed your child-rearing ones. Entering the POP journey with the notion that it will be "short and sweet" will leave you ill prepared for the realities of 21st century longevity, medicine and so much more.

You stand the best chance of having a satisfying and successful POP experience if you can be there for your parents because you want to and you're prepared to make the commitment to do POP from that perspective. Some of you may also have thoughts that since your parents parented you, you "should" do the same for them. Obligation is a motivator for many as is guilt, although neither is optimal here. It will be very helpful to you and developing your POP relationship if you can manage to shift your perspective from obligation/guilt to something more positive, like gratitude and compassion. See if you can focus on what you appreciate about your parents. Or if that doesn't work right now, try focusing your gratitude on your being healthy and strong enough to POParent them.

We do this POP job best if we're clear that we have chosen to go on this journey. Do I think POP is the "right choice?" For most people, my answer is a resounding "YES!" The sooner you discover the breadth of your parents' needs and who and what are available to meet those needs, the sooner you can take responsibility for making your POP choices based upon your own boundaries and your life situations.

It is likely to be getting clearer that your decision to do POP will have long-term effects, planned and unplanned, on your life and the lives of everyone around you. Although the decision to POParent is yours alone, I strongly recommend you also talk in detail with those your choice will impact the most – your spouse, business partner or children who still live with you. POParenting may offer most of you an inspiring life change but no choice is right for everyone. You must search your own heart and mind and then act in concert with them.

If you do choose to invest yourself in POP, be wary to not extend yourself beyond your own "doable" limits. Sometimes it gets hard for us caring POParents to know where those limits are or to ask for help when, or better yet before, we've reached them. You will wear yourself ragged and be of little good if you over-promise and then can't live up to what you've offered. It's critical that while you're POParenting you learn to know when enough is enough for you, too. Your parents may need to hear you say: "that's enough for me for today," when it truly is. You can't do POP well and for a long time unless you also pay attention to caring for yourself and becoming your own advocate. That theme will recur as we do this POParenting together.

Most of your aging parents truly appreciate what you're doing for them, even if it isn't perfect and even if they complain. Your parents really do feel safer once you've intervened and they are grateful. Your parents are also proud of you for choosing to parent them. As you begin to do POP, don't be surprised to notice: your parents are feeling good about how they raised you and how that contributed to your so thoughtfully giving back to them. Although POP can seem to be a gift from you to your aging parents, it may be you're receiving the bigger gift.

Are you ready?

POPlan #2: Helping You To Choose Or Not Choose To Do POP:

Imagine how you would feel if this happened to you:

You're at work and you get a call from your Dad's neighbor that he has taken a fall in the bathroom and has hurt his ankle. You arrange for emergency coverage of your work responsibilities and hop in your car, headed for your Dad's house. There you find him in pain on the floor but with the neighbor's help, you get him into your car and drive off to the ER. There you sit for three and a half hours noting the low priority they have placed on him despite his pain and, of course, in spite of your work interruption. Finally he is examined, x-rayed, treated and released with a prescription you plan to fill after settling him at home, since he is agitated and won't wait in the car while you stop at the pharmacy.

Once at his home, you think to check on his food, given your thought that he won't be able to get to the market for a while. Opening his refrigerator you find little to eat so you decide you'd better pick him up some fruits and vegetables and a few other items at the market on your way back from the pharmacy. While en route you get a call on your cell phone that he will need to start physical therapy tomorrow to prevent the fall from becoming disabling. The doctor told him he shouldn't drive until the ankle heals and your Dad has no transportation to get to a physical therapy regimen.

One simple bathroom fall could add up to all these consequences. For you doing POP, you're concerned about your father and maybe some future falls, it's nine hours later and you now have a missed day at work to make up and a whole bunch of POP things that weren't on your list when you awoke that morning. For your Dad who's being POParented: his ankle is inflamed and hurts; he can't really get around much for the next several weeks and doesn't know how he'll get to market; his new meds have caused him diarrhea and he's depressed just thinking about it. What if your Dad also becomes "too attached" to his pain medications and develops a new drug-related problem that needs to be diagnosed and treated? One thing often spirals into others.

What is your reaction to this "shifting sands" scenario, one not atypical for someone doing POP? Do you have the time, money, energy and stamina to do what it takes to be a good POParent? How does it feel when you listen to the types of expectations that may be placed on you? What if those include alternative roles in your Dad's life, less control over your time, developing more patience and flexibility to respond to him with kindness and appropriate concern? Are you okay with all the unknowns: your tasks and years of

POParenting? How may POP affect your marriage, your routines and your health? Are you committed for the whole journey until the boat takes your "Jack and Lillian" to their final harbor?

Can you also see how parenting your parents can be an amazing chance for you to transform your life?

POP Music

Music has always played a major part in so many aspects of my life and, of course, in how I related to my songwriting Dad. I'm not alone in using music to evoke joy or to "soothe the fevered brow." It's a custom that goes back to King David in Biblical times and probably earlier.

There are many songs – popular, classical and traditional, with words and without – that you can use to help evoke the feelings you desire to experience more of or to assist you while making your various POP choices. One tune I found so special at this time in my POPcycle is the beautiful "Circle of Life."[17] Listen to the words and the music, maybe for the first time and then notice what if anything comes up for you.

Choose as many songs as you'd like and play them often to set the right mood for you and your family to celebrate being together again!

POP music helps POParenting!

---

[17] From Disney's 1994 animated film The Lion King, composed by Sir Elton John with lyrics by Tim Rice.

Chapter 3

Entering POP In The Middle
Of A Crisis

My Story

    That morning showing up on their doorstep when told not to was the unofficial commencement of POP, Wolf Style. Viewed from the perspective of how our parent-child relationship had been up until that morning, going to my parents' apartment when I'd specifically been told to stay away was an act of defiance. But in our newly developing dynamic, arriving there unexpectedly and against my Dad's expressed wishes was an act of responsible POParenting. It felt like it was my first.

According to researchers, when we're trying out new behavior, repetition makes us more comfortable. POP was no exception in the sense that I did get more relaxed with certain "intrusive" POP activities as time wore on. But even then, I was never truly at ease when POParenting looked like it involved "defying" Mom or Dad's stated requests.

Worse yet were those exceptional times when I'd have to verbally "discipline" them for something or intercede to stop my Mom from hitting my Dad. At those times, they acted just like kids! POP would repeatedly make demands on me that were so unexpected that they felt almost "unnatural." My way of responding would be to reach into a place deep inside of me – a place of courage, internal knowing and extraordinary compassion – just to discover how to act as the good parent to my parents. Although the people in the restaurant had faintly resembled my Mom and Dad, that night for the first time they'd also reminded me of young children in their slow and deliberate way of walking and thinking. I considered that I might have to think about my parents differently and sometimes behave differently towards them.

When my Dad opened the door, there were two still "unfamiliar" people standing in front of me in their faded pajamas. "I told you not to come. What are you doing here? Why are you here?" he repeated, as if his questions made any sense.

"I'm here, Dad, because there's something very wrong with Mom and with you and, now that I'm beginning to see it, with the state of your apartment as well. I'm here out of love and because I want to help you. I get that you don't want me to know all that's happening but you need some assistance and I'm here now," I said. I was trying out my calmest, sweetest and best POParental tone. "Please let me help you!" I offered, even more softly. I watched as my Dad just kind of melted in front of me. In spite of his gruff tone and unwelcoming greeting, my Dad seemed – not far from the surface – to be glad I had come.

My Mom wasn't doing a lot of "melting" nor was she capable of lucid conversation or logical thinking. Her attitude was belligerent intermittently and she was disoriented. She seemed highly anxious and hyper-vigilant, as if something were about to be taken away from her but she also seemed too confused to recall what that was.

My first phone calls were to each of their physicians. My parents needed medical care today!! I wanted them to be seen by their own physicians, not by some Emergency Room person who knew nothing of their histories. They had two different internists and I was able to make appointments for each of them for a "quick visit" that day. My Dad's doctor diagnosed pneumonia, gave him some antibiotics, told me to make sure he got ample rest and fluids and suggested that recuperating at home would be healthier than in the hospital. I was also informed that, should he stay at home, my overworked Daddy would need an attendant to care for him 24 hours/day while he was recovering.

My Mom's doctor was concerned about the pneumonia she, too, had contracted. He felt Lillian needed immediate hospitalization but, by now, it was New Year's Eve and New York was being buried under a snowy blizzard. Her physician worried that the emergency rooms would soon be overrun. He reasoned Mom would gain admission faster into nearby Mt. Sinai Hospital if a specialist, a psychiatrist, referred her there rather than if he, a generalist did so or if we just "walked in." I didn't really understand why there would be a speedier entrance process but I took his recommendation: my first of many POP discoveries about how the experts could help "work the system" to my parents' benefit.

Leaving his office, the snowstorm made hailing down a cab a chore but it was getting them into and out of the cab that provided the main challenge. We must have made quite the picture on the streets of Manhattan's Upper East Side. Mom again was looking rag-tagged and was increasingly cold and disoriented. When I tried to extract her from the cab, it looked like I was dragging a dead body.

Then I try to maneuver my Dad out of the taxi and into the cold. He was so shaken up that he seemed off-balance before he stepped outside onto the slippery street. In that moment, I was oddly grateful for Dad's senile osteoporosis, a condition that reduces bone mass, since he now was closer to 5'8" than his original 6' frame. But even with his frailty and loss of height, I was still unable to hold him up. My Dad collapsed onto the street and momentarily appeared to be another pile in the snow. Getting him back up with his dignity in order and walking them both into the building and down the short corridor from the elevator took a good twenty minutes. It seemed more like a bad twenty hours to me.

While doing POP I had the pleasure of finding some truly extraordinary individuals who helped me parent my parents in so many different ways. There were caregivers, nurses, physical therapists and social workers, doctors, dentists, lawyers and neighbors, so many kind and truly caring people I came to treasure along the way. Unfortunately, the psychiatrist who saw my Mother that afternoon was not such a man. He literally screamed at me for bringing my Mom to him. "How could you even consider bringing such a sick woman to MY office?" he demanded to know. No help here, we'd be left with the last resort, going to the ER.

As I was helping my Mom and Dad into their mufflers, mittens and boots at the psychiatrist's office, my thoughts went back to my childhood and I recalled their having dressed me to protect me from other New York winters. Now I made sure they were warmly wrapped up and protected as we all headed back downstairs for our next transportation experience. By the time I'd finished POP ten years later, I couldn't recall a single holiday when I hadn't been in the ER with one or both of my parents. This New Year's Eve was simply the first.

That was also the night Lillian gave me the idea to name what I was beginning to do "Parenting Our Parents." After waiting the expected number of hours, Mom, Dad and I were finally sitting in a cubicle with the ER nurse. When we found out that my Mom was only getting 76% of her oxygen, her bizarre behavior made sense. The reason she'd been acting psychotic or like someone in the late stages of Alzheimer's was due to oxygen depletion from her pneumonia. Lillian couldn't think straight, quite literally, with that small amount of oxygen going to her brain.

But sitting there in front of the nurse, before anyone could give her any additional oxygen, Mom appeared to have "miraculously" transformed herself into a highly intelligent, cogent woman. Asked if she knew her name, Lillian carefully spelled out her full name including her maiden name. "Address?" Lillian was perfect, down to her apartment number and the zip code, thank you. What happened to the woman we'd been dealing with earlier? Previously she'd been biting and scratching, but now she was responding with crisp precision to the nurse's questions.

All of a sudden, I got it! When I was young, my Mom had often repeated one of her scariest fears to me: being "locked up" in a nursing home. Apparently back in the 1940's my grandmother had suffered from advanced Parkinson's disease and, over Lillian's objections, the older siblings had placed their mother in a nursing home. My Mom had always been afraid that she too, would be "locked up" some day by her family. I suspected that my Mother's "survival instincts" kicked in to her oxygen-deprived brain and provided her those precise answers in order to "guarantee her liberty." But I was totally unprepared for what followed next.

Seeking to discover whether the patient was oriented, the nurse asked: "Who brought you to the hospital tonight, Lillian?" With the defiant look of a 6 year old, my Mom wheeled around in the cubicle, screwed up her face and pointed directly at me: "MY MOTHER DID!!" I saw it in a flash: I was about to become my Mom's Mom. What I was facing ahead would be parenting my parents!!

I initially expected that her response was attributable to the oxygen depletion. However, upon further reflection, I realized that her "accusation" and attribution of mothering to me was oddly prescient. I was becoming her mother in the most protective of ways and acting exactly like someone's mother, hers. Perhaps I was even acting like the mother she wished she still had to take care of her.

No matter what Lillian was thinking, she'd given me another name for what I was beginning and she was uncannily on point. I was now the one being her parent, her new POParent. I was there in the ER that night as I would be there for her over the next ten years in the role of her POP Mom.

When they finally admitted Mom into the hospital for her pneumonia that evening, my Dad also was told for the first time that his beloved bride was suffering with dementia. He learned that her illness, which they called Alzheimer's, would become far more serious progressively and, ultimately, he wouldn't be able to handle it by himself. As a result, my Dad came to recognize that together we would have to get more help for Mom and for him, too. Knowing he wouldn't be alone on this sojourn, for the first time on this whole visit my Dad looked me directly in the eye and deeply exhaled.

Later, after the initial crisis and during much of the earlier stages of POP, I was able - and I wanted - to involve my parents in most of the POP decisions. But in those first days and nights, neither parent was physically or emotionally able to participate in those decisions, as is often the case when we show up in the middle of a POP crisis. When I brought my Dad back from the ER and left him with this news and at home without my Mom for the first time in decades, he was very quiet. I wondered how he truly felt but he wasn't one to talk a lot about such things.

Now that I had the time to survey their scene more carefully, I too felt overwhelmed. It was exhausting to look at the myriad of things ahead I would need to "fix." I also felt profoundly alone. This feeling was something different, deeper than I'd known before. I was in the most populated city in the world or one of them. I had a good support system but I didn't even know how to get support for the feelings I was having. My sense of isolation, the overwhelmingly heavy responsibility, a fear of "messing up" and doing POP wrong were some of the thoughts that drifted by. I didn't want any of those feelings but recognized them as authentic. As I look back on it now, I think I was "processing" getting ready to accept the responsibilities of doing POP.

Choosing to become a parent is an awesome choice. Choosing to parent the people who raised me and now were old and needing me seemed nothing less than mindblowing - a full-blown role reversal! I also triggered other feelings long forgotten - like the burden I'd felt as only child, wanting to be "good enough" to make up for the other children my parents hadn't had – or the lonely feelings that had led me to create the proverbial only child's "imaginary friend."

Early on in life, I'd learned how to "convert" the aloneness of an only child and my sense of responsibility into more useful qualities, seeding self-reliance, resourcefulness and an ability to get on easily with grown-ups. Now in order to do this new POP job well, I'd need to marshal all the skills I'd ever developed and apply all the education I'd ever had. But unfortunately, when I began parenting Lillian and Jack, there was nothing I could find to really guide me through this stage of life, this role reversal. Nothing at all!

There were no blogs, no POP magazines offering me any calming advice, no one around to POP Family Coach me. There was no guidance to show me how to work my way through the changes. Back then, there wasn't even anyone thinking in terms of POP nor developing the notion of a POPcycle, seeing it as a time for healing, expanding, even exchanging our roles with our parents. I felt like a geriatric pioneer, cutting brush and laying trails for those who would follow with their similar needs for POP help.

We were fortunate in my family that I had a legal background even more extensive than my geriatric experience. Knowing the law allowed me to be comfortable looking over Mom and Dad's legal and financial documents, talking to their doctors, lawyers and accountants. I used those analytic skills and found that I was empowered when I could put my attention on the things that were known instead of the many unknown, out of control things.

Of course, not everyone POParenting can offer their parents the particular advantages that my education and training afforded Lillian and Jack. Nonetheless everyone doing POP will bring his or her own unique "expertise," talents and background to the POP experience. And now you have the added advantages of my POP "trail" to follow from reading this book and the remarkable contributions other POParents are making on the POP website, www.ParentingOurParents.org.

But I couldn't figure out how much help or even what kind of help my folks would need until I had a complete picture of where Jack and Lillian were at physically, cognitively, financially, legally and spiritually. My parents would only be able to provide a relatively small amount of that data, if they were like most of my older patients. Their ability to recall recent events was less sharp than their long-term memories. I'd need other sources of information from both people and records to verify what they told me and to learn more.

No matter one's professional expertise and no matter whether one has siblings or is an only child, I knew that no one can adequately and satisfyingly care for aging parents as a one-person band. I would need to start forming a team of people, my TEAM POP, those I would rely on both to help me make POP decisions and then help me carry them out.

I'd need someone on my team who could act like my "eyes and ears" for the majority of the time when I was not there in New York, someone who possessed a good set of local contacts for the things my parents would need over the next few days, weeks and months ahead. What I wanted was a mature professional who could reliably check up on Mom and Dad on some kind of a regular basis, although I didn't yet know how often that might be. What I needed was a Geriatric Care Manager (GCM), a professional whose job description involves doing all of that for families like mine.

To find a GCM to help us, I started by contacting some of my lawyer friends who practiced geriatric law in New York. I also remembered that, during a recent reunion, some of my New York high school friends had talked of hiring caregiving help for their parents. I went through my memory bank and "Rolodex," resources that were around before Google was invented, to locate well-respected GCM's.

Wasting no time as I had none to waste, I set several appointments for the following day. Then I sat down to write out questions I thought I'd need to have answered to hire a good GCM. I asked myself: what would someone interested in working for my family in the GCM job want to know about my parents and, from the other side, what would I want to know about the GCM?

I tried to figure out how much information I should supply to the GCM applicants. Were I to prepare an outsider to be my "eyes and ears," how much of my family's usual "let's keep family matters private!" would I have to ignore? So many in my parents' generation shared similar beliefs that no one outside the family should know "private matters" but I recognized that might be highly misplaced here during POP. Should I tell a GCM during an interview that my Mother has a history of being difficult or not?

By doing research and initiating action, I avoided sitting around and "marinating." With little time for contemplation, I decided my best course was to use my energies to take action rather than engage in worrying or trying to figure it all out in advance. I discerned that I'd be forced to figure many things out as I went along and, somehow, that would have to be all right. Doing the research helped me make better decisions and taking action supported my feeling energized and gaining confidence, part of the recipe for POP relief.

Over the course of the next day, I interviewed all the GCMs on my list, checked their references and hired the one who seemed the best fit for Mom and Dad. I hoped my choice would be okay and once having made it, actually felt relieved. Taking these steps helped a lot. It felt good that I was beginning to create some order and I liked the reassurance the GCM gave me that, when I left town, some of the POP burdens would be shared with an experienced professional.

When the GCM arrived to start work the following day, I was almost elated. It was remarkably comforting to have her calmness and, since she did this every day, to feel we were "normal" and like other POP families. I'd been impressed with the GCM's list of possible workers and clearly we needed someone to clean the apartment from top to bottom. I followed all the ideas our GCM recommended that first day. She not only found us a cleaning woman but when we needed new equipment (since Mom's vacuum was literally scotch-taped together) the GCM knew where to go and how to get things delivered quickly.

Our Geriatric Care Manager also had a long list of possible caregiving candidates and I needed to hire several since my Father required round-the-clock nursing. His doctor had insisted on that as the trade-off for not hospitalizing him. The GCM asked me to fully "explain" each of my parents so she could best match her candidates with their personalities.

I then interviewed many women for the initial caregiver positions and even a few men. I understood that even after Mom returned from the hospital, she would need help too. I hoped the daytime caregiver I saw as best for my Dad could also help with Mom. I anticipated that any caregiver working with Lillian would need extra patience and a bit of a thick skin. As far as I could see ahead, which wasn't very far, both my parents would need someone with them for a good portion of their day, perhaps for a long time.

You can imagine that I had misgivings about hiring anyone to help with my parents. Would anyone be as careful or caring with them as I might be? Would my parents feel safe with "strangers" staying in their apartment when they were sleeping? Would these caregivers be reliable to get them healthy food, buy Dad the right socks and take them both to the doctors' appointments that I clearly couldn't attend?

Since I knew from the beginning I was unwilling to uproot my life, move back to New York City and give up my work, I had to find a team of people I could rely on.

I needed to find a balance where I wouldn't be micro-managing everyone but could still have the confidence that I was properly informed and attending to my parents' wellbeing.

I would have to learn to depend on people who were not family to act as families did for each other. I would need to set standards, whatever they might be and provide my aging parents adequate protection from any sort of abuse or neglect. Would receiving regular reports be sufficient? How often would I want to personally visit and see what was happening? With new people in their apartment, how would I safeguard their valuables? I could see that the GCM would be overseeing the caregivers, but I also understood that I would need to have responsibility for everyone, including the GCM.

Our family was blessed when we found Florence. She came to us as the GCM's brilliant recommendation to be Dad's daytime caregiver. Initially when he was recovering from the pneumonia and exhaustion, Dad needed 24/7 help and Florence was hired as the "day" person. For a time he needed three shifts of people doing eight-hour shifts for full-time caregiving but it was Florence who was there through the waking portions of Dad's day. I could see immediately that Florence would be a Godsend. Implausibly, she'd previously worked for another family in our building so she even knew the apartment staff, how to get around the building and our neighborhood, all on Day #1.

When Mom returned, Florence stayed on. She took care of both my parents through some grim days and nights, as you'll read more about soon. Intuitively she seemed to know how to treat both Jack and Lillian: how much kindness or strictness to show and how much warmth or distance. I particularly valued her consistency, grace and patience – qualities anyone should seek out in a prospective caregiver.

Any professional caregiver for aging parents "puts up" with all that goes on over the course of years in a family's life: parents living in pain; people getting grumpy "without reason;" childish behavior and demands. I also felt very fortunate to have someone begin at their POP beginning and work consistently with them until they left New York. That continuity helped me feel safer, especially when I was at such a distance from them.

I'll get to that down the POP journey a ways but what I learned those very first days was that my caring for Lillian and Jack would have to be a "hands-on" job. I could assign tasks to others but, in the end, it would be I who would need to be their parent. And since I was going to stay in California and they apparently would be staying in New York, I would need to discover how this could work.

Your Story

You too may need to get some help for your parents, both for your own wellbeing as well as theirs. You may see getting additional help as particularly valid if you've found yourself in the middle of some POParental crisis and have discovered there are things you need to "repair" that led to the crisis, as well as strategic, long-term POP planning for what lies ahead.

Although you might have preferred carefully planning for the arrival of each of your children, for most of us, neither the birth of your children nor the discovery that your aging parents need your help is ordinarily "planned" optimally. You undoubtedly would have preferred to have had some of THE Conversations and initiated some POP plans before any crisis occurred and maybe that is still an option for you. I certainly hope so.

But if you have an elderly loved one in your life, they will in all likelihood – at some point – do one of the following: have a stroke; take a fall and break a hip; need you to be on their Advance Health Directive form or get someone to install grab-bars in their bathroom yesterday! As you can see, you too will need a TEAM POP to help you and your parents do POP. You'll want to begin getting the members together BEFORE a crisis begins.

To be complete a good POPlan should include how you will take care of yourself as well as your parents, even what should happen in the event you predecease them. Taking care of yourself may offer unique challenges. POParenting may require you to give up doing some things you've cherished. Traveling, seeing friends often or even doing work you've loved may take a back seat for a while. You will need the discipline of prioritizing what's most important for all concerned. Taking care of your parents may cause your social life to dwindle and that may continue for quite some time.

The parents you're attending may well outlive you! The people doing POP and/or family caregiving frequently find they're cutting back on the things they used to do that provided them relaxation and social support. They attend church less often and see acquaintances less frequently. Even more significantly, if you're a family caregiver you may need to reduce your hours at work or cease your employment altogether. If you reduce your hours to less than 20 per week, you may no longer be eligible for certain benefits. You may not even be able to afford health insurance at the very time you're likely to need it the most.

Others of you will need to find paid help to supplement your family caregiving when you're not there. The family member most "qualified" to recruit, interview and hire professional help for your parents will hopefully be available to do so. Having someone who lives close to your parents will make your job of finding caregivers and other workers easier. But you may be equally able to locate a GCM, employment services or in-home caregiving teams online.

Today you can interview potential workers via Skype or Face Time and watch them interact with you and other family members, wherever you all are located. You can use these modern methods whether you're POParenting long-distance or locally and whether they've come recommended by your parents' doctors, the insurance company's Registry or other POParents you've met on www.ParentingOurParents.org.

Once you've hired some caregiving help, overseeing them may take a variety of forms and as usual in POP; one size does not fit all. Your family may want to regularly review written or verbal reports from anyone helping your parents like you did with those who taught or took care of your children. If you have siblings, you may assign reviewing those reports to the most qualified one to respond appropriately. Others may adopt a practice that has been simplified by the Internet: rather than sending reports to only one sibling who will be the "chief communicator," all of you can be placed on a distribution list – siblings, spouses or others intimates – and receive emails with those reports.

If you or a family friend can drop in on your aging parents to check on them and their caregiver "unexpectedly," you might find that very instructive. Some people even get the equivalent of "nanny cameras" secretly installed in their parents' homes to watch those caregiving their senior loved ones and they can receive such videos in real time anywhere in the world. Utilizing 21st century communication tools, you and your TEAM POP can determine the amount of safety you feel is necessary and the amount of watchfulness you can afford.

If you have paid help in your parents' home, you will want to be appropriate about securing and/or removing their valuables. Often family members will give caregivers keys and access to their parents' residence, banks and computers so they can be helpful. Nonetheless, your parents' jewelry, art, cash, identity items, checkbooks, negotiable instruments and even their stamp collections could be temptations. If these things have been left with your parents, it would be wise to store them somewhere safer if your parents have help at home and sleep a lot. You'll also want to avoid giving out unnecessary identifying information, computer passwords and anything that might allow access to your parents' financial accounts unless you consider it critical that your parents' aides know this information. In my experience, it rarely is necessary to share such confidential information.

Again, fellow POParents, remember to trust yourself! You will need to listen to yourself! If you don't have a good feeling about potential employees who will have your parents' minds, bodies and spirits under their care, do not hire them! Legally and emotionally speaking, it's always easier not to hire someone than it is to let him or her go after there's a problem.

POPlan #3: How To Undermine Your Fears That POP Will Require Something You Won't Be Able To Fulfill

Developing the confidence that you're going to be able to do POP and even do it well may be one your biggest challenges. Having that confidence also carries with it some of your most useful rewards. Over time, you *will* feel better doing POP and you'll function more effectively as a POParent. As you succeed in growing that confidence, both you and your parents will be the beneficiaries. You may notice your parents becoming calmer, relieved that you're there and helping make decisions. Especially as you feel more secure in your new role, it's likely your folks will become increasingly appreciative of your involvement rather than resentful of it.

In these beginning stages, you may feel overcome as I was, with how little you think you look like someone who should be parenting your parents. Your mind may bombard you with worry and fears. Some days it may even feel very odd to act POParentally – to set limits, to discipline, even to referee access to your parents' television. It's ironic how this may mirror images from your childhood.

To create a useful vision of how you can best show up in this new POP role, you may need to drop some of the old expectations, fears and beliefs you're still holding onto. For example, during your POP journey you may have to insist that your parents do some things they don't want to do. You may have to force your parents to move across country, leaving behind a now-unsafe environment that was your parents' home for decades, as I did. You may need to put your beloved seniors into institutional settings so they get the nursing care they really need, even when your culture says that's "wrong" and they should stay in your home.

If you focus on your fears, such as "how will my parents react to my being so assertive" or "what if I make a mistake," you're bound to be less effective as a POParent. Moreover, if you think about your insistence as "defiance" of your parents, you've abandoned your role as the caring adult and mistakenly seen yourself as the rebellious teenager.

It is not your goal to do POParenting fearlessly. But after you work on your POP confidence building, you will appropriately see your resolve as the bold act of a responsible and concerned POParent. You will find yourself becoming more respected in the eyes of all concerned, including your own eyes. As you practice expanding your confidence here, you will weaken your fear-filled thoughts and be better able to conform your actions to your desired positive POP role. This is how you build more confidence: undermine the unnecessary fears and act accordingly.

Although your concerns about POParenting one aging loved one, say your Dad, are likely to be different from those about POParenting another parent, say your Mom. But working with this POPlan will enable you to become better at meeting all their needs with consistency and calmness, when the next need arises.

During your family's POP journey a challenge requiring unknown courage may well present itself. Then more than ever you'll need to use the help provided here, on the POP website and from other sources to access this confidence you're developing. Perhaps it is a surprise but sometimes the best way to work with these concerns is to play them out in your mind in advance. Then you can "practice" your responses ahead of time, even modify them to come up with better or new solutions before you're emotionally involved in the real problem.

The Oxford English Online Dictionary describes "Parenting" rather vaguely as: "being or acting as a mother or father ... [demonstrating] ... warmth and attention." In addition to your original two parents, you may also have one or more stepparents, in-laws, aunts, uncles and grandparents or even surrogate parents you wish to – or feel called upon – to POParent. Each one is likely to present you some unique challenges.

Try this when you can set aside some quiet time and space.

Start out by surfacing all the POP "imponderable horribles"[18] that might occur "on your watch." I am certain all of you have already had such thoughts unconsciously or consciously. However, by "taking charge" of your fearful thoughts and bringing them into your focus in a thoughtful way, you can use your intelligence to demonstrate the silliness of some of those fears and possibly usefully "self-talk" yourself out of others.

Ask yourself: what *are* your worst fears about being a POParent? Make sure you list all of them. Get very specific with your answers: what could happen? Then also be willing to feel the feelings you've been associating with your anxieties, whether consciously or not. Try even exaggerating your worries, making them so large you can almost see them. Grow them larger than life. Spend some time doing this work, even though it may be very uncomfortable. It is extremely worthwhile.

If you can't come up with POP fears of your own, you should feel free to work with one or all of the following. Are you worried that: "I wouldn't be a good enough POParent?" Start imagining what would that look like to you? Or maybe you're fearful that: "I won't be able to say 'no' to my Dad for anything after I've said 'yes, I'll help you' the first time?" Are you afraid that: "I don't know how to ask my parents questions so they'll feel I'm on their side

---

[18] A favorite phrase I've "borrowed" here from Justice Oliver Wendell Holmes.

rather than "attacked" or belittled?" Your parents' memories may be getting so diminished they're "an accident waiting to happen" – like leaving on the gas stove or the running tub water and forgetting – but they refuse to leave their home or let help in. Perhaps you feel insecure that your parents will embarrass themselves in public if you take them to your favorite restaurant and "I won't know how to handle that." Or maybe you're disabled and upset that you may run out of energy and ability to POParent your parents before they "run out" of needing your care.

Next, take in a few deep breaths and then exhale longer and more fully than you inhaled. Now look deeply into your thoughts and feelings. Tease out the exaggerations you added in earlier. Dilute some of the drama you've been telling yourself with a good dose of "reality." As you consider your "catastrophes," one by one, focus both your attention and your intention on locating solutions. What it is you CAN do? As you start returning to more realistic conclusions you'll also start becoming more grounded.

Consider: where are there viable possibilities when none previously appeared? For each of your fears, find three ways to remind yourself not to get overwhelmed by your concerns; you *can* deal with them. Then find three possible resolutions for the things you've worried about. If you can't find three during this brainstorming process, make them up. Research reveals that even unlikely solutions will begin energizing your brain and will lead to more ideas appearing.

After you've worked with your anxious POP thoughts and viable responses, you may also find it very helpful to talk over your concerns with others you trust, especially intimates of yours who know your parents' circumstances and share a stake in finding workable solutions. The object of such conversations isn't to fan the flames of your fears nor to make others more fearful. Rather, your goal here it to realistically assess the content of your apprehensions and to promote two things: workable solutions and your sense of capably resolving situations, to the best of your ability. Even if you're unaware of it as you work through this POPlan's suggestions, your mind will continue not only to create solutions but also pictures of your having more confidence of doing POP well.

Chapter 4

Learning More About Our Parents Than We Thought We'd Want To Know: Their Finances, Health, Legal, Spiritual And Other Issues

My Story

I made a series of trips to New York that first year I was POParenting Lillian and Jack. Much of my agenda during those visits was to gather information I would need to help them feel and become safer, now that I was "on board." Like most things POP, it took longer than I'd anticipated to get the information from my folks and then to follow through with whatever else was needed.

When I arrived at their apartment on any day of such inquiry, I'd be immediately struck by the fact that my parents did everything substantially slower than I did. They thought slower, moved slower, decided things slower than most people my age or my friends did. Their experience of time and ability to focus were also different from mine. I saw that I'd need to take lots of deep breaths and literally slow down so that the sheer force of my energy and the speed with which I ordinarily operated didn't overwhelm my parents.

I would show up in the morning, ready to get down to it but my parents might or might not be ready for me or for the next task on my list. I was learning from my parents as we learn from our children how to most effectively parent them. I soon discovered I'd need to speak more slowly, perhaps with more volume, to repeat myself, to make sure they understood what I was asking and, most of all, I'd have to become more patient!

My ultimate goal in gathering all this information was to create additional security for my declining parents, whether that was physical, legal or financial security. Making them safe seemed relatively straightforward when I was having grab-bars installed in their bathrooms or, later, bars on the windows to prevent another parental suicide attempt from their fourteenth floor bedroom. It wasn't always so easy was to figure out other ways to keep them safe.

Since making my parents safe required me to review each document and decision, one at a time, it also involved my asking them endless questions, prying through years of well-worn papers and, generally speaking, intruding into their lives. I had not lived with my parents in over thirty years and, even with me, my parents were private people. When they neglected to ask for my legal advice over the years, I'd tried not to take it personally. I'd always wondered why they hadn't asked my help but now I was finding that keeping me uninformed hadn't been their best choice. Given what I unearthed in some of their documents, I regretted they hadn't sought my counsel earlier but instead had relied on strangers.

My asking them questions, opening up old memories and tens of boxes with papers, not to mention my reviewing their past decisions, was bound to be emotionally triggering for all of us. I saw how my Mom's cognitive limitations were adding to her emotional challenges. She'd try to maintain her focus and stretch to recall answers or compensate by supplying any answer, all the while revealing the very limitations she was trying to hide from herself and me.

Over time, the process got a little easier. But the first day of doing this inquiry was one of the hardest for me. I might have imagined that other days would have been more demanding – like their accidents leading to hospitalizations or the day I put Dad on hospice or couldn't find a mental facility that would accept my Mom. Those were hard days, too. But in the Wolf family saga, the toughest days seemed to be when one parent interpreted events as symbolizing their growing loss of control over life. Usually that resulted in a panicky parent and, almost always, that was my Mom.

Lillian turned out to be much tougher to POParent than Jack. During her twenties, she'd occupied important positions that demanded great organizational skill and she was naturally obsessive. As a result, she'd become their "designated domestic organizer." Mom's bedroom closet was the repository for their most important records. She came from the rubber-band school of organizing. That is, papers were bound together by rubber bands, some worn and stretched out, and others pristine. I'd ask: "how much do you and Dad receive from Social Security each month?" Mom would direct me first to the closet, then to the right box and in turn to the right packet. I'd have to bring it out of her closet and, in front of her, unwrap the rubber band, read the papers enclosed and take any notes I'd need, like the amount of their monthly payments. Then she needed me to re-wrap the rubber band around the packet of papers, return them to the box in the closet and then, return to her for my next inquiry. We would have to go through this process for each question I posed.

When it felt to Lillian like her whole life was swirling out of her control, she did what most people do when they feel helpless. She drew a line in the sand: NO ONE MESSES WITH MY RUBBER BAND SYSTEM!! It went this way for hours and hours. On the outside I was the most patient person I'd ever seen, but on the inside, I was a mess. I tried to be kind and understanding. I even introduced self-talk and thought about how challenging it must have been parenting me. As soon as I could "safely" leave that first day of questioning them, I ran the short block to a nearby cafe where I focused exclusively on a frosty margarita, actually several.

The problem really was with me, not my Mom, I soon saw. She'd been well organized her whole life and my being there now, intruding on her privacy and upsetting her system with my demands, must have deeply upset her and compromised her sense of order and control. As I considered that she wasn't just "trying to be difficult," I was able to evoke more understanding. And more patience.

During January and February of 1998, the bitterest of months in the Northeast, I made four short "hops" back and forth across our wide, three-time zoned continent to be there for my parents. My remembrance of those months consisted of feeling dislocated on both coasts. Even before leaving home for one of those body-bruising three or four day trips, I'd have spent hours re-scheduling my patient appointments and other events. I'd have to book travel and even lodging since it had become clear I couldn't stay in my parents' over-crowded and cluttered space.

On those occasions I'd leave home early in the Pacific morning when it was still dark, hoping the taxi horn didn't wake my neighbors. By the time I'd arrive in New York, I'd have "lost the day" and it would be dark in the City. I would be tired, ache-y from the plane ride and pretty "useless." Although the airlines call it a five and a half-hour flight, it never took me less than nine hours to go between my L. A. home and my hotel in the Big Apple. I also had decided to delay my own much-needed foot surgery while taking care of this phase of POParenting. As a result, the hikes down the long airport corridors, dragging my carry-on and occasionally limping, were painful and didn't make my voyages any easier. By the fourth trip, I began to be a bit concerned for my own safety. I wasn't getting any younger, either. I was also feeling "dislocated" mentally, pulled in the many different directions new parents sometimes describe.

I had liked "my life" before and, even though I'd made the choice to do POP, I was still reluctant to fully accept the bi-coastal life and other ways I now had to adapt. One of the most helpful insights I had about my own resistance during this part of our POPcycle was this: it wasn't nearly as useful to bemoan the loss of "my life" as it was to embrace expanding into a "bigger life," which included POP. Now "my life" and even my view of myself needed to be large enough to include Jack and Lillian as a priority. Sometimes they were the priority. In making these trips to POParent them, I was beginning to prioritize my parents' needs over my patients' needs.

I wondered about the long-term effects POP would have on my new practice, my income, my psyche and other parts of "my life." Only on occasion would I allow myself to muse upon the unknown unknowns. Most of the time, having made the "POP commitment," I turned to my next action step and kept on going. There was always so much to do.

Your Story

You too, will have to get past whatever initial reluctance you might have had to ask your parents THE most personal of questions. If you have siblings, this is a perfect time to divide up different parts of the POP "inquiry" job. Each of you can take charge of one or two areas. If you have some delicacy about money but your sister Sally, the accountant, has none, she's likely the better one to get your parents' answers about their investments, income, expenditures and, later, to locate, organize and evaluate their financial issues.

If Sally is unavailable, has long-standing emotional problems with your parents, lives abroad or for some other good reason, she wouldn't be optimal to lead that inquiry. In each new situation and for each person you are POParenting, you may need to use slightly different approaches. Your parents may have forgotten much and that can't feel good to them or you. Your reminding them of things from their past might result in sadness or even giggling. You'll be asking them a lot of questions and, if your parents are over 85 (part of the "frail elderly"), statistically one in two has some form of dementia. One or both of them may have little left of their short-term memory. All this may generate much confusion and your parents may just shut down.

You don't have limitless resources. Your patience and good humor will last longer if you lower your expectations of what you can get accomplished each time you're with them. You must stay focused and although it helps for you to come there with your agenda ready, they may not be "in the mood." It's likely you'll have a great deal to unearth at your parents' home at this time and perhaps, like me, a job, a family and other responsibilities to return to. But you will want to be thorough and not discover, later on, that you forgot to look at the important boxes in the garage. The questions you don't get answered may rise again to haunt you another day!

Asking your parents the most personal and prying of questions takes courage. You may be way outside your comfort zone. You may be way outside their comfort zone too. You must ask and sometimes even pursue your parents for information they may not remember or want you to know. They may even become oppositional and refuse to grant you access to "their secrets." Here's where you may find yourself face-to-face with the "role reversal," as you demonstrate the courage, patience and determination to get the answers appropriate for a POParent's need to know.

You may be afraid they will get angry with you or feel offended. Maybe they will. Now is the time you can assure them with kindness that it is odd for you too. Instead of "interrogating" them about topics you've never talked about together, remind them (and yourself) that your concern is for their welfare and their future. You simply wish to help; you're not there to judge them. You might even ask them to "be understanding" with you. You can remind them that you are on a learning curve and you'll get more comfortable and confident as time goes by.

Remember too, that it is you who can set – and should set – the right tone for these conversations. You are not cross-examining guilty prisoners: these are your parents.

Brace yourself for the fact that much of their paperwork may not be in "ship shape." Perhaps your parents haven't been thinking very far ahead. Your questions can help them face up to important issues, think through and then effectuate a better resolution of those – this time with you. Your parents may be feeling embarrassed to have you discover their unpaid insurance premiums, unopened bills, how much money they have or the quantity of stored newspapers they're hoarding. You will want to be the calm and patient one, the "understanding" parent you always wanted to have when you were growing up. You'll want to keep your voice raised loudly enough so they can hear your questions but not sound harsh or be "loud-angry" if you have to repeat yourself to be heard or comprehended.

If you're one of the fortunate POParents not facing the drama or trauma I did, you can have your initial conversations with your folks sufficiently early to understand what will be needed and do your research in a more relaxed manner. You can be better prepared than I was. You can take time to evaluate their home for its safety, help your parents draw up the most useful legal documents, meet with their doctors early on to prevent or slow the onset of certain geriatric conditions and discover resources before your POP emergency or crisis arises.

POPlan #4: Discovering Their Issues With The Most Satisfaction And The Least "Disconnection" For All Concerned

Staying connected with your family and improving your parents' lives are what your overall strategic POPlan affords you and them. It's what you can lean back on if you come up against major disagreements or even minor unpleasantnesses with your siblings or your folks. While laboring to find out the array of details you needed about your parents' histories or being refused access to the same, it may have been easy to lose sight of some of these long-term POP goals.

Your family's thorough review of your parents' issues – legal, financial, emotional and spiritual – will help you to flesh out the "tactics" of how to construct and then make your POPlan workable. You'll also want to align with other POP family members to set deadlines so the underlying tasks are completed within set time parameters. Not only will your accomplishing that together feel good but it will also keep your vision clear of what needs to get done, by whom and by when. That's all true as long as you bear in mind that things are always changing with our seniors: learning when and how to be flexible may allows your POPlan to bend rather than be broken.

To help your parents become safer, start by making a list of all the things you'll want to ask them on the first day. Then divide your list by five or ten because you'll be lucky to even get that much accomplished in a single session. As you go through the POPcycle, you'll find that by setting more reasonable expectations for how much can get done in a particular time period, you'll lower your stress and everyone's stress, making your POP time together far more enjoyable.

You'll want to do a lot of the refreshing breathing we've discussed before, during and after each of these sessions of parental "inquiry." I am meaning this literally. Breathing consciously will bring more oxygen to your brain and help your thinking.

Make sure there is plenty of fresh water available for everyone especially when you're doing challenging things with your parents, like asking them about their finances or funeral arrangements. Your senior parents particularly need to stay hydrated, so keep them drinking. Doing so will help lubricate their cells, accomplish a lot of other healthy missions and may even keep the conversation "lubricated."

Very practically, you'll also want to keep in mind that you all need enough light to accomplish all you're trying to do. One of the recurring problems in communicating with our senior loved ones is that often their sensory organs aren't as attuned as yours and mine. They don't hear as well, taste as much, smell as intently or see as well as they used to. Often they're very aware of their limitations but it's still a good idea to check the wattage on the light bulbs where your parents live and make sure there is literally enough light to read, watch the television or even work on a computer without unnecessary strain.

To thrive while you're doing POP, it's necessary to decide you're worth the same loving attention you've so generously been lavishing on your parents. And after reaching that logical conclusion, you must act accordingly. You can reaffirm here the importance of behaving as lovingly to yourself as the people you're POParenting. We'll spend more time later looking at the importance of self-care, especially for family caregivers but, if you're like most POParents, you'll need to repeatedly place that thought in your consciousness.

Many scientific studies report a variety of major health benefits that invoking gratitude provides our bodies, minds and spirits.[19] If one of your goals is to have your POP experience be a journey of love, you'll be more likely to achieve it by frequently activating your sense of appreciating the gifts in doing POP. Even a simple practice – like finding three things you feel grateful for every day when you wake up and three more when you go to sleep – can make you a better POParent. If you can't think of even one thing you're grateful for, borrow these: #1 I have a living parent; #2 I completed the first item on my POP to-do list; and #3 I appreciate being able to remember to do this list.

---

[19] Emmons, Robert A., PhD. "Thanks!: How the New Science of Gratitude Can Make You Happier," 2007, Houghton Mifflin; Seligman, Martin, PhD. "Authentic Happiness: Using the New Positive Psychology to Realize Your Potential for Lasting Fulfillment, 2004, Simon & Schuster; Whitbourne, Susan Krauss, PhD., "Giving Thanks: the Benefits of Gratitude; Why Gratitude is Good for Your Mental Health," Psychology Today, May 25, 2010, from "Fulfillment At Any Age," 2010, Random House.

Chapter 5

Doing And Un-Doing Paperwork To Make Our Parents "Safer" And Become Part Of The 21st Century

My Story

Despite having paid for my education and frequently expressing confidence in me, my parents had excluded me when they executed their wills and made their legal and estate decisions. Now that my parents were finally including me in these decisions and discussions, I would need to understand and perhaps add my own input to what already existed. Maybe they would wish to alter some things to become more relevant to the octogenarians they'd become or the world they lived in?

Hence my first goal in reviewing their paperwork was to offer my suggestions after I'd dug into the details. My other goal was to ensure that, on a go-forward basis, we could all rely on my parents' documents and, should another or more serious illness impact one of them, their wishes could be known and respected. Bottom line: while they were on my watch, I wanted my parents to be and feel as "safe" as they could legally, emotionally, spiritually, medically and financially.

Given my legal background, I knew I'd feel more at ease after I took the time to fully examine their paperwork and discover whether it was all in "good order." I was coming to appreciate that as I became more serene and secure about each piece of the POP puzzle, my Mom and Dad also became more at ease.

When I began the process, I had limited information. I knew things in the abstract, such as: my Dad held various rights and responsibilities from his music businesses that I'd need to learn about. I recalled hearing years before that they'd made a few small "investments," aside from their home and I'd need to know if those were still active and what was involved. I remembered in his early 80's, Dad had proudly announced obtaining long-term care insurance[20] for himself and Mom. "With this plan, you won't be burdened because our care will be assured." It was very important to my parents, as to many of their peers, not have to rely financially on their children, nor to obligate us in that way. I knew I'd need to check the details of their plan's premiums, benefits, waiting periods and terms to see if his dream fit the insurance world's reality.

One day while I was hunting down information, I'd become so upset that I'd thought I might scream. Knowing that such a reaction was not my norm, I paid further attention to it. It wasn't really that I'd wanted to scream - not at my parents, nor even at life. Nonetheless, the muscles in my upper arms burned with the tension I'd internalized and made my own. I felt literally and emotionally overwhelmed, claustrophobic in this storage cubicle, which was actually my Mother's closet. A panicky feeling of not knowing what to do next, wanting to escape and feeling rooted in place, overcame me. As I got quieter, I even heard myself silently "revving" up a host of unwanted emotions: "Ya know, Jane. Given your parents' pace, you might be here undoing and redoing rubber bands and forsaken files for months."

Some of my pressured feeling came from the fact that it really does get overwhelming to deal with some of ours parents and their issues. And these were not my POP Family Coaching clients or my therapy patients with whom I could be the cool, competent professional. The stress I felt to do this POP task perfectly was so intense

---

[20] See Glossary.

because it was my own Mom and Dad and because I had the expectation I should be calm and rational one, even in the midst of chaos.

And oh those endless boxes!! What I found as I got inside Mom's boxes were decades and decades of memorabilia as well as financial, legal and other extraordinarily detailed records. That woman, God love her, had saved not only every bank statement since their marriage but every letter I'd ever written her. She'd even saved the envelopes bearing their five-cent stamps and the debuting of American zip codes.

Jack made his own contribution to the collection of boxes I needed to examine. In addition to his stamp collection and random small coins he'd gathered, most of Dad's things consisted of the remnants of a background music library business he'd developed in his 60's. At that time, writing lyrics became less lucrative for a man his age, but he wanted to keep his hand in music and that provided him a route. It also generated voluminous contracts, correspondence, tapes, CDs, and even vintage vinyl in exotic languages – Spanish, Bulgarian and Swedish.

When I finally got inside the boxes that contained their personal legal papers, I was startled to learn that my parents' entire financial plan was based upon the man owning and controlling everything. Although Lillian had typed each piece of Dad's correspondence and every contract to precise perfection on an old Smith Corona typewriter – when a single error might require her retyping an entire page – my Mom had no money. She had no credit, owned nothing and, despite having worked alongside Jack in all his business ventures, was basically not a "person" from a business perspective.

How could my egalitarian father have structured their assets that way? How could Mom or their lawyer have allowed it? The man I knew never denied Lillian's contribution to his life or business. Quite the contrary. He also wouldn't have intelligently set up their affairs with so little regard for Mom's wellbeing. In spite of having an intense reaction, I decided our developing relationship would benefit if I responded more neutrally to things I was finding out. I'd taught myself and then my patients to "under-react" rather than "over-react" at times with our youngsters. Certainly I could learn to do that with these oldsters as well.

Helping my folks move into the 21st century was part of my POP challenge and it seemed likely I'd be more persuasive with them if I'd under-react more often. I could under-react by "assuming" anything I found that reflected Dad's sole ownership was set up in an "old school" way by a man who took pride in providing for his wife. I could under-react when I reminded myself that Jack had acted out of a traditional *point of view. There wasn't anything mean-spirited in his intentions. As I under-reacted more and reacted less emotionally, I saw myself becoming more successful in obtaining their consents to the changes that were needed.*

Helping myself move into the POParent I wished to become was not quite so easy. On the previous day, as I'd stood amid their things, I'd felt like an alien suspended above Mom's closet looking down on this scene, asking myself: "What are you doing here, Jane – inside this closet in this bedroom sorting through years of these people's papers, photos, stamp collections, shoe boxes, music and books?" Could that bizarre "dislocation" have come from a desire to avoid my feelings? My parents were not "these people." They were THE two people I'd known the longest, the ones who'd conceived me, raised me as best they could and shepherded me through my early life. But thinking about them as "these people" allowed me to distance myself from them and my feelings, feelings I sought to protect myself from having.

Gazing over the boxes, I identified those unwanted thoughts and emotions: exhaustion, sadness, nostalgia and even anticipatory grief about their deaths. In that moment, I felt as if parenting my parents was part of an inevitable march towards their leaving me. Leaving ME. Even my Mom's not being recognizable on that first December night could be seeing as part of MY loss: the Mom I'd known seemed to be departing from my life.

My mind next jumped further into the "scary" future, this time to when I would be the old woman. Would I make similar moves to theirs? What would my life accumulations look like to those sorting and reviewing my things? And who would be there to do this for me, then?

"Whoa!" I told myself, noting I was not in the present. That type of thinking stripped away my positive energy and focus and therefore was actually dangerous behavior. I breathed a few times, deeply in and out. Then I tried another technique I'd taught in my office: helpful self-talk. "Hey, you're not an old woman. Your parents are not dying. You're not operating in real time. Come on back." Breathing deeply into these present-centered cues helped ground me to where I was standing and needing to function: in the here and now!

It was helpful to recognize my own mental patterns of succumbing to emotions of loss and abandonment, obsessively asking unanswerable questions. When I would get lost in them, I'd be unable to mindfully attend to my tasks or my parents. Once I'd uncovered these sometimes hard to identify patterns, I could "intervene" to bring me back to the present since being "absent" is never a good formula for POParenting or any other kind of parenting.

I was buoyed having witnessed the power I had to fight my destructive and enervating thoughts. That evening I continued to work on finding the desired energy and confidence needed to be the POParent I desired to become. I used more helpful "self-talk" to show me how to undermine my distracting thinking.

Conversing with myself again, I reminded me: "you have what it takes to be the grown up here. Surely you can tolerate Dad's having not made your Mom a financial equal and you can live with her annoying rubber band obsession. You can be the calm one and give your parents a sense of wellbeing. Reviewing legal and financial 'issues,' sorting out health matters and listening to people's spiritual concerns – these are all things you're particularly qualified to do. You've performed similar tasks successfully countless times and now it's time to do it for your own loved ones. Calm down, Jane, you know what you're doing. You're fine."

These thoughts did ground me and as I got more centered, I realized that not only had I been obsessively repeating unanswerable queries but also that I'd been asking all the "wrong questions." I'd been dwelling on the "why me" questions and the "am I adequate" fears. These only "convinced" me to feel like a victim and not enough for the job – things that weren't so. I was NOT a victim here: quite the opposite. I had chosen to help Lillian and Jack. Asking myself the wrong questions, like "am I enough?" and "why me?" wasn't helpful to anyone.

In contrast, posing the "right questions" would help me create much-needed empowering and solution-oriented responses. Those more constructive self-inquires would involve asking myself "how" questions. "How can I sort through what I need from these boxes and still return to L. A. fairly soon?" Or "how can I find someone to help me with this?" Or "how could I make this more fun? Would turning on some music help us all have more a better time?" Or, "would it work better to look for things myself and not bother Mom and Dad?"

Working as a therapist, I'd consistently found asking "how" questions to be a great way to generate action-oriented thoughts. Now by interrupting the "why me" type questions and inserting "how" questions, I was not only relieved of unhelpful mental meanderings but also able to focus on getting specific results. By asking myself "how" I could best complete the daunting POP tasks before me, I was actively commanding my mind to find good solutions. It was actually easier to get my job done.

After working with myself on these re-orientations of my thinking that day and later at the hotel, a more mature and confident version of me arrived at my parents' door the following day, a "wiser POParent." I was able to keep my attention mindfully poised on each step of what I was doing. Instead of judging my parents for having so much stuff or myself for not being a more patient POParent, I quieted those voices and just did my job. Very patiently I examined the next box in front of me rather than losing myself in the overwhelming responsibility of "endless" boxes and work.

During the days that followed, I found more ways to motivate myself to clear out my stale unwanted thoughts. I could clear my head quickly by going outside to take a brief and conscious walk as a personal "time out." Literally putting myself into a different space and moving my body offered a simple, non-toxic solution. Something else I tried to put me into another time and space was inviting my mind to clear itself of the remembrance of their apartment as it was today with its endless boxes, anxious parents and disarray. In its place I brought in another scene from years ago, a specific and happy memory of what it had been like to live in Manhattan with my parents when I'd been young. I saw I had many happy memories to choose from and after allowing myself some time to linger to savor a good memory, I could return to my tasks in their apartment refreshed and surprisingly efficient.

Unfortunately even after I'd found the time to review my parents' paperwork and offered them some suggestions we incorporated, I was not peaceful. I suffered from a condition I seen so often among POParents that I'd even given it a name: "Insufficient Information Syndrome" or I. I. S. Although no one in business or law would advise making important decisions without hard data, there was no hard data on many crucial things. Instead I suffered from I. I. S. as I had no idea, of course, how long my parents would live nor how their needs might expand. How long would any funds my parents had set aside for their late-in-life care last? How fast and often would the escalating cost of everything geriatric rise?

I closed my eyes, took a breath and asked myself the question I'd often heard Oprah ask others. "What do you know for sure?" I did know this: I was "in" for the long haul. I had whatever resources I could locate and it was my responsibility to figure out how to use those for my parents' wellbeing. I knew for sure that I'd keep them safe as best I could. I'd just have to find a way to live with my I. I. S. and make the best decisions I could with whatever data I possessed.

These early POP days were a wealth of training opportunities for me, demonstrating clearly that what I'd been telling others was right for me, too. I saw that when I'd return on future visits, I'd need to come "prepared" – calm, purposeful and focused – since showing up like that "allowed" my parents to be clearer and even better able to help. I was appreciating that I could only accomplish a limited number of tasks during any one visit. If I tried to do "too much," tempers would flare and the quality of our time together would suffer. People my parents' age moved and thought at a slower pace and it was I, not they, who would need to do the adjusting.

It became clear I would benefit from further practicing "emotional neutrality," under-reacting and that I could use some additional work on my patience. I'd found it hard to keep serene and didn't like how little emotional stamina I'd recently experienced. I would need to get help from my friends and family, the people who ordinarily let me "vent," to talk through things without censoring. Hopefully doing all that would allow me to re-emerge stronger.

Eventually we redid the paperwork where that was needed. The Wolfs were now logging into the 21st century. Mom became a full partner in the family funds and developing a credit status at age 85. I gained access to their accounts and, should they become unable, to making medical their decisions. I assured my parents that all their new documents were properly executed and stored and we all breathed another sigh of relief. This POP stage had been successfully completed.

Finally able to look up from the boxes, I gazed towards the ceiling in their bedroom and saw anew the state of their apartment. My Mom had refused permission for workers to come in to repaint and, over time, the discolored sheetrock on the ceiling had become visible. That would have to wait for another visit.

Your Story

You too, will want to find, read, consider and then discuss with family members what your parents have set in place, legally and financially and beyond. Depending on their circumstances, you may wish to include your parents in that process. Thereafter you'll want to examine any reasonable alternatives to see if there are more "current," less expensive or other better ways to modify your parents' existing situations. You will want to do this sooner rather than later, since making and executing these decisions often takes time, an unknown here, and your parents may have a limited window to possess the mental competency[21] necessary to change their documents.

First you'll need to find out all about your parents' finances. What are their assets and where are they located? Just because your Dad says he has an interest in an oil well in Texas or one of those certificates of ownership in Jack Daniels' land, doesn't mean its value is what

---

[21] It's most prudent to discuss these matters with estate or other qualified lawyers and financial advisors in your parents' home state as these standards vary and are determined by state law.

he's thinking. Do you know if your parents' assets are insured? If so, by what company and under what conditions? That information may also help you evaluate its worth. What are your parents' premiums, deductibles and benefits for all their insurance? Do your parents have debt or mortgage obligations? Do they have a reverse mortgage and is that working for them? Who are they paying, for what and from what source? We all hear about older citizens getting ripped off. Has that happened to your parents?   Are their bills being paid on time? How do you know that?   Do they have debt and if so, how is it being managed? Is it at a good rate? You will need to see their paperwork for yourself and attend to what is necessary.

Your parents may have become more forgetful, gotten ill or just had trouble keeping track of their mail and so much more.   As a result of their forgetfulness, for example they may not be paying money they owe to some federal agency or their non-deductible portion of a hospital bill. If so, you'll need to understand which of your parents' bills must be paid immediately and what may be re-negotiated by you later. You will want to ensure that no bills "get lost" lying around at your parents' home somewhere. Your aging parents' "priorities" may sometimes surprise you: to them, being late for dinner may be unthinkable but being late on a car insurance may be "no big deal."

If you can't get reliable answers from your parents about their existing monthly payments, you'll want to create a theoretical list of their likely obligations. For example, if your parents own their home, they may owe on a mortgage or two, an equity line or a reverse mortgage. You will then need to go find such documents and seek out specific answers. If your parents are still driving, they may owe payments on an auto lease or a loan. A car registration or a smog check may be coming due soon. Once you've gotten a handle on their bills, it would be helpful to put reminder cues in place on a central calendar you create for recurring events so that whoever starts to pay their bills can do so in a timely manner.

If your review of their current situation suggests your folks are unable to continue managing their finances without ongoing help, you may need to take over some or all of it. You also may wish to consult an attorney and see about filing a petition in court seeking a conservatorship of their money or whatever their state requires for you to manage their finances, especially if you're concerned about your parents' signing checks or making poor financial choices. A power of attorney may be sufficient but you will want to have certainty to best protect yourself, your parents and their estate.

Having The Conversation with your parents about your taking on more control of their money or other aspects of their life usually has many levels of complexity to it. Again, harkening back to parenting children, you have a moral obligation, should you choose to accept it, to protect your parents financially. That may mean that your being on their bank accounts is necessary at this time of your POPcycle in order to protect them from scams, missed payments or other unattractive consequences. Under more unfortunate circumstances, you may even need to protect your parents from a sibling who's living under their roof and "conning" them out of their Social Security moneys.

After having reviewed your parents' obligations, resources and foreseeable needs, perhaps you will suggest that they obtain a personal loan or a reverse mortgage on their home. When interest rates are low, that may present an attractive solution to finding the funds you need to hire caregiving assistance. Perhaps you'll advise your parents to make some short-term investments to extend the life of their savings. You will want to keep current regarding taxes, Social Security and Medicare. There are many resources available to help you including, of course, www.ParentingOurParents.org.

It's wise to spend small sums in the beginning of POP to have experienced professionals guide you and your family – evaluating what's in place, legally and financially, and deciding what might be better. Perhaps someone on your TEAM POP already has these skills but if not, find qualified people licensed in the state where your parents are planning to live out their days. There may even be legal or financial professionals providing free advise for the indigent elderly in their state; your parents may or may not qualify for these services. In making financially prudent choices, it's often sage to expend some money now to ensure future savings and avoid stressful worrying. Even if you and/or your parents have concerns about the expense, you may find it useful and comforting to consult with seasoned professionals.

Over the course of your POPcycle, you will find yourself hiring, firing and supervising lawyers, doctors, accountants, GCM's and others. They may have far more education and certainly will have far more experience in their areas of expertise than you do. "Supervision" of these professionals in the form of oversight and "follow up" is part of TEAM POP's job. The best-qualified or most local TEAM POP member is often the one to be assigned such overseeing. I urge you as POParents to not become intimidated by professionals who are helping your family. Speak up! Ask a lot of questions! Better safe asking too many questions than sorry asking too few. It's your job to ensure that your parents are getting the best service possible, so don't let your old fearfulness stand in the way of good POParenting.

Knowing that you've become involved, that their paperwork has been updated, that they're not alone dealing with their hospital bills or balancing their bank books *will* relieve your loved ones' stress. That can literally extend the number and the quality of your parents' days and nights on the planet!

POPlan #5: How To Undo Or Redo Our Parents' "Important" Documents

Start the "difficult" talks, The Conversations, with your parents by making sure they can hear you. If they wear hearing aids but don't have them in, ask your parents to put them in. They may be resistant or grouchy about that, but it's critically important that you be heard and understood. You may need to explain the POP ideas you're suggesting slowly, patiently, loudly and clearly.

You will need to speak so they can hear you. Be aware that sometimes your loud voice, the one you're trying to project so their elderly ears can understand, may sound like you're angry with them. Having to repeat yourself may also cause you to feel frustrated and sound angry. Therefore practice raising your volume and lowering your emotional tone simultaneously. Invite your parents to ask their questions and even if they repeat the same question many times, find the part of you that is most patient. Have that kind part of you answer your parents.

You may be feeling overwhelmed by the whole of this POP task. I certainly did. I recommend you break it down into manageable pieces. If you begin early enough in the POPcycle, you and your parents will be able to incorporate any desirable changes more slowly, incrementally and that will likely evoke less resistance. If you can make even one small modification that makes them less vulnerable and improves the quality of your parents' lives, they're likely to be more cooperative about the next change.

For example, if your parents are leery of anything electronic, suggest they agree to directly deposit their Social Security checks into their bank account. At first the notion of electronic depositing may seem foreign or "too tech-y" for them. Talk with your parents about how this small thing will help them. For your parents, getting to the bank each month may involve much effort and some physical risks: arduously walking to the bus stop, waiting in the cold for the bus, getting up and down steps those bank steps. Then there's avoiding exposing themselves to the elements and everyone on the bus during flu and cold season. Let your parents know they can skip the trip they now have to make to the bank each month and their benefits will be in sitting in their bank account faster and more dependably.

You might recall an incident that will help them better understand your point. For example, remind your parents of the time last winter when they'd both had colds and couldn't get out to the bank on time. Since they'd already mailed their payment to the Water and Power Company, their utility check had bounced. Luckily, you'd seen that pink bill on their desk and called immediately or else your parents would have lost their heat and electricity, potentially suffering far worse respiratory consequences than their colds.

Once you've clearly and patiently explained things, your Mom and Dad may be willing to try direct depositing. When having conversations with your aging relative, avoid using the word "change." This is a term that subliminally suggests they've done things incorrectly up until now. Try using the word "expand." It suggests newness without fault, not having to give up on what they liked from the past. In the subtle dynamics of parenting your parents sometimes using just the right word can make your POP idea far more appealing to them. Have the patience and take time to talk with your parents so they understand anything that's different. That will make it easier for them to feel more secure. Once your parents "accept" your first good POP idea and see how it helps them, they'll better appreciate your suggested changes will often be advantageous to them. Then they'll be more willing to allow you more POP changes. Your POP successes *will* build on themselves and perhaps they'll be more open to the next idea you propose as well.

All too often your parents may be hesitant to ask you for help or even refuse it when you offer. Some parents, like my Mom, are fearful that you and I will come in, alter their world and they'll "lose control." This is particularly challenging if they already feel like much is "out of control" or their bodies feel that way to them. Not only that but older people often have become very set in their ways and are not comfortable with things that are unfamiliar.

Nonetheless like my Mom, it's likely your folks will be grateful for the things you do that relieve them of feeling stressed. While doing POP you need to stay alert to discover what, when and how to make suggestions to your parents. "Slow and steady" is often a good approach to making changes here as elsewhere when you're POParenting. "Slow," since your parents tend to do things at a more deliberative speed and need time to feel comfortable with your new role and your suggested changes. "Steady" since you will need to be thorough if you've seen a number of things you believe need "fixing."

Therefore, in choosing where to suggest your next POP "expansions" (as we're renaming "change"), look at what and how you've been able to alter in the past with your folks with the least number of problems. Learn how to leverage your POP successes to update and improve more in the future.

POP MUSIC

Listen again to the familiar lyrics of the Beatles' song, "Taxman"[22] from your new POP perspective. Consider how your assistance – reviewing and possibly up-dating your parents' decisions and ensuring that all their paperwork is "in order" – can help your parents financially and otherwise. Maybe because you stepped up to the plate for POP, your parents can avoid the frightening implications the song suggests.

---

[22] "Taxman" was written by George Harrison and published by Sony/ATV Tunes, LLC.

Chapter 6

Facing Down The Life-And-Death Mission Of Pop – Theirs And Yours

My Story

I was at home one afternoon doing nothing in particular when an unrelenting voice said: "Call your Dad." Ordinarily when I thought about him, I'd smile and remind myself to call. "Gee, it'd be nice to speak to Dad. I must remember to phone him later, when I get the chance." Unlike those times, I kept hearing something in my brain urging: "CALL YOUR FATHER NOW!"

I obeyed.

Florence, our caregiver, picked up the phone and formally announced: "Wolf Residence."

"Hi, Florence. I'm looking for my Dad. Is he okay? Will you go tell him I'm calling, please?" I sounded cool, but my heart was beating loudly in my chest. I was focused and uninterested in chatting with Florence as I ordinarily would have done to gain her view on the current situation with my folks. But now, I just wanted to feel the relief of hearing my dear Daddy's voice. I had a very cold feeling crawling up my back and chest.

Florence got back on the line to tell me she couldn't find him.

Now, my heart was jumping out of my chest. "NO, No! Go find him! It's not a very big place." He couldn't be lost! They only had a two-bedroom apartment!! What the ...!!!

Florence returned breathless. It seemed that Dad had quietly slipped into my former bedroom, aka his music business office, locked himself inside and then placed a plastic bag over his sad baldhead. Just as I called, he'd been trying to end his life!!! Responding to my demands, Florence burst in on him and removed the weapon of personal destruction that plastic bag might have become.

OH MY GOD! What if I hadn't been alert to my own internal voice? What if I hadn't honored the relentless driving voice and followed its command? What if I had not phoned? What if Florence not been there to pick up the phone and stop Dad? Everything would have turned out ... differently.

I am so grateful I heard and heeded my nagging voice on that otherwise "do-nothing" afternoon. Somehow I'd felt it, that "instinctive signal" parents describe getting when their kids are in danger even thousands of miles away. Perhaps similarly my close POP attachment to my Dad had now alerted me that something was very wrong, even at our distance.

I was already having serious doubts about the long-distance POP I was trying to do. Maybe it wasn't my finest idea. In fact, the afternoon's events seemed not only a blessing in having saved Jack but perhaps also a wake-up call: I would need to be watching more carefully than before, more than I could even imagine. And since my parents didn't want to leave New York, my greater "oversight" would have to come from a distance.

Dad's behavior had truly shaken me up. I'd been totally unprepared for him to become so beaten down by life's stressors that he'd contemplate suicide as his last life statement. He'd been "the rock" for everyone else since his childhood, helping his kid brothers, buying up my uncle's cleaning business. "Dependable Jack," they'd called him. "Mr. Moderation," as Jack sometimes called himself, wasn't the guy to take his own life. But somehow over the prior several months, when I'd expected Jack and Lillian to settle into their more protected life, my ever-stable parent had been acting in dangerously uncharacteristic ways.

Even with the abiding humility he cultivated, Jack had always seemed bigger than life to me. Maybe most girls felt that way about their Daddies. Looking back, I remembered how his being ever curious about everyone and everything had meant I couldn't pull my dates away from talking with him. When had he stopped being curious? He had always seemed so comfortable being the strong, invincible one. Had he tired of the role? Only once in my whole life had I ever seen him cry. Dad become totally frustrated over something rather small but it had gotten to him and he just sat and wept. It was eerie to watch as a child but the incident also humanized him for me. I'd never seen a serious break in him before. Nor had I foreseen that it would be Dad of my two parents whom I would need to rescue from a suicide attempt.

I was both shocked and profoundly saddened that he'd felt so desperately to want to end his life. Of course, I jumped on the next plane to New York. I had no idea what I would do when I got there or what I'd actually say to him. I'd figure those things out when we were up close and personal. Now I just wanted to hold his hand, take him on a walk in Central Park and offer him the peacefulness he used to give me when I needed rescuing as a child.

Maybe Dad would share his burdens or disappointments with me. I also felt badly for not having known more. I'd been unaware he was so unhappy, as he'd never confided that to me. I was shocked that he'd think suicide could be a solution. I wondered if he'd been thinking at all or just reacting. Maybe he was just feeling forlorn and overwhelmed. I feared that even when I was by his side, my Dad – like so many men of his generation – wouldn't communicate very much about his emotions. I also wondered how much, if at all, I could help him.

By the time I got into the City from the airport, my Dad had been calmed down from his suicide attempt. He was grateful to have me there and told me he'd appreciated my answering his "call for help." I'd naively hoped that some of the fatigue, withdrawal from life and absence of joy I'd seen at Christmas time would clear up after his daughter and the caregivers improved his life. However this depression had not abated much at all.

None of it had truly lightened the internal burdens Jack had placed on himself, it seemed to me now. Trying unsuccessfully to be his wife's caregiver, Dad had to face that his wife and life partner had been diagnosed with Alzheimer's and there was little he could do about that but watch the decline and love her. This news had taken its toll on the resilient man he had always been.

Depression is often hard to detect for family members, even if you're living nearby and even harder long distance. As I looked back, there had been clues that my Dad's stress and life changes could turn into a major depressive episode. And statistically there is a remarkably high rate of suicides (and attempts) among men in their eighties. But even I, the thorough professional therapist, had wanted to believe things were getting better and had not been looking for signs of depression in my Dad, my strong parent. And of course, I wasn't there to observe him. But even had I been physically closer, suicide attempts complicated phenomena and not necessarily "predictable" despite someone's depressed mood.

At this point in life, my Dad was entering his late 80's and still working at his background music publishing business. It was very detail oriented work involving foreign rights and domestic contracts. My folks had been a team in that business from the beginning. As my Mom's cognitive decline became more apparent, she was less able to keep up her end of the tasks. I could see how her condition might have distressed and challenged Dad, demanding additional unknown skills from him at an age when he was finding it harder to learn new things. A man half his age would have had problems carrying on their projects (without my Mom) and persevering despite grieving.

When I began POP so much of my attention had been focused on my Mom and the impact of her dementia on her activities of daily living,[23] her moods and her functioning. Now I'd been forced to pull the camera lens further back on the scene and see the effects of my Mom's conditions on our larger family dynamics. Jack had aged too over the past visits. Caring for my Mom had stressed him and made him more vulnerable first to pneumonia and later to depression. Despite Florence's continuing attention, it was mostly Dad upon whom my Mother relied for real support and her long-term cognitive illness also seemed to be impacting Dad's emotions.

It couldn't have been easy for him. I tried to get my Father to talk with me as we walked through Central Park. It was not his ordinary way to "burden" his child. But after I'd so quickly returned to be with him in New York, Dad began to talk more, although in a limited way, acknowledging feelings of confusion, loss, resentment and even shame. I listened, offered an occasion interjection and listened more. I held his hand, kissed his baldhead and reminded him of my steadfast love and appreciation. There was only as much I could do for him even as I wanted to do more.

---

[23] See Glossary.

When Dad became his wife's primary "emotional caregiver" during her long cognitive decline, he'd needed to give up a central part of their marital arrangement, the team they'd had as a working partnership. Dad was beginning to learn that medication could slow Mom's dementia for a while but that as time went by, she would become less and less his wife. Florence's calming demeanor was very helpful for both of them around their house. Her quiet consistency and the predictable patterns she created worked well for both my folks in spite of their very different personalities and needs.

On this visit more clearly than ever I'd come to see that, since I couldn't rely on my parents to be accurate reporters of their own conditions and since as a POParent I had a pressing "need to know," it was my job to develop more reliable and regular procedures to oversee them at a distance. Florence and I created a protocol in which I'd be alerted sooner to any observable changes in my parents' behaviors or health. She prepared written reports weekly. I advised their building's superintendent to have the staff on the lookout for anything "unusual" with my parents, especially on the weekends when my parents were "home alone." I was "battening down the hatches" around the boat carrying my fragile folks.

Even though I held the hope that Dad would feel like his former self after his suicidal attempt, he clearly needed more help. I checked into some psychiatric referrals for him and set up an appointment a few days later. Then I went home. Flying back to New York to be with him had only provided a temporary fix, it seemed. I returned to California, enjoyed a good night's sleep in my own bed and heard the phone ring the next morning, very early L. A. time. It was Dad.

"If you don't come back, I'm going to kill myself."

Oh my Lord! What would I do now? What would the experts advise? Oops, I'm supposed to be the expert!! This is why doctors don't treat their own families, I reminded myself. I was hardly objective.

Nonetheless, I looked to see how I, the geriatric expert as well as the daughter who adored him, could best help. I recognized that I must take his threats seriously, especially after his recent episode, but somehow this didn't feel like it had before. This time it felt like a familiar feeling parents get when your child needs more of you. Was Dad truly suicidal or testing me manipulatively? If he were truly suicidal again, the day after I returned home, then I'd need to have Florence get him to an institution! If, on the other hand, he just needed more of my attention, then I was in parent-child territory and I had some good ideas of what to do next.

I went with my gut as I considered my new role-reversing mantra: "You're their parent now!" It didn't really feel like Dad wanted to kill himself despite his words.

It really sounded like he wanted me around more. I asked myself how could I best respond to him lovingly but also with appropriate limits, like a practiced POParent. I wanted him to know I was there for him but couldn't be "bounced" back and forth across country. And I couldn't afford to be wrong.

Instinctively I decided to employ a couple of techniques I'd developed for my patients and the POP families I coach. The first is an opening "test question:" "what age is my Dad now?" I'd found that asking that question calms people down by allowing them to put a little distance in place. Taking a moment to consider their parents' more "childish" ways, recall similar ways their kids acted and then fitting those two into an actual number has been a very powerful tool. Over time I'd also seen how helpful it was for me and lots of POParents to use the technique of "under-reacting."

Somehow I thought to ask myself: "what age is Jack now?" And somehow, quite naturally, my mind answered. I instantly "knew" the age that seemed closest to how Jack was acting. It was about 8. If you've ever seen an 8 year-old boy act somewhat irrationally, desperate for his mother's attention, that was pretty similarly to what my Dad was evoking in that moment. How does a parent treat an 8 year-old boy who's feeling needy?

I took the deepest cleansing breath I could find and made myself sound as kind and normal as I could: "do you think you could wait all the way until next weekend, Dad, for me to come back and for us to spend some time together? I've just returned home and that means I just can't turn around and return to New York without at least seeing my office and some of my patients. I know the weekend may seem like a long time, but I promise that if you won't be too sad until then, I will come back this weekend. Can you work with me on that?"

I set a boundary but was still holding my breath to hear his response. I had no idea if my approach would work or if he would hang up and try to hurt himself. I hoped he would give in to the reasonableness of my request, get that I'd heard his neediness and would soon be back.

"Okay. I'll wait. And Jane, thank you."

As it turned out, my Dad's depression was not yet healed. Over a period of months, he would try to kill himself on three separate occasions; once by plastic bag and then twice more, by leaning out the window of the fourteenth floor duplex apartment he'd fought so hard to get into. The last attempt he almost jumped knowing I was in a cab on the way across town to see him. But he didn't jump, thank God!

Over those months, I'd unearthed various specialists that Dad met with in addition to his prescribing psychiatrist. He saw psychologists, clinical social workers and religious men. He took biofeedback treatments, psychiatric medications and herbal supplements to prevent future harm, alleviate existing symptoms and function better. But, poor man, he still seemed to be crying out for additional help.

One way I hoped to provide him help was to relieve Jack of the burden associated with his music publishing business. Perhaps if given the chance, I could sell off the valuable assets he'd written and published but now lacked the energy to exploit commercially. After having appropriately compensated Dad for his copyrights, perhaps the new, younger publisher would also want to use Jack's considerable "veteran" expertise to further advise him. With fewer responsibilities, the pride associated with unexpected funds in the bank and the respect that came with being a "consultant," Jack could experience, as my beloved so beautifully termed it an "R.T.L.," a Reason to Live[24].

It took me a long time to accomplish but eventually I was able to sell Dad's publishing to people who continued to share his life work with the listening public. His joy in that transaction and all the accompanying benefits of it lit my world: the R.T.L. helped us all a lot.

Another way I hoped to relieve some of Dad's emotional burdens and Mom's too was through the mentoring and support I got from colleagues. Throughout my POP journey, I was blessed to have Dr. Michael L. McGrail, "the physician in our family," as my geriatric guru. A devoted friend and my office partner, Michael was a highly gifted psychiatrist with an amazingly kind heart and a devilish sense of humor, beloved by his patients and students. Having him by my side while parenting my parents was a gift as Michael always provided me both the information I needed for POP and the wisdom to interpret the data accurately. I would call him day or night from the emergency rooms of hospitals in New York and later California – sometimes desperate and always grateful for his sound advice.

After so many attempts to treat Dad weren't helping, Michael convinced me that Dad's form of depression would best be halted by carefully administered electroshock treatments (EST). No longer the frightening experience portrayed in 1950's movies, EST had become an acceptable "last-ditch" way to permanently relieve intense psychological pain. When my Dad tried to suicide a third time, I agreed and tried shock therapy. I recall few sadder moments in my whole life than leaving my Daddy being prepped for shock treatments.

Tied down to a "geri-chair" – one of those hospital high chairs where old people look like young children waiting for lunch – Jack's eyes were deeply sunken and radiated

---

[24] See Glossary.

terror. I wanted so badly to comfort him, to make it all better for the man who'd been there to comfort me and my "boo-boo's" in his day. I let Dad know that he would feel better again soon and would function more like himself after the treatments. I suggested he talk frankly with the nice young woman who was the social worker, "confiding" she shared my training and might become one of his best allies on the road to recovery. He said he would try.

With a very heavy heart, I left him sitting in that high chair and headed back to their apartment. There I bid farewell to my Mom who was a bit confused with all the psychiatric attention now focused on Jack. I checked in again with Florence, to be on the lookout for Mom's need for some special attention. Then I went down to the building superintendent and instructed him to install bars on the windows of my parents' elegant apartment. That would assure that neither parent could use their fourteenth floor windows as an exit point from this world. Then I boarded another plane, thankful to escape back to my home.

How much any of those treatments or professionals helped my Dad is frankly hard to assess and may not matter. I was grateful for anything that brought him some respite. Participating with these methodologies provided Jack a variety of tools to manage his stress and the more "single" life he would increasingly live as Mom retreated into her dementia. And Jack never suffered a recurrence of his symptoms, to my great relief.

Your Story

Hopefully, you will never have to be on a call like mine rescuing a potentially suicidal parent or loved one. I would never wish you the helpless feeling of seeing your parent in such emotional distress. But you, too, may unexpectedly be called upon to prevent a suicide as a part of doing POP. If it does happen to you, hopefully reading this will alert you to handling it more effectively.

If you or your parent are having a personal crisis and need help right now, call this toll free number: 1-800-273-TALK (8255). Your call goes directly to the National Suicide Prevention Hotline[25]. Even if it seems totally unlikely, you should keep the number handy for future use.

---

[25] This toll-free number is available 24 hours a day, every day: 1-800-273-TALK (8255). The National Suicide Prevention Lifeline encourages us to call for ourselves or a parent or anyone else we care about. All calls to this line are always confidential.

POP in reality is a life-and-death mission with the end point your parents' departure from the planet. There will be times when, for everyone's sake, you may wish the end to come sooner rather than later. Watching people you love in any kind of pain – physical, spiritual or emotional – is hard and sometimes you may want the suffering to end. Do not feel badly, repeat DO NOT FEEL BADLY if you have had such thoughts. They are just thoughts. Thoughts are things and they are measurable, but they are not actions. Research teams have counted as many as 90,000 thoughts each day. And we all have thoughts from time to time that don't represent our finest hour. So, don't start punishing yourself for your thoughts.

If you are doing the primary family caregiving, like my Dad felt he was, there's a lot of information and many resources available about taking care of YOU! Family caregiving may often result in depression or some other health issue to the caregiver who rarely pays sufficient attention to him/herself. This is not an exaggeration. Like my Dad, one of your parents may already have joined the more than 65 million Americans (more than three in ten households) who provide unpaid care to an elderly or disabled adult[26] family member. These family caregivers provide an estimated 80 percent of the long-term care in the United States.

It is not at all uncommon for live-in family caregivers to develop serious health problems. Research has shown family caregivers are more likely than non-caregiving family members to:

- display symptoms of depression or anxiety

- have a long-term medical problem

- show higher levels of stress hormones

- spend more days sick with an infectious disease

- have a weaker immune response to flu vaccines

- heal wounds slower

- carry around higher levels of obesity

- show a higher risk of mental decline, including problems with memory and concentration (the precise areas one doing POP would most want most to have)

A few years ago I tried unsuccessfully to set up a support group for people doing POP. Prospective members told me they definitely wanted to feel better, could absolutely use support from fellow caregivers and knew they *should* give some loving attention to themselves. But they were unwilling to commit to regularly attending a group whose focus would be on their

[26] From "Caregiving in the U.S. 2009," a report conducted by the National Alliance for Caregiving (NAC) in collaboration with AARP, and funded by the MetLife Foundation.

own wellbeing and not their parents. Just as you and I, when we were young parents, set our "default" to attend to our baby first, when parenting aging parents, many family caregivers similarly take care of parents first, bathing, feeding and attending to ourselves well later, if ever.

Promise yourself you won't fall into this pattern of self-neglect. Find ways to set some boundaries or space between you and the loved ones you take care of. Schedule at least some activities that are focused on you alone. Make some time every day to attend to you, even if it's only a quiet cup of tea as you listen to a favorite piece of music. You will recall that on airplane flights, they always remind parents: put your own seat belt on first! Similarly with family caregiving: if you don't take care of you, you may not be ready when it's time to help your parents!

If you're a spouse to a senior or the older adult child yourself, remember that your poor self-care may eventually make you more "at risk" than the person you're attending! Yes, some caregivers will die before their charges. After all, what good will you be to your loved ones – and what sort of model – if you become ill or disabled and then need a caregiver of your own?

If your senior parents are still living with a partner, the fact that people age at very different rates may have an effect on them as a couple as well as individuals. People decline at different rates, partially because of genetics and particularly, as we age, because of the life styles and mental attitudes we've had. Even if your Mom and Father have the same number of years on the planet, as mine did, they may now be functioning at and feeling themselves to be very different "ages." I see many situations and maybe it's like this in your family dynamics, where the husband persists in his "provider role" by taking care for his same-age or even younger wife. Contrary to many of our stereotypes, one in every three American family caregivers is male.[27]

Your parents may "conspire," consciously or less so, as mine did in the beginning to keep their limitations hidden from you, the "outsider." That may take the form of covering up what's forgotten and then "compensating," where they "fill in the blanks" when they can't recall details. For example, your Dad may claims he phoned you yesterday as promised, even supplying details, when he doesn't really remember. Partners will often camouflage each other's disabilities, making your detection of conditions like depression harder. This is a version of how your teenage children may have acted, although for different reasons. Perhaps back then you honed your "parental detectors" and can utilize them again these days for POP. Your aging parents may be falsely reasoning that they can hold onto their autonomy, their home and their lifestyle if they don't let any "outsiders"

[27] Research provided by "Caregiving in the U.S. 2009," a report conducted by the National Alliance for Caregiving (NAC) in collaboration with AARP, and funded by the MetLife Foundation.

know about "weak links in their chain." But as we've seen, that is rarely, if ever, in their best interest.

Depression among the elderly is a very serious matter. It is widely associated with suicide. Older Americans are disproportionately likely to suicide. White non-Hispanic men over 85 pose an unusually high risk for self-destruction.[28] This phenomenon is under-recognized and under-treated. Disturbingly, some health professionals and even some seniors themselves mistakenly believe that persistent depression is a "normal" way to live, because of the serious illnesses and financial hardships that often accompany aging in our society. Many older adults who die by suicide have visited a physician within a month before death, yet those alarms appear to have gone unheard. As a result, it's even more pressing for those doing POP to be alert to our parents' wake-up call.

This underscores the urgency of improving your ability to detect your beloved elderly parents' mood disorders. One of your goals in being a proficient POParent is to train yourself to use your "observing eye" in service of your aging loved ones. As you become attuned to the symptoms of geriatric depression, perhaps you can help avert a family crisis. Take the time now to review your parents' reactions – over the past several weeks – and note if your parents have had any or many of these symptoms of depression:

- Changes, if any, in:

    Appetite
    Weight
    Energy
    Concentration
    Sleep
    Mood Patterns;

- Feelings of:

    Hopelessness
    Helplessness
    Lack of pleasure in things usually pleasurable (called "anhedonia").

Elderly people with severe depressive bouts are still overwhelmingly in the minority. If a number of these symptoms persist for two weeks or longer or they get worse over the weeks, your parents may be abnormally depressed. It is always worth checking out your concerns with their doctors since depressive disorder is *not* a normal part of the aging process. You will likely want to re-evaluate any geriatric professional who tells you it is.

---

[28] www.nimh.nih.gov/health.

While everyone may experience "normal" sadness, grief, feelings of loss and an occasional "blue" mood, persistent depression is different and it is not normal.   And although your parents may be very sad if and when their partners and long-standing friends die, generally speaking as we mature, people in this country and abroad often feel more secure and content. Those who lived into their 80s and 90s reported that their emotional happiness increased as they aged.

In general, despite the high valuation we place on youthfulness, older Americans report being happier with their lives than younger people. A sample of 28,000 of our seniors, from aged 18 to 88, interviewed from 1972 to 2004, revealed the happiest sector of Americans are the oldest![29] Research presented at the 117th Annual Convention of the American Psychological Association showed people actually become happier as they age, experiencing more emotional control over their lives.[30]

A big part of POP involves your becoming watchful of your parents in a different way than you've ever been before. That may look like your doing "watchful" things – examining their home, papers and refrigerators in ways that might have seemed like an imposition on their privacy when they were younger. You might keep track of the contents of their medicine chests for information about undisclosed diseases and a better understanding of how much and which medicines they're actually taking. You may even wish to do some POP research by going online to read up on their prescription drugs and their side effects.

When you chose your POParental role, your "watchfulness" may have begun to take a more subtle form as well. The next time you're around a caring parent with their very young child, follow the parent's eyes as they track the eyes, the smile and any change in the facial movements of their baby. Similarly, as you watch a caring POParent mopping the brow of a Dad whose forgotten his or her name, it is likely the POParent's eyes will also be tracking her father's eyes, his smile and any changes in his facial movements.

If you're going to do POP well, you may also need to supplement your own eyes and those of other family members with professional help, full-time or part-time. If so, your TEAM POP will need to address these questions now and again over time.

- **What do our Mom and Dad require help doing now?**

- **How many days or hours/week do they need this help?**

---

[29] Yang, Yang. Social Inequalities in Happiness in the United States, 1972 to 2004: An Age-Period-Cohort Analysis. American Sociological Review, Volume 73, Number 2, April 2008, pp. 204-226(23)

[30] http://selfawareness.suite101.com/article.cfm/older_adults_enjoy_happier_lives_research#ixzz0uBZLWGRv.

- When do we need to start to give them that help?

- How much will that cost and how are we/they going to afford it?

- If there isn't enough money, how else can we use our talent and resources to get them the help they require?

In order to oversee these various POP tasks and your parents' aides, you or someone in your family will soon be learning the "in's" and "out's" of these systems: Medicare; Medicaid[31]; long-term care insurance; pensions from employment; geriatric dosages of medication; home health care workers and more. I placed these terms into the glossary and provided you updated resources, links and blogs at www.ParentingOurParents.org so you can further explore what you will need for your folks. Online governmental resources also make it easier today for POParents to become conversant with terms like: eligibility guidelines, waiting periods, deductibles and waivers. Your designated family member can apply for many programs online[32] and get much helpful information directly from the providers of the services.

You will want to be creating a TEAM POP contact list. Over-include on your list so that you have as many people as possible. Make sure you get the cell phone numbers and email addresses for your parents' neighbors and close friends for the TEAM POP contact list you're developing. You may be pleasantly surprised at the kindness of neighbors who've lived across the hall from your Mom and Dad for the last twenty years. They can sometimes add extraordinary eyes and ears where you can't be. Remember to keep your contact list updated with changes and to send the updated lists to everyone.

But no matter how many people you hire or who they are, YOU are still the one leading POP. As such, you need to remain watchful as things change and they will change, of that you can be certain. If your parents have a good geriatric care manager (GCM), you may only need to be in regular and ongoing contact with one centralized source of information. Even if they have a GCM, you may be the type of POParent who wishes to have more direct and/or written protocols with your parents' caregivers and others to better monitor any changes. You may watch as carefully as you can but be aware that sometimes things change quickly in little ways that end up changing everything.

---

[31] See Glossary.

[32] Even applying for Social Security and making benefit payments by direct depositing can be arranged online.

POPlan #6: How To Avoid Risking Your Own Health While Doing POP

I have designed the POP quiz below to help you assess the extent to which caring for your parents and your other responsibilities may be affecting your own wellbeing. The quiz will help you see how your POP life is wearing on you. Thereafter you can figure out how best to "beat" the stressors before they beat you. The most important part of your taking the quiz is to educate you and your family so you can prevent risks to your own health while POParenting. I recommend that you and the others in your core POP group fill out your answers and share them with each other.

Your answers will reveal what in your whole POP picture is adding most to your stress and where your relief could come from. Are there "out-of-the box" solutions that will require you to sacrifice your important POP goals? For example, if you're traveling more than 30 minutes one way to do a particular POP task and that's wearing you down, maybe you could find a closer but equally good solution?

Doing this POP quiz will inform you whether you could reorganize your POP visits to avoid rush hour thus reducing your time on the road and unnecessary strain. It may suggest to you that biking over to see your Dad could be faster and healthier for you than driving your car during rush hour. It may help you see the benefits of moving your parents closer to the primary person doing POP.

The goal is not to set yourself up to complain about your POP woes, get annoyed at your siblings' insensitivity or acknowledge how much you've sacrificed. The therapist in me agrees that we all need a few minutes of moaning and groaning now and again but the purpose of doing this POP quiz is practical.

I want you to have some hard data on how much POP you're providing and how that is affecting you. For example, using this quiz may help you see that you have been unconsciously resenting unequal work distribution. This is often a recurring complaint among siblings doing POP. Rather than let that festering feeling grow, this quiz will invite you to figure out how to equalize some of your POP burdens without blame or finger pointing. Knowing these answers will allow you and your family to get on better with each other and to accomplish your POP jobs with more enthusiasm, energy, group synergy and satisfaction.

POP Quiz

A. How many people are you POParenting? What is their relationship to you and to each other and how long have you been doing POP?

B. How disabled are your parents, physically, cognitively and mentally?   How long have they been at this stage of their POPcycle?

C. How many hours per week are you doing POP and what is the nature of your POP jobs? (Your answer might be: "I do it all and my Mom lives in my house. It's 24/7," or "I'm the one responsible for the bills and record-keeping and that takes me three hours per month plus one hour for their bank reconciliation.")

D. Who else helps with your POParenting and what do they do in terms of the nature of their jobs and number of hours/week? Who supervises your parents' help – family and professional caregivers, lawyers, accountants and doctors? Are you and your POP family satisfied with the current help you're receiving from these people?

E. How old are you? Are you employed? Do you have a spouse who is healthy? Is he or she employed? Do you have children still at home?

F. What is the state of your current health, money, energy and satisfaction and how has any of that changed since you started doing POP?

G. How has doing POP affected your ability to work at your employment, including your attendance, time and focus there?

H. How had doing POP affected your involvements with your family and friends?

I. How has doing POP altered your interest and ability to do other things you value and planned to do before POP?

J. How far from your parents do you need to travel to do POP or do they live with you? Is this arrangement working for all concerned? If not, what sorts of changes would you, your parents and those in your household like to see? Are those desired changes consistent with each other and if not, what resolution do you wish to see?

K. How would you describe the nature of your emotional relationship with your aging parents recently? How is that different from the past? Do you feel acknowledged and appreciated by your parents for POP?

L. How would you describe the nature or your emotional relationship with your siblings since starting Pop? How is that different from the past? Has your relationship with any of your siblings improved since POP began? Do you feel acknowledged and appreciated by your siblings for your POP work?

M. What else do you think is needed, wanted or missing as you're doing POP now? How can you improve things in your current POPlan by adding or removing things?

N. What do you believe makes your POP job the most satisfying? Who is supporting you through the POPcycle – a partner, support group, your religion or spiritual practice, a child, neighbor or friend? Are they sometimes resentful, envious or thankful of the time you spend doing POP?

O. What do you believe makes your POP job the most difficult? Are your parents still resistant to being parented? Do you need more physical help or more time for yourself? What changes, if any, in how you POParent would afford you more time?

P. What sorts of backup do you have and how often do you actually use your respite care to refresh yourself? When was the last time you took a day off from POP? What does that mean to you?

Q. Might you be getting depressed? How are you currently sleeping? Do you get physical exercise regularly? When did you last see your physician? What emotional feelings have you been having recently? Do you find yourself generally anxious without a specific reason? Are you sad and tired, not enjoying those things you used to enjoy?

R. Is POParenting causing you financial strain? What alternatives can you find in care, housing, benefits from the Veterans' Administration or other programs to lower your costs and stress? Is there someone who could help you find more?

S. What do you believe you need to do POP better that you may be missing? If you had a magic wand, what about POP would you make different?

T. What about POParenting gives you the greatest joy? How can you attract more of that?

Chapter 7

Discovering Our Parents May
Need To Leave Home

My Story

Jack and Lillian were "home alone" each weekend for several years. From Fridays night after Florence left, having given them their dinners and medications, until Monday morning when she'd arrive in time to make them breakfast. My parents were insistent that they would not accept a second caregiver after Florence left for the weekend. Even though I never supported this part of the POPlan – and it was the one real "hole" – I'd gone along to keep the peace.

Back at home, I was hardly peaceful. More accurately I walked around on egg-shells every weekend during those years, worrying about them alone for all that time and waiting for my phone to ring. Although I wanted to, I knew I couldn't call every hour. A few times I actually chuckled, thinking this was my "payback;" as a teenager, I'd poo-poo'd my parents' demands to let them know I'd arrived somewhere safely. Now it was I who wanted them to call and check in. How ironic POP was turning out to be! But I had laughed and during POP laughter is almost always a real gift!

When I'd walked into the middle of the crisis that first Christmas, I had been required to respond immediately and with an infusion of massive help. In addition to the obvious need for a clean-up crew, the GCM introduced me to a number of qualified professional caregivers who could be available for 8-hour or 12-hour shifts. The GCM's suggestion had been to assign Dad a primary daytime person, Florence, and then use others to "cover" the remaining hours she would be gone.

The GCM talked of wanting to "train" my parents to accept that they needed regular caregiving help even after they'd recovered from being sick. The GCM further argued we would need separate, additional full-time staffing for my Mom after she returned from the hospital. How much would all this cost? Would each of my parents need a full-time individual attendant and, if so, why? I couldn't even figure out where all these people would stand in my parents' relatively small apartment?

On a more philosophical level I also recognized that no matter how many caregivers I supplied my parents, I could never truly keep them "safe" forever. And what was "safe?" I saw that doing POP would have to involve my "re"-discovering the right balance any good parent aims to find: enough assistance and attention to provide safety and enough "freedom" to promote their doing what they can for themselves.

Supporting as much self-reliance as was appropriate seemed to encourage my parents to do more for themselves. It also supplied a subtle but positive message that they still had much living left to do. This approach appropriately challenged my parents and seemed to be as helpful for POParenting as it had been for parenting my stepchildren when they were young. But it did require me to stay continually alert in order to achieve that right balance.

I would also need to discover how much caregiving assistance was right for them. Even before the thorough housecleaning was accomplished, I could see that my parents would require ongoing assistance. At the least, they'd need someone to keep their apartment clean and help them with their laundry, marketing and meals. I intuitively sensed that too much help might be worse for my parents than not having enough but knew I didn't want them to be at either end of that continuum.

Upon Mom's return from the hospital, the GCM again expressed strongly her view that Lillian needed her own set of caregivers and needed them 24/7. Frankly I was concerned. Having that much help in my folks' home felt wrong for a series of reasons. My immediate reaction was that it felt like far too many eyes on my folks and they would hate that. They lived in a 2-bedroom apartment with a modest amount of space. They'd feel overly watched with two caregivers there all day and every night, I suspected.

But I deferred to the GCM's superior experience. For once, I didn't listen to me. My private parents never liked much "oversight" and as a few days went by, I could feel them bridling under the rapt attention of ever-present caregivers. Hell, for years my Mom hadn't even let in the guys she knew from the building to plaster the damaged ceilings.

Noting their current medical conditions and ages, I easily saw they'd need more help as time went by, so from a financial as well as other perspectives, I needed to find a level of help that we could maintain. If I spent what they'd set aside for their future care too quickly, we'd encounter a problem in the long run. Since I couldn't estimate how long a future we needed to plan for, that always made for complicated monetary planning.

My parents were receiving Social Security and Medicare, the two entitlement programs all U. S. seniors are eligible to receive. But because of those programs' limitations in terms of health and long-term home care benefits, they also had to supplement the benefits they received from the government with additional coverage from private insurance companies. One covered them for the infamous Medicare "donut hole" lapse in medication coverage[33].

Fortunately for everyone concerned, Dad had purchased a Long-Term Care (LTC) insurance policy for himself and Mom before they got into their 80's. If they'd purchased these policies earlier, when they'd been younger, their premiums would have been lower. Nonetheless having their LTC benefits helped out a lot and doing POP led me to sign up for my own LTC policy. As soon as I saw how it helped my parents and made other POP choices more affordable for our family, I became an advocate. When I applied for my LTC policy, I was still young and took care to get the right policy for my predictable needs.

One "wrinkle" was that their LTC policy had a waiting period of 90 days after their claims were filed and their eligibility verified. During that waiting period, no benefits "kicked into" place and my family had to pay out-of-pocket for all their help – domestic, GCM, caregiver, whatever wasn't covered by Medicare.

After my parents' LTC benefits commenced, we encountered another series of restrictions under their particular policy. First, their insurance company wouldn't pay

---

[33] This is set to be fixed under ObamaCare.

for more than one caregiver.   Second, Dad had mistakenly signed up for a policy that required him to continue making payments even after he and Mom were deemed sufficiently disabled to receive benefits. Third, Florence wasn't on the insurer's listing of accepted employees, known as their "registry." Only registry caregivers could receive payment under their LTC policy. And probably most troubling, the hourly fee paid registry caregivers was less per hour than what we'd been paying Florence through the GCM.

Once I understood the contractual limitations of my parents' policy, I was left with several decisions. Should I continue paying for multiple caregivers with our funds or go along with the terms of their policy that afforded them only one caregiver? If I paid privately for two caregivers, clearly the funds we'd have for my parents' care would run out far more quickly.   I decided to ask my parents' opinions.

Like many others who'd grown up or lived through the Great Depression of 1929, they lived with the fear that their money would run out. They voted for one caregiver and that the person be Florence. Even before I'd asked, they'd complained that having people watch them sleep was an unnecessary waste. My Mom particularly didn't like people "underfoot," as she called it and neither of them felt two people were necessary for their level of limitations. I found myself agreeing with their reasoning on this.

I'd hired the GCM to be my onsite "eyes and ears" and we talked at length. The GCM was so unrelenting that I retain two caregivers 24/7 that she threatened to resign if I didn't follow her counsel. I felt really confused by the intensity of the GCM's reaction and was unnerved she would talk of abandoning my parents over this decision.

That left me with a difficult quandary. I wanted sufficient attention for my parents but not excessive help that might actually weaken my Mom and Dad. I didn't want to run out of money for their care but didn't want to deprive them of what they needed because of funds. I appreciated the GCM's "high standards" for care if that was what she was arguing for. Maybe my folks and I were wrong. Perhaps they were so disabled that they needed that level of care? The last thing I wanted was to provide them insufficient caregiving attention.

And I felt particularly vulnerable: were there no GCM on the core team, I wasn't sure how well we'd do with our long distance POPlan. Who would do the GCM's bi-weekly oversight visits?   Since Mom and Dad seemed to be doing so well, I'd been feeling a bit more confident with my parents living so far away. Would I be putting their recoveries in jeopardy were I to cut back their caregiving to a single person, as was covered by their LTC insurance?

To my part, I didn't find it supportive to have our GCM threaten to "cut my parents lose," if we didn't chose her decisions. Where could I go for other "reliable" points of view? I talked with my geriatric mentor, psychiatrist Michael McGrail, who urged me to not "overstaff" my parents, given his experience with their personalities and his professional insights. I contacted my parents' long-standing doctors and even some of the people from their building to get an idea of what they were currently observing about my parents.

Finally I listened to myself. I got rid of the double caregiving, let the GCM fire herself and narrowed their "staff" down to one. That decision left me with my next set of challenges. Should I work with the insurance company to get Florence on their registry or start all over with one of the company's cheaper caregivers? If I were able to get Florence on to the insurer's registry, could I ask her to work for less money per hour than we'd originally agreed? And were I able to get Florence on their registry in order to keep her working with my folks, could we afford to make up the difference between the insurer's hourly wages and the original hourly she was being paid through the GCM?

I saw how valuable Florence was and how well she worked with both my parents. They greatly encouraged me to find a way Florence could stay on with them. I got into "POP mode" and started negotiating with the LTC insurance company in order to get Florence on to their registry. When Florence agreed to do my parents' housecleaning and laundry, I was also able to cut back on the cleaning lady. By this point, we also weren't paying for the GCM. These changes left us in a budgetary position where I felt more comfortable supplementing Florence's registry hourly rate, which turned out to be a fine resolution for all concerned.

But like so many seemingly easy developments, little was easy when I was parenting my parents. Now I discovered there was one small wrinkle in this new "Florence only" POPlan. Lillian and Jack had drawn a line in the sand: nobody watches over us on the weekends. We like Florence and that's okay but "we need our privacy" too. When she was there from Mondays through Fridays, Florence now became my long distance "eyes and ears" but after she left ... they were still HOME ALONE every weekend!

My parents were adults and they lived 3000 miles away. So it appeared I had little choice, once they resisted my strong suggestions to have help for them on the weekends. What could I to do if they refused? It wasn't like I could demand they take a time out or ground them. But, were they hurt then due to any lack of attention, I would feel terrible and I would feel responsible. I would never have dreamed of trying to parent children long distance but here I was with all the feelings of being a parent and nothing I could see to do to rectify this out-of-control situation.

As an interim solution I added "extra" trips to visit them to the POPlan. I reasoned that, by increasing the frequency of seeing my parents in New York, I would provide them more direct attention and could also spend more of their "sunset" time with them. In one two-month interval I "transported" my body across our wide country eight times and it was exhausting me. I wasn't that young myself and I'd postponed some badly needed foot surgery. I couldn't imagine having my procedure and then walking around on crutches in the midst of my parents' "situation." Instead I hobbled up and down the corridors of hospitals and airport terminals that seemed to grow increasingly long, ignoring my own medical needs.

Looking back to that time I can see that once I'd taken on POP, I wasn't clear how to stay true to that commitment while also giving myself permission to take care of me. In my office I had seen too many POParents continue down this "sacrificial" path I seemed to have found myself following. I even taught stress management seminars so I knew for sure that, if I didn't attend to myself, eventually I'd not be able to properly care for my Mom and Dad. I would have to practice what I'd been preaching and walk the walk.

Then one day I got another phone call from Florence. When she'd taken my parents to their doctor visits, they'd instructed her to have me call as soon as possible. The bottom line was this and Florence as well as the doctors were in agreement: no help on nights and weekends was exhausting Jack and insufficient oversight for Lillian.

With that phone call I saw that things were about to change again. In that moment it was clear they really might be leaving New York. My wish to end long distance POParenting might now be granted. I aimed to realistically appraise the whole situation I told myself: "Breathe! Breathe deeply enough to have sufficient oxygen go to your brain to think clearly." There was a lot to consider and more things that I didn't know.

Dad and Mom were 87 years old and might easily live many more years; I certainly hoped so. Predictably they would require increasing hours of help not fewer. Our family resources were hardly limitless and reviewing them at this juncture was important since any decision would need to be grounded in what was financially possible.

We had their LTC insurance benefits, which they were using at the maximum number of hours already, their monthly Social Security checks, occasional music royalties and the savings my parents had set aside for their latter years. Plus I had a small amount of money saved but I'd changed professions from attorney to psychotherapist. I was just starting over in mid-life to build my new practice when POP had popped into my world. Although the fear of "running out of funds" loomed and I wasn't certain how we'd work it out, I knew I'd never give up on my commitment to do POP.

Since everyone but Lillian and Jack agreed my parents needed more help, the simplest new POPlan would have to have them accept additional hours of caregiving help on weekends and nights. Such a plan afforded them continuity with their physicians, Florence, their home and beloved City. But that plan also had long-term down sides. I had to consider not only what my parents would be "willing to accept" but also whether and how we would "afford" their accelerating care needs.

Were my parents to "age in place[34]" – that is, stay in their New York home – the number of hours of care required might soon increase drastically, especially because of my Mother's diagnosis of Alzheimer's. Her illness would likely require full-time nursing care eventually. Both of my parents might require live-in aides in the future and any hours of care, beyond what Florence already provided, would all be our out-of-pocket expenses, uncovered by LTC.

My other problem with this "aging in place" POPlan was that if we continued living at this distance from each other, my capacity to share my folks' sunset years would likely decrease. I might even see them less often than I was now, with the added pressure on me to bring in more income for their escalating care.

An alternative POPlan was that they move in with me. That alternative had much downside. I was gone all day at work and my Mom and Dad would need a caregiver to help them at least during those hours I was away, if not longer hours. That might have worked out since they still had home health care benefits under their LTC policy but several other factors made that option unworkable.

For one thing, a few months prior to Florence's call, when it seemed Jack and Lillian were "forever" settled in New York, I'd purchased a house that was not well suited for doing POP. You entered the house by either climbing 47 irregular steps in the back or 38 even ones in the front. The first time Dad had gazed down at my amazing view after slowly huffing and puffing his way up those stairs, he'd said: "Terrific view! You should move!" There was nothing about the house's physical setting that would have worked well for my elderly parents. Likely they would have felt "trapped" because those daunting steps made going anywhere burdensome. The floor plan was compact and they would have had very limited privacy. There wasn't even a convenient place for a caregiver to sit down and rest.

---

[34] The Center for Disease Control defines aging in place as "the ability to live in one's own home and community safely, independently, and comfortably, regardless of age, income, or ability level." For additional information, see chapter 8.

Another reason moving in with me wasn't a good choice was because I didn't believe my parents and I would get along well living together while I was also parenting them. Many families find that when their roles become reversed doing POP, it's challenging to live together, especially when there have been decades of living far apart. I didn't think we'd operate as well under the same roof as separately after living a continent apart and observing my parents' generational "do it our own way" approach. Although we never had a formal discussion where any of us formally rejected this choice, Jack, Lillian and I shared the understanding that the place I sought for them – even in a senior residence - would be their own home. They wouldn't be uncomfortably "borrowing" mine.

A third POPlan – and the most realistic – was that my parents would move into an attractive senior facility. In such an environment they could get sufficient "Florence-like" individual attention to be comfortable and protected while living more communally and maybe socially than in their New York apartment. They would get a chance to dine with others and could become involved in various social and recreational activities with their peers.

If they lived at a facility in New York City, I would again be relegated to long distance POP. If they to going to leave their NYC apartment and have to face that loss, it would be just as easy to move them out to California as to some east coast facility. Since most of their friends and living relatives had already moved to warmer climes or to be nearer to their kids, bringing my parents to my neighborhood wouldn't deprive them of their social support as it might have earlier on.

But the biggest advantage of their coming west was that we could become more involved in each others' everyday lives! Once I formulated this "doable" POPlan, I began to "see" them living in California. Lillian would be smiling and relaxed, a shawl lightly draped over her shoulders as she basked in our year-round warmth. Jack would be holding an iced tea in one hand, a music business weekly magazine in the other.

I imagined my Dad and me at the end of my workday, talking like we'd done so long ago at the end of his. Then he'd recounted his exciting trips to the music business' Brill Building or news of another Frank Sinatra recording of one of his songs. I wondered what I'd recount to him about my day at work? In my mind's eye more California sun and glasses of iced tea floated by. I could finally stop the bi-coastal POParenting I'd never been comfortable with. This would be good, I found myself thinking.

I also was feeling proud of my ability to adapt to the needs of my parents' changing circumstances. I was congratulating myself on making good modifications to our *initial POPlan and thoughtfully moving forward. I thought this new arrangement would give us everything we wanted. They could have their "independence," a good climate and a healthy life. We could be closer, making it easier to see each other and be in each others' everyday lives again after so much time spent apart.*

It wasn't long before the next phone call came in to burst my daydream. This time it was my Dad who issued the bad news: "We're not coming. Your Mom doesn't want to move to California." That was all he said.

Their Story – Mom

I'd never thought much about death and my religion of origin didn't provide a lot of guidance about an afterlife. And whenever I had considered the end of our lives, it was almost like Jack and I would age but stay pretty healthy and eventually we'd sort of fade away in our apartment. One day we'd just be gone – off with our families in heaven. But like so many things these days, as I've gotten older, life has been turning out far differently than I ever imagined.

Since that first December when Jane started helping us out, she's been the one making more and more decisions for us. I didn't like that very much but, since I couldn't focus very well and Jack clearly wasn't himself, it seemed that would have to do. I'd long been concerned that moving to California might mean my daughter would run my life and had always been apprehensive that my family would put me in a home for the aged someday. My siblings had done that to our Mom when she had Parkinson's and Jane was just born.

When I came back home from the hospital after my horrible bout with pneumonia, I was surprised to see that the house had been cleaned from top to bottom. It was a very different place from how I'd left it. The fact that it was spotless again felt good. But by the same token now there were also strangers who seemed to have taken over my home. In the beginning these caregivers Jane had hired had been there all the time, even when we slept. She'd insisted that I have a caregiver watch over me and that Jack have one too. I'd hated having so many people in the apartment all the time under foot and watching me.

I also didn't like that these caregivers cost so much. They didn't have that much to do for Jack or me, so they sat around much of the day anyway. Jane had refused to let us be alone until I'd laid down the law and wouldn't let her get her way on that point. After a little while Jack and I were able to work it out with Jane so we could have fewer people and more privacy in our home, which was a relief. We prevailed on her: no one there late nights or weekend.

That left one person helping us, Florence, whom I liked quite a bit. She had a good sense of people and wasn't too chatty, which I enjoyed. Florence just seemed to know when I'd be okay with her helping me and when I could do things on my own. She'd been there with Jack since the first day and he was comfortable with her too. Florence had even worked for another family in our building, which I appreciated because she'd known our maintenance staff as well.

Yet despite our physical recoveries, our clean home and attentive caregiver and in spite of Jane's numerous visits, as time wore on I watched my husband get more exhausted and agitated. Those had never been his ways. I was usually the more anxious one. It was disturbing to see him become so easily upset and so often. Psychiatry had been my refuge while Jack had always been the consistent and calm one. When he needed to go see a psychiatrist for the first time in his life because he had ringing in his ears and, later on, obsessive and suicidal thoughts, I became panicked too. I feared that unless Jack straightened himself out, we might have to leave our home and move into some old aged people's home or out to California. Jane had begun presenting these alternatives but none of the options looked good to me.

Jane had been suggesting for a long time that Jack and I move out to California, her home state. It's very pretty out there and has been a lovely place for her to live and us to come visit. But I don't picture myself as a "California gal." I've never surfed and I'm not even sure I know what that involves. I've never been blonde or even particularly suntanned. I am a New Yorker and by choice. I moved here after Jack and I were married in 1941. We both harkened from Paterson New Jersey where we'd been born and raised but we'd become died-in-the-wool New Yorkers. And we New Yorkers don't particularly crave the sun all day every day and don't necessarily want to know from beaches and surfing.

I watched Jane very carefully in those early days of her caring for us. And it didn't seem that she wanted to put us anywhere we'd hate. In fact as our daughter started visiting more often and doing more things for Jack and me, I saw a different sweetness come over her. Jane was sincere in wanting to listen to us. What we wanted or didn't want mattered to her and I saw her struggling to find "the best way" to manage us and everything else she had on her plate. I eventually realized that she didn't have an agenda that involved controlling us and was trying to do the right thing. Much of her challenge was in figuring out how to protect Jack and me but still let us do things "our way," reprising Sinatra.

But I definitely didn't like what I was now being told. Our doctors had said it was "unmanageable" and "unacceptable" for Jack and me to stay in our home in New York without more caregiver help. Probably it would be best to move closer to Jane but I didn't like anything about what I was hearing. It was just too late in life to turn into a California girl. I wasn't going, so there.

Your Story

The only predictable part about POP is continuous, unpredictable change. Make a plan and see. You'll need to get comfortable with change! If you want to thrive doing POP – or even survive it – you'll have to keep up with at least two abilities: a) discovering the changes to your parents' conditions or their environment and b) responding quickly and wisely.

No one wants to learn that the existing POPlan, the one you worked so hard to make viable in all its details and everyone likes, needs "tweaking" or worse yet, total reconstruction. Your POP experience will benefit if and when you develop a more "objective" set of eyes and ears to detect changes in your parents' health and home, even if you're hesitant to see it. You *can* train yourself to become more "scientific" in order to view more analytically any alterations in your parents' environments, physical bodies and cognitive states.

If you're living at a distance, to some extent you'll need to rely on others to discover incremental changes, people who see your parents more regularly than you do. A professional caregiver, a doctor, a surrogate daughter, GCM and/or even a good neighbor will often be that person. You will want to keep those in your core POP group apprised of everyone's contact information and schedule regular communications with them. Today's technology allows this to occur with ease as you can copy family members on emails, reports, texts or even Skype up the core POP group for a quick video conference call when needed.

Because of visits and/or your talking with those physically close to your parents, you will have updated, objective and accurate information. Use it. You'll still need to regularly re-examine your current POPlan. Is it still viable today? Avoid the temptation to fix what's working well but be willing to expand your ideas and fix what isn't working. Does your plan allow for your responding in a timely manner to observable shifts in your parents' circumstances? Are you "guilt-tripping" yourself into promising something more than you can give or are willing to follow through on?

To know the difference, look at your current plan from both sides of the POP equation. From your aging parents' perspective – does the current POPlan provide me an optimal balance between "self-sufficiency" and "safety?" What, if anything, do I not like or find objectionable about the current arrangement. How might this situation be improved for my greater comfort or enjoyment? From you, the POParental perspective – does the current POPlan take more out of you than you're comfortable giving – in terms of lost income, time with young grandchildren or whatever else you value? What did you plan to spend your retirement resources on before POP happened? Does the arrangement give you the optimal balance between sufficiently protecting your parents from harm and your ability to "have a life?" What if anything do you not like about your current arrangement and how could it be improved for you?

If you want to do better than survive during your middle stages of POP, you will want to maximize some of your personal qualities that have shown themselves critical for your successes parenting and POParenting so far. At the least, you've needed your flexibility, your resiliency and your ability to laugh at "the small stuff" in life. Now you can work to make these traits even more available to you as a POParent. You will find that focusing your intention and your attention on responding less automatically and allowing patience and "out of the box" thinking will add to your flexibility.

A powerful tool to do all of that and more is something I call "under-reacting." By teaching yourself to respond less automatically and less intensely, you will have learned a technique you can use over and again during challenges in your POPcycle, when parenting your kids and with your boss. You can "under-react" to disappointments and unplanned-for events. After all, these happen all the time and practicing your "under-reacting" will contribute to your resilience. By under-reacting, you'll be able to lighten up and find humor in the midst of these challenges. When you and your parents can laugh more, everyone around has you more enjoyment.

You're right if you've decided that many things are out of your control during POP. You probably spent a lot of time and effort making a good POPlan. Perhaps it was a great plan. But if your Mom or Dad refuses to go along with it, what are your choices? If they refuse to see your point of view, it's never a great POPlan. Even if what you want to achieve is in your parents' best interest, how will you be able to impose if they disagree or are at a distance?

Here as in so many POPcycle challenges, the ideal POPlan for one family won't necessarily be yours: one size does not fit all. You will need to listen to your parents' wishes as best you can and perhaps make some compromises you're apprehensive will work. In some of your POP decisions, you may even need to do what POParents (and all parents sometimes do) – that is, take some protective action you believe is right when it's contradictory to their expressed desires. You've seen that I had to do that. Ultimately you too may need to choose for them, especially if your parents are gravely incapacitated or otherwise not able to think clearly.

POParenting is neither for the faint-hearted nor for the easily discouraged. It's tricky because unlike when they parented you, you can't "insist" that your charges eat their vegetables or turn off the TV. But don't underestimate your powers of persuasion. Having chosen to be POP responsible, those powers to "convince" your parents may include the rightness of your position, limited finances and, of course, your excellent reasoning. Or maybe it's really your love and concern that finally convinces your parents to follow your well-reasoned POPlan.

POPlan #7: How To Make Your Parents' Moving A Win-Win: Letting Their "New Life" Unfold Safer And Even Better

How do you use your powers of persuasion to get your parents to "buy in" to some of the big and smaller parts of your POParenting?

For example: You think your parents will live a healthier and longer life if they eat more nutritionally. Their doctors agree. You go out and get specific suggestions to benefit their needs, learning that eating more low salt foods will improve some current medical issues. You research the possibilities and determine the best plan for them is the "easy-to-prepare and clean up," no shopping, low salt options that can be delivered to their home through Meals on Wheels. So you order it, pay for it, have it delivered to them and inform them that your new POP approach to their eating is on its way. You have a great plan.

One problem: when you call their next-door neighbor, whom you've enrolled to "check on them" every few days, she tells you there are about 30 packages of uneaten Meals on Wheels in their street garbage, right next to the empty boxes of pizza. The problem? No one had included your parents, the "lucky" recipients, in formulating the plan. In business schools, professors speak of the effectiveness of a program as being related to the consumer or employee's "buying in" to it. Without your parents' "buy in," POP management can't easily impose its wishes "from above."

Instead, after your research is done, try giving your parents a clear and intelligent explanation of what the Meals on Wheels program is all about and how it will help them. If you want their "buy in," use a loud enough voice for them to hear, allow time to answer their questions and patiently provide examples of how they will actually benefit. Try to have some good responses, perhaps your plan serves up some special cuisine they like.

To be most useful, you'll want to have the answers your parents are likely to ask: when does the food arrive? Where will it be stored? What if it goes bad? How will the program know to send us low salt food? What if we don't like some of the food? Your parents may be repeating themselves a lot or having difficulty understanding new things you present to them. If you can explain this new POPlan to them clearly, your parents will appreciate your patience as well as your cleverness in accessing a good idea. Emphasizing your parents' ease in Meals on Wheels' program with its "no fuss, no muss" approach may be more impactful than extolling the benefits of a "low salt diet."

Since your goal is to encourage your parents to choose the eating plan that's most healthy, obviously if you can get your parents to agree, they will likely comply more fully with your proposed POPlans. However if you can present helpful data in a tolerant and interesting fashion, you can also teach your parents nutritional facts they might like to know. When your parents were growing up, "meat and potatoes" was an American way of life. Some of what we now call "healthy eating" may never have been a part of their life-style or lexicon.

You can take this as your opportunity to share things you believe your parents would benefit from knowing. Go online and read a little bit about hypertension and salt. Discover some compelling point that might catch their attention. For example, one ounce of salt in their bodies requires three quarts of water to hold it in its solution or how their hearts may be damaged by excess salt. They are unlikely to know that pepperoni pizza is very high in salt and can contribute to their hypertension and bloating. You may find your parents are far more interested in complying with "your plan" to limit their salt intake if they can see it will help them feel better and lose some unwanted weight,

Use your enthusiasm and your other positive feelings towards your folks when you try to convince them to try your POP suggestions. Remember when your children didn't want to eat certain foods, and you said: "TRY IT! YOU'LL LIKE IT!" After they've become willing to encompass your "good ideas," listen to your parents' reactions respectfully and see how you can accommodate or incorporate them. Maybe once a week, a small pizza would be okay? For some of your parents it may be a relief, even a joy to have you making their decisions. As you continue to do POP successfully, your parents' confidence in your choices will grow and their willingness to follow your POPlans is bound to increase.

Nonetheless your parents may continue resisting. They may tell you how much they "really enjoyed" their healthy food but you know from the neighbor that they've still been chowing down on pepperoni pizza. Do you confront the situation, cancel the Meals on Wheels or wait until you get the call from their doctor, reporting digestive problems? Your powers of POP enforcement are often limited. However your most successful POPlans will be those where you've taken the steps so that your parents see the wisdom and "buy in" to the plan. As your parents and you advance from the middle stages of POP towards the latter ones, they will have fewer powers to resist your POPlans.

Chapter 8

Finding The Best Fit For Our Parents' New Home

My Story

In spite of the apparently unconditional nature of Dad's announcement, I knew that eventually I would bring my parents to California. It was the only responsible way for me to continue doing POP. I found I had an unusual sense of clarity, confidence and determination in that moment.

My initial task was calming my Mom down. I knew that when she was calmer, she would agree with what had become apparent to me, Florence, their doctors and I presumed, to my Dad as well. POParental rationality would need to take precedence over my parents' fears, concerns or any other "good" excuses they might ante up to avoid leaving home.

I was fueled by the unanimity of opinion that moving near me was their wisest option – unanimous that is, aside from Mom's veto and Dad's apparent acceptance of her choice. I aimed to hold on to that feeling of competency and confidence. That was especially important since I would somehow have to "override" my parents' decision. Had I not previously confronted my Dad at his door as I stepped up for POParenting, I might have been more reticent to challenge my parents or more concerned about their reactions. Perhaps I would have even backed down.

I knew that I must not personalize any aggressive or hostile-sounding remarks I might hear when I'm "forcing" people to do what they don't want to do. And the truth Jack and Lillian didn't want to accept was that they needed more help than Florence could offer.

All things considered, that meant they would need to come live in California. The move wasn't only for my Mom. I'd also seen my Dad decline, getting weaker psychologically as well as physically because of the stress of caring for and gradually "losing" my fading Mom.

Lillian and I would talk many times before she was finally convinced. I knew I'd need to allow her to express herself as best she could for as long as she needed. My mother shared her fears about moving and how it evoked her long history of loss and abandonment. She told me of her concern that moving to California would alter her relationship with my Dad and with me. I tried to reassure her that those changes could be wonderful, better than she could imagine and I meant it. When she saw I was listening to her and, thankfully, she was cogent enough to get my message, she softened.

In spite of my own lingering hesitations, I reassured myself that their moving closer to me was the most intelligent, prudent and loving POPlan for all concerned. All right! I'd just pack up their remaining stuff and we'd be on our way. Done with partial caregiver coverage and done with long-distance POParenting! At last!!

As we all settled into the idea of the move becoming reality, I noticed an old twinkle return to my Dad's eye. I hadn't seen it there for far too long. Jack was excited. He was relieved to be leaving the apartment and his heavy responsibilities in New York City. He looked forward to living closer to me after all these years and to my sharing his burden. In fact my Dad looked lighter and younger than I'd seen him in years. I thought I heard him whistling a tune that sounded like "California, Here I Come ..."[35]

---

[35] From the 1924 release of Buddy DeSylva and Joseph Meyer's song, written for the 1921 Broadway musical "Bombo," starring Al Jolson and published by Brunswick Music.

If my parents had lived closer, I'd have first gone to scope out a bunch of places, narrowed my favorites to the top three or so and produced a "short list" for us to visit together. But since I wanted everything to be ready when they got off the long plane ride from New York, I had to make all the choices without any input from them. I had to figure out where they might like to live and that was not necessarily where I might have chosen, were I choosing for me.

My goal was to find a facility where Lillian and Jack would "do best" – feel at home, remain content and maybe peaceably pass away some time in the future. Their level of care already mandated some caregiving so the purely Independent Living (IL) model for seniors was too unstructured for them. Nor did my folks yet require the more serious medical care available in a skilled nursing facility (SNF) where people need nurses.

So my search became focused on finding them either an intimate, pretty home-like setting where they would get some personal attention – a six-bed board and care facility (B & C) or an assisted living facility (AL), a larger structure where everyone lived inside their own apartments, as they had in New York, and shared meals and activities.

Which type of setting would my parents fare better in – a small facility, a six-bed B & C or a more populous and private AL? In a B & C, they would live in a quaint California converted home. Each resident had a separate room but all shared meals, facilities like a lovely garden and a reading room and much of their time together every day. Everything about a B & C, including the number of staff, residents and size of the facility would be smaller.

An AL sounded like what my Mom and Dad had known and loved in New York. I liked that "ring of familiarity." But I wondered if they might not prefer a more traditional California bungalow-type setting? Maybe they would enjoy living in a small B & C facility with just 6 bedrooms where they could walk out on the grass and read in the garden outside on a warm winter's day.

Either way I had to imagine that I knew my parents' current tastes and preferences in location, type of residence, décor and furnishings. Eventually I chose their residence, most of their furniture and furnishings as well. I bought many things to make it "homey" for them when they landed at their new place since hauling a lot of their heavy items cross-country didn't prove a great idea. In a way, my "nesting process" before their arrival was another symbol of our role reversal – my doing for them the equivalent of what they'd done for me when they'd first brought me home, their newborn baby girl, all those years ago.

To narrow my search for the most suitable facility for my folks I found help in the form of a geriatric placement agency[36]. Happily using their services didn't cost our family anything. Senior residences pay these firms who function much like employment firms, offering interested families a menu of prospective residential choices. I chose this particular firm based upon recommendations I'd received and upon my intuitive sense of the woman who ran the company. I liked her questions, the way she posed them and her professionalism. Like earlier on in the POPcycle when we'd needed a GCM, now it was the placement person who needed to understand a lot of background information concisely expressed to best counsel our family.

When the placement woman and I spoke, she reminded me of several significant criteria in settling aging parents into suitable facilities. Later, when I had to re-settle each of my parents, I'd return to speak with her and I'd be reminded of the validity of her basic points. One key was to locate my parents near enough to my home and/or work so I would visit them frequently. Another key was having good and caring staffing, if possible of long-standing.

Regarding proximity, I was well advised to be realistic. Longer distances do discourage even the most diligent and loving of POPParents from visiting as often as they might like. When seeing my parents added a lot of drive time to my schedule at the end of a particularly challenging workday, I might end up not going. Moreover if they lived close by me, visiting would be far more accessible. Not only could I be more casual and spontaneous but dropping in on my parents unexpectedly could prove useful. If some of my visits to my parents were "unplanned," I might obtain a more accurate view of how they "really" were or how the facility actually attended to them.

Many other factors came into the mix. I tried to put myself into the heads of my parents. What did Mom and Dad like to do? Who did they wish to get to know? How did they spend their time? What would Jack most enjoy in a new home? My Dad had become far more introverted than my memory of him when we were both so much younger. What did he like? Unless I turned the radio or stereo on, he rarely listened to music in New York. Maybe he just enjoyed the quiet? My Dad read a lot and watched his TV shows. Jeopardy and The Tonight Show were his favorites. He ate, did some stretching at home, meditated and talked to my Mom and to me. That's basically what I'd seen when I'd visited in New York and I expected he'd be similarly quiet once he'd settled into the west coast lifestyle.

Lillian was far more outgoing. She had previously enjoyed crossword puzzles, listening to music, taking drives through Central Park and watching plays. Still

---

[36] See Glossary.

beautiful at age 87, she could be gracious and friendly with others. Much of the time she still appeared engaged and very affable. But she could become hostile, haughty and demanding, aggressive and unreasonable – sometimes without any apparent triggering events. I suspected Mom's discovering that her mind was increasingly beyond her control resulted in much of her frustration and bad behavior. Although I sympathized with her pain, her condition made it challenging to predict which type of senior facility might be best.

During our New York POP years I'd witnessed my Mom's volatile temper manifested in pinching, punching, bullying demeaning and scratching my Dad and threatening to jump from her 14th story bedroom window. It was painful to watch. Dad had become frailer and never acted aggressively with her. On a few occasions when Mom's disorders would overcome her, I had to intervene between my parents. As the emerging disciplinarian it was now becoming my job to set the limits of my parents' acceptable conduct. That felt like role reversal gone wild.

So far most of Mom's aggressiveness had been directed at Dad but I wondered if she might act out with others in her new place, particularly when the dementia would further take her over. Telling the placement professional this history was important so we could find a facility that would most suit all my parents' needs, emotional, physical and mental.

I had concerns about placing them in a smaller B & C facility with my Mom's history of being a difficult patient. I'd seen her "blow through" a series of hard-core veterans caregivers in those early 24/7 care days in New York. I questioned how soon her fellow residents and the small number of caregivers in any B & C might become a problem for Lillian? I kept returning to the notion that such an intimate setting as six beds could provide too many opportunities for Mom to become upset and/or to upset others.

With this in mind, I turned my sights to locating a serene, nice-looking larger AL facility. With the list of ten in hand that my placement professional had given me, I drove from one to the next, checking out all of them. None proved quite right for Lillian and Jack. Nonetheless, while visiting one on my list, someone there recommended an eleventh place that I liked immediately.

This AL seemed to offer the right blend of serenity and activity, was geographically "pretty good" and, I would soon discover, it had the additional element I sought: a caring and long-time staff. I respected the people I talked with who worked there and liked their attitude towards "their" people. The staff I met seemed genuinely interested in expanding the quality of life, not just babysitting the residents.

The more I heard about this independently owned and operated AL, the better it sounded. Mom and Dad would be provided much on-site in terms of exercise, recreation, holiday celebrations and even health monitoring. A van took interested residents daily to the local mall for shopping, banking, and sundry errands. I even saw other transplanted New Yorkers whom I imagined might become friends with my parents.

To do my due diligence, I visited the facility a number of times. I went at different times of day. I tasted the food, smelled around a lot and asked a lot of questions. I wandered about, talked to the residents, their families and to more of the staff. I questioned people I knew in the community about the facility. It all sounded quite fine.

Although I went about the tasks methodically and as unemotionally as I could, I mistakenly thought I'd become inured to the sadness and other emotions that got stirred up while I looked for a place for my own parents. This was how they would end up" living their final days... I guess I'd convinced myself that my clarity about the decision to move them to California and my extensive professional background would "simplify" my feelings.

I soon found that choosing a residence for my own parents was very different from visiting similar facilities for my patients. Even walking into the first senior residence felt emotionally wrenching for me as I contemplated what it meant to be "institutionalizing" my own Mom and Dad. I plagued myself with unanswerable questions about where I would end up? What would it be like, when my turn came?

POP provided me the chance to ask myself questions about how I wanted to age. There was longevity in my family on both sides. I began to recount the list of my aunts and uncles who lived into their 90's. Even my maternal Grandmother with Parkinson's had lived until 78 and that was over fifty years ago! My relatives had been healthy people with little obvious dementia and few physical disturbances. I could see that being ill while old could deplete me of much of the joy of being alive. Looking down the road ahead, I re-committed to my own healthy living.

It would be a good life for them, I assured myself. I made the decision and filled out the application on their behalf. Before I could sign the paperwork and seal the deal, I needed them to be accepted by the AL. I understood that different facilities had varying requirements and was relieved and thankful when they told me my parents met theirs.

The apartment I chose for them had a small balcony where Mom and Dad could sit on comfortable patio chairs with blankets and gaze over the magnificent oak trees. Or so I envisioned. Next, I went around town furnishing their new home right down to purchasing their favorite toothpaste and bedside books. I so wanted it to feel like home when they got there after their long plane ride and, more importantly, leaving their home in New York.

I was elated when I found a good place for Jack and Lillian. It was the answer to my POP prayers that we could finally end the long-distance POParenting. However, as their move was actually upon us, I was surprised to discover I had some mixed feelings that weren't all positive. On the one hand, I was reassured that I could better monitor my parents' wellbeing from up close. But on the other, I felt clueless about how it would be to have them living so close and, as a result, I became anxious.

When I get anxious, my mind starts feeding me questions. How would the triad of my Mother, Father and I do living in close proximity at this time in our POPcycle? How often would I see them: once a week or every day? Would they or I want visits to be more frequent? How would I find them decent physicians? Would I take them to their every dentist and doctor appointment and if so, how would I afford the time? Would they even want that? How would they get to the drug store to buy toothpaste or would that task and so many more now become mine?

I was full of unknown information, speculation and unanswerable questions. I even had some fears that, doing POP up close and personal, I might "fail." Although I intellectually knew that time would answer all these questions, sometimes it was particularly difficult to replace my anxiety with the faith in myself and the universe's goodness I usually experience.

Most of the time I was able to use my thoughts constructively – to support me in dealing with knotty POP challenges such as unnerving instances of "role reversal." I defined those as when I was "being the grownup" instead of the child in my relationship with my parents. At this stage of the POPcycle "being the grownup" had meant taking care of all the physical details of finding their new place and helping them settle in, much like when they'd taken me to settle into summer camp or college.

"Being the grownup" also involved securing a solid emotional base for my Mom and Dad to lean on. One way I was seeing I could use this role reversal to all of our benefit was to remember what I had craved from parents when I'd been the child and then shower it on them. I'd wanted my parents' unconditional love, acceptance, permission to lean on them without shame and a spiritual rootedness. And whether or not they'd been able to give me all of that back when I was young, I saw this as my chance to offer those very qualities to them, now that I was "being the grownup."

There were other times when I was less the consummate adult, times my mind created unnecessary problems for me. For example, when I attributed a fearful meaning to this stage of the POPcycle, I found myself succumbing to a deep sense of loss. Similarly I'd make myself upset when I obsessed over thoughts of my original "protectors" needing a "protected environment" or my beloved parents "descending" a winding road toward increasing attendants and then death.

Lawyer Jane would even try to argue me out of my sinking sadness. I tried to convince myself it wasn't logical to be upset now since I'd long accepted that my folks needed a fair amount of help from Florence and now they just needed more. Psychotherapist Jane jumped in and encouraged me to observe my fearful and sad thoughts rather than allow myself to get drawn into or paralyzed by them. Sometimes that was hard to do since my feelings seemed to want to "run me."

POParenting required me to pull myself back into the present as quickly as I could because it was in that authentic present – and without drama – that I made my most sensible and wise decisions. And right now my parents were not leaving the planet or me but just New York and they needed to live in a place precisely like the one I'd worked so hard to find.

Doing POP is, by definition, bittersweet. My folks seemed so vulnerable now, not the "invincible" examples they'd been years before when they'd been "the parents." I was POParenting older parents whose aging genetically programmed them to become less capable of independence and ultimately more childlike. This is strikingly opposite to the experience of parenting children who are genetically programmed to do the opposite – they become more independent and less infantile. When we "launch" the children we've raised and fallen in love with, we're shipping them off to (presumably) bright, shiny careers, schools and marriages to fulfill what they learned originally when they were with us. But when we "launch" our beloved parents, we're sending them off to apparent emptiness and the big unknown.

Anticipating their moving closer, I recognized that proximity would also allow me to observe my parents' day-to-day declines. It seemed to make the time we had left together especially poignant. None of these times could ever be recaptured but I most often noticed the bittersweet taste when my parents seemed most like "their old selves" again. It was as if I could "see" through the old people they'd become to the individuals I used to know. Those remembered parents sometimes seemed more real than the aged couple in front of me.

In the early 2000's I spent time studying with Dr. Martin Seligman and his extensive network of researchers and clinicians I named the "Happiness Scientists."[37] Their rigorous studies validated some conclusions I'd also reached while working

---

[37] See, e. g. January 17, 2005 Time Magazine, "The Science of Happiness."

with patients in my office. Doing certain practices regularly and repetitively can and will re-train a brain's connections. I learned that we can expand our capacity for real joy in life by consistently engaging in three activities – being grateful, granting forgiveness and savoring the good in our lives. As a result of doing so, we can re-set the level of our "happiness thermostat," that internal mechanism that operates to regulate our emotions much like a thermostat regulates the temperature in our homes. One thermostat "raises" our environmental temperature and the other our internal happiness level. It was apparently up to me to move that dial, but I could raise it!

Once Mom and Dad moved into my world in California, I reminded myself that I could – and probably should – adopt this happiness formula for myself. So on a daily basis I began to invoke all three: gratitude, "forgiving" my parents and myself – mainly for being human – and delighting in gift of this moment. I made the conscious choice to focus on the sweet side of the bitter-sweetness while doing POP.

While not denying my real sadness, especially when I "anticipated" the future of our POPcycle, I didn't see much utility in bathing in it either. I would remind myself: live in the present, Jane! Your parents are very much alive! After 35 years of living apart I now had the chance to become closer and more loving with my family and to accentuate the positive in all of that would add to its sweetness.

The three of us needed me to be enthusiastic and to share with Jack and Lillian how attractive the move and their new place would be for them. I'd be no good for any of us if I continued to concentrate my thoughts on their "inevitable descent" or talk about this upcoming phase as "institutionalizing" my folks. Those words sounded very dramatic but didn't really represent my truth.

Instead I could more accurately and helpfully work with myself by applying a tool from cognitive research called "reframing" my thinking. "Reframing" involved examining my thoughts and noticing how else I might think about the same topic, perhaps more neutrally and less emotionally. Here what I'd been telling myself was that moving them to the AL was "putting them in an institution." What if I thought about the same activity as "picking out my parents' next home?"

Interestingly, shifting my way of looking at that and thinking about it differently helped quite a bit. Afterwards I was more energized to settle them happily in their new environment and accomplished my POP decorating tasks with more ease and confidence. "Reframing" became a reliable technique I would return to often during my remaining time with my parents, especially so when I found myself feeling stuck in repetitive unwanted feelings.

108

The AL facility I chose for Mom and Dad was only a few short miles from my home. The eucalyptus trees just outside their patio provided beauty, shade and a distinctive aroma I've come to associate with southern California. Downstairs the food smelled great and tasted even better. My Mom would soon be looking forward to a sitting yoga class while Dad would enjoy reading undisturbed in the quiet library.

I wondered: "... is there a minimum age to move in?"

Your Story

Most families will have many options for where your parents can safely live out their final days. If your parents need to move from their current location, hopefully you can choose a place that will remain a viable residence through the course of their illnesses and declines so you can avoid moving them multiple times. Multiple moves add to everyone's turmoil, present particular challenges for those in cognitive decline and have occasionally appeared to trigger the death of some aging loved ones. Moving from home to AL to one SNF after another, as my Mom did, involved multiple traumas each time: physically moving, readjusting and having to re-learn.

Essentially your POP choice comes down to three approaches: aging in place; moving to a relative's home or choosing a senior "institutional living" facility. None of these is inherently superior to any other. Each type of living experience is very different and each has its advantages and disadvantages. In deciding you must face the uncertainty of not knowing the number of years your parents have left. If you have limited resources – and who doesn't – you'll need to consider price as you look over these alternatives. One factor you will use in weighing your options will be financial. Other costs, such as your own emotional, physical or cultural demands, may be even harder to calculate.

If your parents want to "age in place" (stay in their home with extra measures taken to protect them) and your TEAM POP agrees they can do so without much apparent risk, that may be your best option. There are some great advantages for your parents if they *can* stay living where they've resided for a long time. By staying where they actively engaged in life and everything is familiar, your parents may experience stability and community that are irreplaceable. Having to adjust to a new home, to new neighbors, new routines and to so much else that is unknown can be taxing at any age. During their senior years such a move can be overwhelming.

It should come as no surprise that most Americans over 50 would prefer to remain living in their own homes than have to move. My parents did and yours may too. Certainly one reason people don't want to move involves the series of upsets associated with it: the loss of familiar people, places and activities and the anxiety of the unknown ahead. Experts claim moving is one of the highest stressors in life. It's also hard physical work to prepare, sort, pack up, cart, haul, unpack and re-place things in new places. If moving is hard on a healthy adult, you can only imagine how much more traumatic it might be to your parents. They rarely have the mental or physical energy, stamina and level of recall you do.

But neither should you underestimate how upsetting, sad or depleting moving your parents may be for you. Some of you, like me, will be packing up homes where you grew up and lived. During this process you may find yourself caught up in nostalgia and other emotional memory jogging. It may bring tears to your eyes to watch your sweet, maybe shorter, loved ones go to their favorite haunt together one last time. I choked up watching Jack and Lillian at their local deli savoring their last NY corned beef sandwiches on corn rye with sour pickles. Seeing your parents leave behind friends or siblings with whom they shared both happy and tougher times, knowing they'll never see each other again, can wrench you apart. Many of these moments can be avoided if your parents stay in their home.

Should your parents be able to "age in place," you will find a growing industry to help you create in-home environments that support staying at home as a decent and safe alternative to institutional life. Unlike the POParents who will need to find a new setting, your challenges will be to help make your parents' current housing become even "better." If you can avoid having your parents move late in life, their successfully "aging in place" will also necessitate more work for you. You may need to make modifications to their environment, discover how they can access sufficient safety and hygiene methods as well as obtain good nutrition, stimulation and social interaction. Then you will also need to see that those things actually are happening and, later, also check that they are working well.

Those who advocate "aging in place" remind us that many senior parents can stay happily and safely living in their homes, even living alone, *provided* certain modifications are made and/or certain technology is available. Others point out that "aging in place" may also require assistance from occasional or full-time help. If your parent or parents served in the U. S. military, they may qualify for a program called Aid and Attendance (A&A) Pension. It provides benefits for veterans and their surviving spouses who need another person to regularly attend and assist the person in eating, bathing, dressing and undressing or taking care of the needs of nature. To check if your parents qualify for this program, no matter if they are living in their own homes or in an assisted living facility, go to www.veteranaid.org.

Another group of modern geriatric professionals, Certified Aging-in-Place specialists ("CAPS"), is available to help your parents remain at home. Their offerings can be particularly useful if your parents' need for modifications is a result of a traumatic event (usually a fall) or a more progressive decline in their function or mobility.

Falling is the leading cause of injurious events to older people. The two major goals of suggested home "modifications" are to prevent falls and to allow seniors better access to their possessions and daily activities. Some repairs involve taking steps that are as simple and inexpensive as removing clutter and dangerous "throw rugs." Other modifications may include installing hand-held flexible showerheads, grab bars and non-skid flooring in appropriate locations. Increasing lighting, railing and accessible light switches near stairs are also often recommended. In general, adding more light to the environment of our seniors is very helpful – whether that be replacing bulbs with stronger ones and/or adding additional lighting and lamps.

Other modifications may be a bit more costly and require hiring someone with tools, perhaps a contractor, electrician, plumber or a handyman. You may need help if you wish to create sliding shelves and drawers, walk-in closets and showers or to widen entryways or build ramps for wheelchair access. Your out-of-pocket cost for these installations is likely to be well worth the long-term savings to life, limb and everyone's stress levels. Perhaps there is also a program where you live that will help pay for such "fixes."

Technology's contributions to your parents' ability to "age in place" grow with every moment. Smart houses are being developed to address the variety of hazards associated with the cognitive and physical declines of older adults. "Elder cams" run on the same surveillance premise that "nanny cams" offer concerned parents watching their children. Even now, apps on your smart phone can allow you or your parents' keyless entry and cashless payments for needed POP items. In all likelihood, all sorts of new tech tools will come along to help your parents remain as independent as possible in their own dwelling.

If your parents are 55 or older and meet certain conditions,[38] they may be eligible to stay living in their community and receive comprehensive care at home rather than in a skilled nursing home under a federal program entitled PACE. This began as a pilot project and because it was so well received, it has been expanded to many American communities. Over time, we may see other programs that support "aging in place" becoming even more accessible.

But like the other options, "aging in place" has its disadvantages too. There is a toll that having your parents' stay in their home may take on you. As you've read in My Story, when my parents were "aging in place," I had numerous long-distance POParenting concerns and distressing weekends until their conditions left our family without that option. "Aging in place" is complicated when all the adult children live at a distance or when those who live close by are already occupied caring for their children, homes, jobs and lives.

Another problem with your parents remaining at home is the danger of their becoming socially isolated there. As your parents age, several factors coalesce to make this period a potentially lonely one. If your parents no longer go out to a job or senior daycare, they may

---

[38] Check online at pace@cms.hhs.gov and also www.Pace4you for those conditions and the benefits available.

spend many days or much of every day sitting alone in their homes, having no contact with other people. Your parents' closest friends and relatives may have died, moved or divorced. Now there may be few if any of them left "in the neighborhood."

Your parents' diminished senses of sight, smell, hearing and/or taste may affect their interest in and enjoyment of other people's company. Being in pain or having little energy similarly makes socializing a strain. Some of your parents will even experience shame or embarrassment if they have become forgetful or can't easily learn new things. All of this has the potential to have your parents further insulate themselves and remain within the so-called safety inside their homes.

At this point in their development your parents may have little inclination to leave home to meet new people or make new friends. If they remain living in their own home, your parents are likely to relate to fewer and fewer people and live in a smaller and smaller world over time. Exceptions exist and perhaps your Mom's attending her years long-Tuesday night Canasta game with "the girls" might be one. Hopefully something unexpected and wonderful may happen in their lives, like your parents becoming best friends with a couple who happened to be seated near them in a restaurant. However predictably, your parents will have diminishing social support and engagement if they "age in place."

A part of your POParenting responsibilities will be to discover how to encourage your parents to get out of their homes, "hang" with their friends and attend activities they enjoy. It is part of your job to be keen to symptoms that may look like depression. Loneliness and isolation can lead to clinical depression and even suicide. If they will allow you to, your finding interesting local activities or arranging the equivalent of senior "play dates" might lift your parents' spirits.

If your parents can stay in their home, you may be able to undermine some of the loneliness by staying in "better" communication with your parents than I was. Skype, the Internet, FaceTime and the many other communications developments since my parents were long distance can help you mitigate the potential danger of your parents becoming too cut off. Sharing family events they cannot attend and keeping up with their grandchildren on the computer can bring your parents immediate pleasure and keep them involved in your life and vice versa.

The second major approach for where your parents can age comfortably is for you or your siblings to offer them a place to live in one of your homes. If you're thinking you might be willing to step up for that, stop and ask yourself: is it optimal to bring my parents to live in my home? And if your answer is a clear "no," whether immediately or after much soul-searching, consider whether your sister or brother's home would be any better. If you or your siblings answer "yes," you will need to assess whose home would be best for your parents and why. If you and your siblings have responded affirmatively, all of you should read these next paragraphs carefully. If your answer is "no," for all your homes, you will need another alternative altogether and can read below about institutional options.

But just because you and your parents *can* "make it work" to bring an aging and/or ill, disabled and demented parent into your home doesn't mean its really the best choice for any of you. You need to discover if POParenting in your home is viable for you and whether it is the optimal place for your parents over the long haul. Realistically evaluate your parents' current and imminent needs. You may think you can watch your parents more carefully if they live in your home than in theirs or in a residence but maybe not. I believe it is crucial to search your heart and mind before you answer, perhaps in the way you did before deciding to bring a child into your home.

Analyze all the elements involved before committing to a potentially life-altering transition for everyone living in your home. Look at the many different aspects of your current life including your employment, relationship with your spouse, your health and your home's configuration. Recall your long-standing history with your parents and how you've all fared more recently together.

If you work full-time or part-time, would you have to sacrifice your job or its benefits to care for the parents in your home? What if your parents' disabilities eventually require two to three aides to transfer them from their beds to the bathroom commode, as my Mom did towards her end? If your parents' cognitive declines require increasing hours of professional care or even more caregivers, would your home still be optimal or even an acceptable location? Would that be affordable in your home or would you need to move your parents again?

Consult a variety of family caregiver support programs[39] and other organizations focused on family caregivers and their special needs. Find out the costs, financial and emotional, and learn about the benefits. Talk with others who brought their parents into their homes and listen carefully to what they have to share. Go online to the POP website and blog with other POParents who are doing that in real time. You may be "exposing" yourself and your family to the rigors of living with chronic disease and/or dementia. Hearing details of how doing that affected other families may provide you with very useful insights. Even if your spouse, your children and your siblings all believe that "everything will be just fine and we'll help too," listen carefully to your own wisdom!

As you assess your own limitations and those of your parents, you want to think in detail and be alert to the most likely possibilities. For example, is there enough security in your home for your Dad with Alzheimer's as such patients often wander off without securely locked exits? How will your parents negotiate the steps in your home if they need a walker and have to go to the bathroom in the middle of the night: will they be waking you?

---

[39] See National Family Caregiver Support Program in the Glossary.

Can your marriage survive, if it's already in a stressed state, and your parents move in along with your "boomerang" adult children? If everyone ordinarily is away from 8 AM until after dark, can your parents prepare their own lunches, go to their doctors unaided and be alone all day? Will they need a caregiver for some hours in your house? Will you be able to "hold your head up" in your family if you refuse the traditional dictates of your culture that "require" you to bring your parents into your home?

If no relative's home is right for your aging parents, where will you and your family look next? Your third approach for today's senior residences is the wide range of attractive institutional options. Although the term "institutional life" may sound off-putting, like you'd be shipping your parents to the back wards of some old dank hospital in the 1950's, quite the opposite is true today. At one end of the spectrum some institutions are simply private apartments in buildings or communities with other seniors. At the other end are locked settings where the residents' mobility and care is provided by staff.

What type of out-of-home experience is most suitable for your parents? The first step, which you've already begun, is to become clear what level of care your parents require for their safety. Since you rarely want to see them as weak or needy, beware not to underestimate the extent of your parents' disabilities or their need for assistance.

The institutional setting for seniors with the fewest needs is termed Independent Living (IL).[40] These facilities permit "as needed" caregiving services to be added to your parents' bill or allow POParents to hire "outside" assistance. If your parents were able to care for themselves fairly well in their own home, this might be a good choice. However, if they need "more" care or you envision that happening in their near future, your parents may be better off living at the next level of caregiving, an Assisted Living (AL) facility and avoiding the necessity for multiple moves.

Some AL's and Independent Living facilities have very specific restrictions. Most won't admit a resident who has a gastric feeding tube or require a resident to be able to evacuate the building without assistance in case of an emergency. Some offer flexibility by having different levels of care provided residents on different floors in a single building. If your parents become more "needy," one or both of them can stay in the same facility but move to a different floor. This allows for continuity in location and staffing as well as permitting couples to have much contact in spite of being at different levels of aging. Entities called Continuing Care Retirement Communities ("CCRC's")[41] offer families a contract that allows for continuity

---

[40] Although this term also represents a philosophical position about people with disabilities, when we're speaking in this eldercare context, IL is a step on the continuum of care requirements with "assisted" living – help from others – being the next rung up of care.

[41] See Glossary.

of residents at a single location during the entire POPcycle with fluidity in the resident's housing and nursing care available.

TEAM POP can meet to clarify and prioritize the desired characteristics of the new residence that meet your parents' specific needs and desires. Then you'll be better equipped to concentrate your efforts on precisely what you're looking for and know when you've found it. You'll also need to check out which facilities have space available and what is affordable for your family. Cleanliness, the number of residents, proximity to family, privacy, accessibility to your parents' doctors, churches, bus-lines and stores are certainly likely to be relevant features in your evaluation. It will be helpful for you to consider the attractiveness of the setting, size of the rooms, closets and bathrooms, the extent of the recreational activities, the attention you observe that is given the residents by staff and, of course, the quality of the food.

You will want to inquire about the quality of their professional people. I liked to hear that the staff remained working at a facility for a long time since that longevity probably represented satisfied employees and my parents could get "comfortable" that the staff would be there with them over time. In some states like California, senior facilities are required to maintain and make available to consumers a book in which all "problem" situations and their "fixes" are noted. If you have that advantage, you can look at any remarks or history and are likely to find it highly instructive. You can see if governmental authorities issued any orders or negative reports and ask lots of relevant questions. Consider moving on if you're not okay with their answers.

Your POP role will be evaluating the alternatives and making your parents' transition as seamless as possible. It will begin with your helping them accept that their "leaving home" is necessary and end after you've settled them into their new home. As you begin to look at these residences, you will develop a nose – often literally – for one that is likely to work best for your parents. And where else can you go to find your parents' new home? Fortunately there are lots of methods to locate senior living facilities. Word-of-mouth, online searches, governmental reports and professional referrals can each prove helpful to you. Increasingly, online entities provide their take on what will be good for your family[42] but beware that many websites are commercially-sponsored or supported.

Your parents may protest. They may wish you to believe they need less attention than is really warranted. Many will be concerned about the cost of all of this. Maybe your parents are embarrassed at the loss of some of their faculties or mistakenly see that as a weakness to be hidden. I always recommend that you treat your parents' aging limitations with respect and kindness and that you honor your parents' intelligence even in their last days. However if your

---

[42] For example, see www.helpguide.org.

Dad repeatedly can't remember to turn off the water when he runs his bathtub, you will need a facility that makes sure that happens either by requiring you to hire additional help or providing it.

Professional placement agencies, such as the one I used, are another link in the geriatric service industry. They will need to interview you or your family's representative and maybe your parents as well. They will be discovering your requirements and hearing your preferences. After that, they will generate a list of maybe 10 facilities for you to visit. Similar to how employment agencies work, their services are generally paid for by the residential facilities and are therefore complementary to the families, They can help you face where on POPcycle your aging loved ones really are, clarify your priorities and provide up-to-date information on charges, availability and facility requirements.

As with other "real estate decisions," the three watchwords for your POP housing choice may be LOCATION, LOCATION, and LOCATION. When you start visiting your parents often, it will be clear why it's easiest to do POP locally when they live close by. It also might be advantageous to find a facility near to a freeway or on your route to work. Proximity to public transportation for your parents who may not drive can also be wise.

Our government regulates today's senior facilities. Most you will find are respectable and some are so elegant, you'd bet you were in a boutique hotel. Nonetheless, there are still some institutions that have significant problems that can pose a concern for POP families. How will you be able to know which is which?

In addition to the ways already suggested to check out facilities, you now have two specific websites to help you learn about their defects and governmental inspections. The Centers for Medicare and Medicaid Services surveys and certifies the nation's roughly 15,000 nursing homes. It has made available online the full text of reports that nursing home inspectors have filed for each of these facilities, a step many have urged for years. By going to www.medicare.gov and navigating your way to Nursing Home Compare, you can access this useful data. You can also do POP research at http://projects.propublica.org/nursing-homes, a website set up by a nonprofit organization of journalists. This site allows you to specifically discover nursing home defects in a simple, state-by-state manner.

There are always scary stories when people with some vulnerability, like our elderly loved ones, are living in institutional settings. And you must always stay vigilant when your parents are living in such places, but few are anything like what my Mother had dreaded from the 1940's and 50's.   These days most senior residential facilities pose few hazards and the majority of people who live there are grateful for the companionship, care and activities afforded them in these residences.

POPlan #8: Getting Yourself Ready To Accept And Then Effectuate This Chapter's POP Decision-Making

While performing the "field" research to find your parents' facility, don't be surprised if you become flooded with thoughts and feelings, as I did. Perhaps you've noticed throughout your POPcycle that doing tasks for your declining parents often evokes many unexpected reactions, some of which may feel decidedly undesirable. Worrying about your emotions or getting further into your inner drama can distract you from accomplishing your purpose and are rarely useful ways to spend your valuable time.

Not only that but you have better choices as to how you will respond to these triggering events. To stay in your role as the POParent and not get off track, try some or all of these.

1.) Stop! Notice exactly what you're thinking and feeling. *This is a way to slow down, listen to yourself and get back into the present moment.*

2.) Calm yourself with the thought that your reactions are normal, even if you don't like them or they're uncomfortable. *Most POParents become flooded with fearful thoughts and sad feelings at this stage of the POPcycle. You have an advantage, however, in that you are mindfully attending to your thoughts and feelings. This will help you focus on the task at hand.*

3.) Inhale deeply at least five times as you consciously breathe in fresh oxygen, light and thoughts. Exhale twice as long as you inhaled. *Doing this helps you eliminate stuck and bothersome thoughts, feelings and other physical wastes like carbon dioxide.*

4.) As you keep breathing in and out fully, remind yourself that you need to live in the present, not in the unknown future and not in the recollections of the past. Be here now! *This will keep your focus on the current task and this moment, where you can do POP now, moving your attention away from fears in the future or other imagined events.*

5.) Separate out what you may be feeling or thinking from what's actually happening. Then find something occurring now for which you are grateful. *One of the most powerful ways to positively redirect your energy and attention is to rouse your latent gratitude.*

6.) As you continue breathing consciously, expand your feeling of gratitude even more. Bathe yourself in it. *The healing power in gratitude has been validated scientifically over and again. Now you can melt into its supportiveness.*

7.) When you feel you're ready, return your consciousness first to yourself in the present and then to the POP task you're wishing to accomplish. Observe how refreshed and alert *you've become. You've been on a mini-vacation and can complete your job more effectively and less emotionally.*

8.) Promise yourself to find the time soon to process any feelings that may still remain incomplete.   *By following through on this promise, you're developing the good habit of attending to your own reactions, rather than engaging in the dangerous habit of denial. You're also learning about and respecting your own responses and not just your parents' feelings.*

9.) Remind yourself that you can return at any time to this energizing place of gratitude and then do take the time to keep practicing and attending to your own energy, health and wellbeing. *The cycle of giving and receiving requires that you too receive at least some of your own loving care. No one can give forever without this type of refreshment and respite.*

10.) Congratulate yourself: you've learned another useful technique to support yourself being a great POParent!

Chapter 9

Dealing With All Our Parents' Stuff

My Story

Laughter has always served me well. When I was confronting my toughest POP challenges, I needed to rely on humor the most. Sometimes when I was doing some aspect of POParenting with Lillian and Jack, comedy routines from my childhood would "come to me," seemingly unbidden but usually very helpful. At precisely the moment I needed to begin examining all my parents' worldly possessions and decide what to do with them, a classic George Carlin routine appeared. In it, he had warned us of people becoming dominated by their "stuff."

Carlin claimed that, without being aware of it, we could end up making all our life decisions based upon our stuff. We could use our stuff as the basis to choose our homes ("looks like a good place to put our stuff"), know when it's moving time ("we've too much stuff, we'd better move on") and even pick our line of work ("that's the way we get to buy more stuff"). I particularly loved the part where he pointed out the vast divide between other people's so-called "garbage" – although he used a different word for it – and our own valuable things.

Carlin's routine not only made me laugh (one of my "life tools") but also made me think about how best to manage my parents' life-long collection of possessions. Maneuvering them and their things across country was an enormous undertaking. For a fully functioning forty-year old who's lived in a small apartment for only a few years, relocating across town can be taxing. Moving and/or disposing of everything two eight-seven year olds ever acquired and schlepping them and their remaining things across country was, to put it mildly, huge. When I reminded myself that my parents would never return here, that awesome thought added even more weight to the impending drama I was primed to experience.

As was my way, I made a list. That helped me keep myself organized and on target. I loved making lists because I loved checking things off. Completing this list was particularly satisfying since, as I crossed off items, it meant we were that much closer to getting them settled in their new home.

The first thing on my list was to "prepare" Mom and Dad physically and emotionally for what was ahead. My goal was a bit delicate. I wished to enroll them in the excitement and momentum of their move without getting them fatigued or overwhelmed. I explained to my folks the general scenario.

1) Jane looks over all of Mom and Dad's things to get a good picture of the overall situation.

2) Jane sorts their possessions into categories – things they'd need on the plane or immediately when they arrived in California; things I'd ship to their new home; items to be given away; larger or more expensive pieces of furniture, antiques or non-memorabilia I would sell.

3) Jane consults as appropriate with Mom and Dad on these categories so they don't feel they're losing control over their stuff.

4) Jane packs the items to be shipped (with some "manpower" help), organizes the giveaways and arranges to sell the valuables.

5) Jane ships, gives away and sells those things.

6) We three fly to Los Angeles together.

I explained my list, that we could bring much of their everyday clothing by air and that they'd be able to take their treasured and familiar things to their new *place.   Then I asked if they had any questions but they didn't. I sensed their appreciation that this was a big job and they had confidence I would do it well. That felt good.*

Later, when the apartment was emptied of all my parents' possessions, I would write another list. That second list was for me to begin hiring people to clean, paint and refresh an apartment that hadn't been well maintained for many years. It had been a decade, maybe two, since Mom had been willing to allow anyone in from the building to re-plaster and paint. As a result of these years of neglect, the metal screening behind the plaster, ordinarily several layers below the paint, had become bare and exposed to view. It was a bizarre contrast to look up from the elegant antiques in my parents' beautifully decorated home to the ceiling and see sheetrock.

Eventually I hired a real estate agent to rent or sell "their" apartment. Years before POP began, my folks had transferred their interest in the apartment to me as part of their estate planning.   Technically it had become my apartment back then but no matter what the ownership papers said, it always felt like my parents' place to me. Like so many of their generation, my parents' apartment had been their major life investment. By age 47, Jack had worked hard to achieve some commercial success in the music business and was finally in a position to purchase (along with a little financial backing from his relatives) a home for "his girls," as he called my Mom and me in those pre-women's liberation days.

My folks had been very proud to be able to buy their home and fulfill the American Dream.[43] And what an American Dream they'd found! Our Manhattan high-rise was beautiful! It was erected on the site of a lavish mansion and rose twenty-two stories high, above lush Central Park. The architect had won awards for his vision of our lobby that retained the antique marble columns and fountain from the former building and entwined them amid the ultra-modern glass doors and windows of the new one.

I'd been in seventh grade when the building was in construction. The three of us eagerly visited each Saturday, excited to discover what the workers had accomplished during the previous week. Had they put up the new walls yet or installed the air conditioners? Was the carpeting laid and how did it look? Later on after we'd moved in, my friends and I watched a major motion picture, "Butterfield 8," being filmed in our lobby.   We were pre-teen girls and tried to imitate Elizabeth Taylor's

---

[43] Jack revealed some of his patriotic ideals in his songs. One of these, co-authored with Robert Colby, was called "The American Dream" and it was the theme song for a major New York Festival starring Howard Keel.

sultry walk in her Oscar-winning performance, probably providing much humor for the building staff looking on.

Decades later when my Mom had become old and was bored being in the apartment, she'd ask Florence or me to take her down to sit in that lobby where she enjoyed chatting with her neighbors and our building's workers. Now I wondered if they'd had a laugh at her expense too? So many memories!

As I started taking the paintings off their walls, sorting and packing up my parents' possessions, I felt an odd sense of comfort. For forty-two years that apartment had been my parents' home. Originally it had been my home base too. I'd only lived there for five years, back in the late 1950's and early '60's but a piece of me always considered it my home. Since my parents had stayed there after I'd gone on to college, law school and other pursuits, even after I'd developed my life in California, their apartment had remained my historic domicile.

We had been the only family to have lived in and loved inside those apartment walls. If there were secrets pressed into the recesses of those peeling plaster walls, they were our family's secrets. I wondered what those walls would have revealed, had they been able to speak. The familiarity of working among their things seemed to ground me at the time when what lay ahead seemed so unknown and shifting. I knew my focus should remain on completing these tasks but my emotions sometimes proved demanding and distracted me. My lists were organized but my feelings were dizzying all over the map.

Some days I'd arrive ready to work on my self-assigned tasks only to discover that Mom and Dad had more pressing things for me to do from their perspective. Most of the time, I'd stop and divert from my lists because I felt I should attend to something they felt was more immediate. Other times I could only work for a limited amount of time because my emotions did take hold of me, almost weighing me down. As I sorted through their boxes of life "treasures," I felt like I was watching a soap opera – but the characters weren't strangers, they were the nearest and dearest members of my family. I would unearth photos of my family or myself when we were all younger and reminiscences would be triggered "from nowhere." Unearthing some of their memorabilia, I'd find myself traveling down memory lane.

Now that I was eyeballing and handling all their stuff, I was surprised at how much new information I was learning I'd never been aware of. Could it be that I really knew very little about these two people I'd thought I'd known so well? I remember having a momentary epiphany, childlike in its simplistic nature: my parents were people with lives before I knew them and before they even knew each other. They'd had lives before – and aside – from being MY parents.

Trying to remind myself that these emotional "side trips" added time and delayed my efficiency, I often found myself taking them anyway. I was speechless when I came across the boxes that contained thousands of love poems. My father, the lyricist, had penned his poetry inside monthly "anniversary" cards he sent to his bride every month for six decades! The romance of that took my breath away. For a moment, I wondered if I were intruding ... But even as part of me was wiping away my tears, the work-driven part was feeling inundated.

Too much stuff! I didn't want the responsibility for making all these decisions. Trying to figure out what to do with pounds and mounds of their memorabilia was complicated. One thing I discovered was unopened, unused items Lillian had collected over time – clothing, shoes and even some expensive perfumes that, of course, had evaporated over time. I wondered what this "saving things" was all about. I'm just the opposite, a woman who often wears new clothes directly out of the store, asking the sales clerk's help to detach the labels for me. So Mom's saving things for her future enjoyment wasn't something I had in common with her.

But like many of those young adults who survived the economic deprivations of the Great Depression after 1929, my Mom was left with a condition some term "Depression Mentality." These folks save things "just in case" they might someday need them, should there come a time again when they wouldn't have enough. While cleaning out my Dad's closet, I found that he too had amassed his own collections, although they were not of unused items. Dad's collection consisted of coins, stamps, albums and tapes.

What of all of this should I save and what do I throw away? How long should I keep the three copies of Mom's high school yearbook displaying Giggles' photo? Or even one of them? Who will ever want to look at them again? George Carlin was right: one person's treasure is another person's garbage. After we're gone, our treasures may seem worthless to our kids. And those love poems, should I even read them or were they too private? How many of the poems and cards should I keep? Five? Ten? Should I keep all of them? Would my parents ever ask for them again? Did they even know they had them now? And where would I put all this stuff?

I found the whole process very stressful, fraught with the chance for me to err big time. I feared my parents' future crest-fallen faces: "Jane, you threw out my precious...." These were hard decisions to make, harder still because it wasn't my stuff.

I felt an odd sense of something that resembled betrayal when I let go of things that once seemed to have meant so much to my parents. Sometimes when I made these decisions about their stuff, they were resting in a nearby room. Most of the time they weren't present at all. On occasion I consulted Jack or Lillian about how I should deal with a certain item, but most of the time I just decided.

I sought to show my parents the appropriate deference and respect for their possessions. But my parents were never very materialistic people and, for all my concern of disappointing them or mis-categorizing their things, it turned out to be a non-issue with them. I recall having only one conversation about how I'd dealt with their possessions. It was with my Dad and occurred right after their move. Apparently I questioned his wearing an olive colored shirt. He responded that he was at a bit of a loss to know what to wear, since I'd thrown out or given away all of his favorite shirts. Nevertheless he reassured me: "That's really okay with me, honey, they weren't that important. I guess this shade of green isn't my best color, huh?"

Despite my ordinary point of view that worrying is wasted energy, I so often found myself worrying during POP. There was also so much I "mis-worried" about, so many apprehensions I had about events that never actually came about. Upsetting my parents by how I handled their stuff was apparently one of those. When it came down to it, my parents' stuff mattered relatively little to them ... what really mattered to my Mom and Dad was how I treated them.

Their Story – Mom

It's strange how I felt as I watched my daughter go through all our boxes and total strangers pack up our belongings before our trip. I'd never liked having a lot of people in the apartment. That was why I let the ceilings and painting remain like that for years and why it was so hard for me when the caregivers were here all the time.

In my younger days I might have been shocked to watch Jane read the love poetry Jack had written for me. Years ago I might have taken offense having these moving men paw over my teenage photographs or our clothes. It might have felt like they were invading our privacy or that Jane was gaining access to my secrets but today I find I don't mind they're being here in the same way.

At this point I can't recall all the things that I've collected over the course of my long life. There sure was a lot of it. When I was amassing the contents of all these boxes, what was inside them mattered to me – a lot. They represented pieces of my life. I cared a lot about what was inside these boxes, or, at least, I cared about the meaning I'd attached to them. But I've come to see many things differently since I piled these objects into the boxes. Today I care about the kindness Jane and her moving men have shown and the gentleness in how they treated me, Jack and our "treasures."

Of course I still value the wonderful cards and poetry my husband sent me each and every month on the 25ᵗʰ, our anniversary day. I'm also happy to have the letters Jane sent us from camp, school or wherever she was. I kept lots of photos of our baby girl, she was so adorable. And I held on to the sweaters I'd knit for Jane and her dolls. I also had pictures of my parents and siblings from when we'd been young in those boxes. In the past, looking at some of those things had made me sad. But now, when Jane would come to us with Playbills from the Broadway shows we'd attended or the other memorabilia of times we'd had together, I was pleased to be reminded of things I had long forgotten.

I looked up and Jane was there, standing in a corner near the light, examining a shot of Jack and me when we first met. She was eying the photo carefully and I wondered what my daughter was seeing in it? I have a clear memory of that day but I can't recall what I was like back then. Who was that young woman in the photo? I look so naïve, so unsure of what I was to become or the life that would be ahead for the two of us. And Jack – his face is so unbelievably carefree and young! He's wearing those rimless spectacles that were so popular back in the 1940's. He looked handsome in them, so intelligent as he gazed at me with those kind eyes that won me over. I still love my husband's eyes and his intelligence. Can Jane see the love that was just starting that day between us? Is she imagining Jack and me before we'd even thought of having her?

As I look over all my things from the perspective of being an old woman, I feel detached from sadness or even nostalgia in a surprisingly good way. After years of working with psychotherapists, I've come to finally understand that I was really the one who'd attached any negative meaning to the events in my life. I probably cared too much that my things and I be "just right." My sensitivity to what others thought or said caused a lot of unnecessary pain. These days I'm trying to put a more uplifting meaning to my past. Jane says we can be calmer, Jack and I, if we focus less on our losses and more on savoring these moments we have together now and the good times we can recall. So, I'm trying that.

I'm even getting more relaxed about Jane's telling our story. If seeing the poems Jack wrote for me or reading about how we worked out things together as a family when Jack and I got older can help Jane help other people like us, where's the harm in that? I'm beginning to accept a lot of what's happening, maybe even our move to California.

Your story

Almost everyone has some emotional wounds left over from their childhood. You've already seen that my doing certain POP tasks, like packing up my Mom, Dad and my childhood home or looking for an AL, activated both remembrances and feelings that sometimes seemed "unreasonably" intense or even inexplicable. Perhaps that has happened to you as well. Despite sounding innocuous, dealing with your parents' stuff can be a minefield. It may surprise you how powerfully you react as you delve into your parents' belongings and memorabilia. You may unearth items you've never seen before and memories you may have long ago forgotten. Discovering childhood photos of you and your siblings or home movies of times when your parents were younger than you are now may "blow your mind."

Like me, you may be mid-box somewhere among your parents' items when you spot a grainy photo of your Mom looking unrecognizably young and carefree, smiling up with wonder at her new "boyfriend," your Dad. He may be wearing a wide grin or a hairdo that was fashionable decades ago. You may stare at that shot for what seems like hours, imagining how your parents were when they first met or decided to have you.

When you've completed your POP tasks for the day and are available to fully listen to them, you'll learn a lot if you sit with your aging loved ones and invite them to tell you of their life joys or accomplishments. Since you and your parents may be sharing many feelings and memories, this time could prove a good one to strengthen your new POP relationship. You can "mine" your historic and loving connection by asking your parents to share their early memories. Even those parents with memory loss from dementia may recall their "long-term" memories. Do your best to be curious and have a non-judgmental attitude. You will want to honor their stories or memories with compassion and perhaps a sweet appreciation for all they've have been through in their lifetimes.

When you're examining the things that your parents saved over the course of their lives and talking with them in these ways, you may find that you're engaged in a kind of life review[44]. That can elicit a variety of sentiments for all concerned. As a caring POParent you'll want to be sensitive in your responses, recognizing that sometimes a life review can result occasionally in your parents' emotional distress.

It's important to give yourself time and space to experience your own feelings during this "stuff-deciding" part of POP and other stages as well. Emotions like grief, nostalgia, regret, resentment and others you didn't realize you had may come to the surface for you, too. Once they get triggered, you're likely to find it liberating to permit yourself to feel whatever comes up for you – be it the passage of time, your losses or the irony of parenting your own parents.

---

[44] See Glossary.

126

In the moment, your feelings may challenge you; however denying or avoiding your emotions and reactions eventually will inhibit the flow of your healing.

Even if you get sad or tear up, "owning" your feelings can connect you with your authentic self. You'll never want to short-change giving yourself what you need to process what's been going on for you. Nonetheless, you can also decide to "delay reacting" until you're in the right place to take care of your own emotions. You may need to wait until you return to your home, partner, POP Family Coach or friends to do so. Earlier you learned the value of "under-reacting" while POParenting. "Delayed reacting" is another technique you will find useful as it will help you regain a feeling of power over the things that *are* under your control – your own responses.

Even if you're only sitting at your Mom's desk trying to make sense of her Medicare insurance premiums, don't be surprised to find you're having a lot of feelings. As your parents have gotten older, chances are they've acquired and kept a lot of papers. As attentive POParents you'll need to be discriminating as to what should be kept, filed, cleaned or tossed. Perhaps lately your parents have been less attentive about filing. You may encounter a lot of disorganized papers, bills and other notices. You may also find yourself distressed at some of their recent decisions and want to undo some things your parents did late in life that they thought would be helpful – perhaps a reverse mortgage that isn't sound or a life insurance policy that makes little sense to you.

What your parents collected or chose to save reveals a great deal about them. Looking through their stuff may offer you a window into understanding them better and, in turn, help heal your relationship. Do their boxes contain your parents' finest memories or their darkest secrets? Have they turned into hoarders whose possessions have overtaken all available space and light in their house? Will they be offended by your disposing of their "proud" possessions?

As POParents you and your siblings may well be deciding which of their things to keep and which to give away or even sell. If you're moving your parents to smaller quarters in a senior residence or in one of your homes, you can rent storage space for some of the things you or they can't stand to part with. You may discover that your wanting to hold onto their things is an unconscious way of holding onto your parents. There's nothing wrong with doing that but you won't want to overdo it.

Parting with your parents' belongings can be really challenging. In general, we Americans like to keep our stuff. In 2010 the self-storage industry in the United States earned $20+ billion in annual revenues. I "confess" that I paid to keep some of my parents' things in storage after they moved to California and even after they'd passed on.

You will also want to be attentive to the fact that packing up their home and looking over their "stuff" may stimulate irritability or even irrationality in your elderly parents, from your perspective. If they've already reached age 85, like mine had a few years earlier, statistically one out of two of them will have some form of dementia, including Alzheimer's type. They will be least alert and least able to help you after the sun goes down (known clinically as "sun-downing"). They may demonstrate behaviors of people with dementia like "compensating," which may involve providing you answers when they don't know them and "perseverating" which is repeating themselves over and again.

It may disarm you when you first discover their long-term memories of events from the past are far sharper than their short-term memories – like what they ate for lunch. How else might these factors impact this part of your POP job? If you're pulling some golf trophy off the shelf and trying to decide if it stays or goes, you might ask your Dad about its history. As he's recounting some long story your Mom may be grinning but not letting him see. She knows that those events never happened as he's telling it.

When they have certain diagnoses that affect their memories, your parents will do their best to remember but when they can't recall a real answer, they may make one up. It's their way of dealing with not remembering at a certain stage of memory loss and shouldn't be seen by you as lying. Later on in the course of their dementia, your aging loved ones won't recall and won't try to pretend they do. Later still, they won't try to recall and you won't ask them to. Understanding their conditions and where they are progressively if your parents' diseases are progressive will help you make better POP decisions as well as be less perturbed by their seemingly quirky behaviors.

Similarly with "perseverating," if your parents repeat themselves, ask you the same question over and again in the same conversation or call you with the same query several times in the same hour, it can try your patience. They're unaware they're perseverating but you are. Even if you've heard the story about your Dad's golf trophy often in the past, when you bring it down from the shelf, you may choose to patiently hear it again. And you may hear it again a short time later if your Dad asks: "honey, did I ever tell you about the time I won that golf trophy?" Employing the compassion and patience you've been "growing" will help you deal with these moments.

Even if your parents don't have a form of dementia or debilitating disorder, your "poking around" in their things may be frustrating or upsetting to them and they may not be happy with the whole idea. Your parents' reactions may even be inconsistent from one day to the next. Like your children, they may react differently to your good ideas from one sleepy night to the next rested morning. Or on Saturday your parents may seem grateful for your help in packing them up but on Sunday, they may have become upset or confused at what you've done with their things. If you are in a hurry with this part of your POP tasks, you may prefer to not ask them for much "help" or do this when your folks are out of their house or sleeping.

Certainly your parents are likely to have many feelings about parting with their home and the possessions they spent a lifetime amassing, some of them both positive and negative. For example, your folks may like having fewer things to be responsible for and may appreciate your downsizing or de-cluttering them but still resent your "intrusiveness." Resisting giving away certain things – like their 45 records with no turntable to play them on – may be your parents' way of holding on to their memories or of retaining some control to offset feeling overwhelmed and full of grief.

Even if your parents' possessions seem old, out of date or unattractive to you, they may turn out to provide great comfort or joy to your Mom and Dad. Those 45's may turn into an unexpected "gold mine" on EBay and provide them a great way to share their memories with young people who are interested buyers. Just as your daughter's beloved blanket was such a consolation she refused to let you wash it, your Mom's silk pillowcases may be a treasure you shouldn't "mess with." Some of you have parents of my generation who still carry around the fearful "Depression Mentality" from 1929 and they may be reluctant to let any stuff go, no matter how much they have or don't have or its "street value." That will make this POP job all the tougher for you.

You might be able to turn some of your POP sorting and organizing into donations for needy individuals and charitable entities. Giving things to others less fortunate can feel good for your parents and you. Plus, those deductible donations may also help them when tax time rolls around. Well-planned and advertised garage sales could yield some money for things you and they don't want to trek far. EBay, Craigslist and many online sites offer opportunities to turn your parents' items into cash for them. Selling your parents' business, coin collections, vintage clothing and vinyl records can become a source of unexpected income. Your parents are likely to be grateful for any increase to their finances and proud of you for demonstrating your ingenuity to "see" money where they did not.

The division of your parents' stuff can pose a serious hazard for siblings who are co-POParenting. Don't be surprised to find yourselves disagreeing with your siblings, sometimes over emotional things and sometimes over the stuff itself. Since family members have a stake in the outcome, they're likely to have their own ideas of how and what to do with your parents' "keepsakes," vintage items and their stock portfolio, too. Various siblings will want some things and some of you will want the same things. Some may think items should be sold and others will have different opinions. This is where I like to point out the advantages of being an only child: you get to take all the stuff you want and nobody argues with you about it.

When you have siblings, however, everything is a bit different and may require delicate negotiating. All of you may want to own the special tea set your Dad brought back from Japan after World War II and only one of you will end up "winning" that round. On the other hand, there would be no negotiating if you see the torn ticket stub from your parents' first date as future trash while your sister sees it as a nostalgic "treasure" she wants to keep. Over the years your parents may have promised to leave some of their things to you or to various siblings. Those bequests may now create unpleasant friction within your family, a family who is also operating as TEAM POP.

Consider: how you and your family can avoid the foreseeable risks of family discord. Talk with each other candidly and kindly. Utilize today's technology like Skype and FaceTime to set up family meetings, not just to deal with POP issues, but to share yourselves with your distant siblings on holidays. If you think your family could benefit from some help, try some POP Family Coaching or other family counseling with a pastoral or counseling professional. The seeds for future controversy and much misery, even litigation, can be planted or uprooted before they root at this stage of your POPcycle. When your parents have left the planet, your siblings will hopefully be a source of continued love and devotion; it's important to pay attention to your family's well being and not expect the healing and good feelings to "automatically" occur without your paying them some focused attention.

Another good way to avoid such potential infighting is to discern when "unfinished emotional business" is overtaking the place of rational discourse and choices. That is, notice carefully if you and/or your siblings are bringing "unrelated matter," into your conversations about what to do with your parents' possessions. That may hypothetically take many forms. One may include such catty remarks as: "Sure, you want Mom's mink coat. You always liked those luxury items Mom had. But why do you need her coat? You found a husband who buys you lots of them. It's just like when we were kids, you thought you were entitled to all Mom's pretty stuff that she didn't use anymore. You remember the pink taffeta dress…"

Family relations will improve if each of you separates out the past issues from the present time. Everyone needs to stay on POP purpose as intra-family squabbling over inequities or antiquities from the past will only serve to undermine your efforts. Talk about how to make wise decisions together today and focus on your parents' best interests. What's wanted and needed today among you POParent-siblings is family unity. Avoid making comments that interpret people's behavior rather than resolve the issues. Stay away from trying to prove something about the past with your siblings. Don't attribute a meaning to which sibling gets what possessions from your parents' estate or who is allowed to do whatever with your parents' things since doing so can easily divert your collective attention away from the main thrust of POP.

My advice is to do all you can to avoid seeding more family problems into your future. Since your siblings will predictably be here long after your parents are no longer around, aim to be considerate to their sensitivities even as you're learning to be a more loving POParent. Every family has its strengths and limitations. Greed, bitterly spoken differences of opinion, sarcasm and disdainful judgments can undermine or even destroy the very harmony you're trying to construct.

It might be you're arguing when you're really just sad that your folks will eventually leave the planet and abandon you. It might be human nature to argue about stuff if anger is easier to tolerate than sadness. We need to face that some people in every family are more concerned with money and material things than others. It's likely they've been acting that way for decades. If that conduct reappears now in this setting and it's likely it will, use whatever tried and true "techniques" you've developed, if you have any, to weaken the damaging and divisive impact of this on your family. Staying on target with your POP mission will help you to do that: after all, POP's not about the money; it's about your folks.

POPlan #9: Five Tools To Strengthen Family Ties When Dealing With Your Parents' Stuff

TOOL #1: Your "assignment" at this stage in the POPcycle is to find, sort, take, clean, give away, sell, store, fumigate or otherwise deal with your parents' things. A good way to start tackling this is to "huddle together" with your TEAM POP and discover who among you is the most skilled in doing this type of organizational work. Designate that person the leader. Knowing who's "in charge" will help bring this POP task into the present rather than automatically relying on former family roles and assuming the oldest is in charge. The team will want to learn what practical tools have worked well in the past for its members with detail-laden projects? Was it lists, online apps, a buddy system, Excel spreadsheets? To optimize results, the team's quarterback may wish to: include everyone's good ideas, present clearly defined tasks, with agreed-upon goals and reasonable times to quit working each day.

TOOL #2: Examining your parents' possessions can provide the chance to argue or, better yet, to sit down with your family for some intimate interactions, even re-bonding. Taking some time together around the proverbial fireplace or the kitchen table during this phase of physical labor to share about your collective past or more recent challenges can turn out to be enormously beneficial. It may help you feel like a family again. You might even invite your children and grandchildren to join your parents in a series of conversations called "life reviews." Your parents' re-telling of their old memories and the family's listening in a non-judgmental way can be very satisfying, resulting in renewed closeness.

TOOL #3: Your family may be more physical and less talk-y. Maybe "life reviews" aren't your style. For you, strengthening family ties is likely to involve engaging in activities together. You like cooking your favorite ethnic foods together and then eating them, playing board games from the old days, like Monopoly or Scrabble, or taking a stroll in the "old neighborhood" (even if some of you are in wheelchairs) can be a comfort, linking the known from the past with the current moment.

TOOL #4: Aiming to "meet your parents" as if they were new people can strengthen family ties by showering your parents with the attention and curiosity you might show a stranger seated next to you on a plane. By doing so, you might learn your parents had interests you were unaware of or had expanded themselves in ways never before known to you. More importantly, when you use this tool, you're committing to live in the present as much as possible by grounding yourself and your family relationships in today's reality. Maybe you've had the experience of walking in on your Dad as he was actively engaged with someone who was a stranger to you. You may have been surprised at how much more lucid and passionate your father seemed with the stranger than he sometimes acted with the family. Sometimes we feel constrained and ironically act more inauthentically around our family than around strangers. This tool can help.

TOOL #5: Finally, you may feel closer to your family after you do some work on yourself. Rather than trying to change anyone else which is essentially hopeless, you can focus your energy on becoming more peaceful and satisfied with your own performance. Strengthening family ties is easiest when you're already feeling content, confident and proficient as a POParent.

Find the right circumstance for you to be alone and undisturbed. Turn off your electronic devices and other interference opportunities. Allow yourself the time and space to get clear by asking yourself these questions about this stage of your POPcycle.

- *What thoughts and opinions did you have about yourself and you parents when you saw their possessions and knew you'd have to decide what to do with all of them? Did you wonder why they'd kept certain things and not others? Did you learn things you'd never known about your parents? Were you shocked or maybe upset that "no one had ever told you" or maybe that your siblings knew things about your parents but you didn't? Is there something more you need to do, forgive or say to someone to become more peaceful?*

- *Did you learn anything new about yourself doing this part of POP? Can you feel your emotions – like sad, mad, and glad – and distinguish them from your opinions, which are thoughts not emotions? How else might you like to think or feel about your parents' stuff and this phase of the POPcycle? Remind yourself of the fact that humans have in excess of 60,000 + thoughts every single day. Then tell yourself you can find out how to be at peace even while you're holding some conflicting judgments and feelings.*

- *In order to function in a more loving way with your family and be more peaceful within yourself, maybe you can re-frame the parts that are troubling you regarding your parents' things, your siblings' attitudes or this part of your POPcycle? If you can reframe it, do that now. If not, "make up" some thoughts that will allow you to see the current situation in a more compassionate or acceptable light because that will actually help calm you.*

- *Intend to savor the happiness behind your memories that were recently stimulated from viewing your parents' collectibles? Can you separate out and then release the parts of your recollections that have remained painful all these years? If so, do that now. If not, contemplate and then express to yourself what you're most grateful for at this time in your life and your POPcycle. You will then be able to move on with more peacefulness, closure and compassion.*

POP Music: Listening To The Right Music While "Dealing" With Your Parents' Stuff

I "prescribe" putting on upbeat music you all enjoy while doing your "stuff-related" POP tasks. Playing the right kind of music can distract you from your unwanted thoughts and feelings. It may even transform those into more enjoyable and productive ones. Doing that should improve everyone's mood and even your efficiency.

You may like "rockin' and boppin'" to music you've downloaded on your iPod or mp3 while doing your POP "sorting and packing." You and your parents are likely to enjoy listening to radio stations that broadcast music from categories termed "retro" or "the music of your life." Some online radio stations even stream your parents' era of musical favorites live online.[45] Never underestimate how the right choice in music can create the right atmosphere.

---

[45] You can find them by going to http://www.1260.am and www.retro1260.com.

Chapter 10

Settling Our Parents Into
Their New Lives

My Story

    Both by training and inclination I'd always been fascinated with how the human brain works. Now I wondered about Jack and Lillian's minds. Why had they tolerated eighty-eight snow-numbing east coast winters when they could have lived in the sunshine where their joints wouldn't ache and their only child could come by for lunch? Had they seen themselves as pioneers from New Jersey or "survivors" of challenges, like Frank Sinatra had crooned of New Yorkers: " ... if I can make it there, I can make it anywhere...?"[46]

---

[46] Paraphrased from a line in the song, "New York, New York," written by John Kander and Fred Ebb and published by EMI/ Uniart Catalog, Inc.

But years of practicing psychotherapy had taught me that people have different values and therefore other people's minds seem a bit inexplicable to us. I'd also learned that my road to greater contentment lay in being grateful that my parents were here now rather than understanding why it had taken so long to get them here. Upon their arrival at the AL there were innumerable things I'd wanted to do so my folks would feel welcome. Now that I'd started making many of their important decisions, my main goal was to help them enjoy healthier, richer lives in their California setting.

While doing POP long distance, my default position had been to be "overly protective." In the past, I'd erred on the side of doing more than was necessary for my parents rather than less. I'd thought long and hard and always planned ahead. I had lots of Plan B's, C's and even a few D's. I was the POPoster Mom for "Be prepared!" Maybe that had been my way of compensating for not being in the same city where they lived. But now that I was virtually "down the block," I wanted to "get it right" and avoid doing too many things.

How would I know when I should help? How could I accurately hit the mark and do neither too much nor too little for them? The last thing I wanted was to undermine my parents' dignity or skills. Particularly when they were first getting used to their AL and to our new relationship in this California location, I wanted my Mom to feel comfortable that I wasn't going to micro-manage everything or "run her life." I wanted Dad to know that I'd stop "helping" him long before I'd automatically cut his food into little cubes.

My goal was to see what worked for Lillian and Jack in their AL and then do more of that. I figured that the three of us would do our best, were I to stand back a bit and take a little time to observe how they were doing "on their own" at the AL. Breathing through my anxiety to have everything "figured out" immediately, I reminded myself that was impossible as things just took longer with aging parents. Ah how wonderful, for I realized that I too could slow down! I just needed to better observe how they were faring in their new environment.

When I slowed down and held the intention to observe rather than assume I knew what would be best, I was in the best position to discover what was actually occurring. And by doing that, I also learned to be more discerning. I found I could more clearly hear when my parents needed me and when they didn't. Maybe I could even wait until they asked for my help? I wanted them to feel confident and to keep "stretching" and now I wondered again: if I didn't run in so quickly, would they and could they do more for themselves?

Since beginning POP, I'd always encouraged Mom and Dad to be as self-sufficient as possible. I knew that by being too protective, whatever that was, I might be undermining their ability to do things for themselves. That could also make them lazy, become depressing to them and weaken the very "muscles" we all wanted strengthened.

Finding that "fine line" of where "not too much help" was located and then living up to it was challenging because it was ever changing. In spite of starting many a visit promising myself to do no more than was warranted, I often found myself drifting into "autopilot," as I now termed it and "over-parenting" them. I'd be lifting something they could move or offering to make a dinner arrangement when they were perfectly capable of doing that for themselves. When I saw it, I'd stop myself in my tracks. I felt I was beginning to treat my Mom and Dad like they were children, not the adults with some limitations they truly were. I knew that my continuing to act in that way wouldn't be good for our relationship. So, in addition to subtlely watching them, I kept a watch on myself as well.

As I aimed to make their transition "seamless," I reviewed what they'd needed Florence to do. When Jack and Lillian had still been in their NYC home, they'd needed minimal physical help from Florence on the five days each week she was there. She assisted with a few of their basic activities of daily living (ADL's)[47] like taking baths and dressing. But most of her work had involved assisting them with their instrumental activities of daily living (IADL's)[48] like seeing they took their medications, food shopping, preparation and cleanup, house cleaning and laundry. She'd also been the one who accompanied and transported Mom and Dad to their doctor appointments, rehab, haircuts and trips to the accountant at tax season.

Many of those tasks would now be done for my parents by me or at the AL. Their bathrooms would be cleaned, healthy meals prepared and other domestic matters attended to. Mom and Dad would also be furnished a variety of new recreational and health opportunities such as exercise programs, outings, lectures and trips to the mall. I'd anticipated having to pay for a fair number of extra hours of caregiving once they were at the AL and was pleasantly surprised to learn how little additional they seemed to need.

Before long Mom and Dad were participating in their new life and community. The AL had its own rhythm and schedules and they seemed to have no trouble adapting to it. They were happily taking the van to the mall to do some small shopping

---

[47] See Glossary.

[48] See Glossary.

trips, remarking on how good the food tasted and Mom was even attending some chair yoga classes.

Now that they were finally close by, I looked forward to more direct contact with their medical providers. I went about the process of interviewing and hiring a small medical team for them and then watched it grow. They needed a dentist, cardiologist, eye doctor, audiologist, geriatric internist and a geriatric psychiatrist. I also wanted my parents to go to my longevity specialist, hoping that seeing him would lengthen and strengthen their lifetime with me. Eventually they both would also have to undergo the cataract surgeries that almost all older parents have, requiring another specialist. Dad's fall would need us to have a brain surgeon and a whole rehab team; Mom's fall would require an orthopedic surgeon and several rehab teams as well.

I was recommended to a kind dentist who had retirement in his future in a nearby town and set up an initial appointment there for Lillian and Jack. I researched a good local optometrist and arranged for them to get new glasses. Repeatedly I took a frustrated Mom to her very patient audiologist. Improving the quality of hearing can be an almost impossible goal, as I have discovered with even my very wealthy older patients who would pay anything for better hearing aids but the audiologist tried over and again.

I trekked my aging parents the hour and a half drive each way to work with Dr. Barry Fox, the well respected "longevity doctor" I used. Getting Mom and Dad to make the long ride into downtown Los Angeles to see him was tough. I insisted. By the time my folks came to town, a contemporary of theirs, Barry was still actively practicing medicine and dispensing sage advice, dietary supplements after testing for their body's deficits and other "disease prevention" routines. Barry was always inspiring and I wanted them to receive the same high-quality holistic care I sought for myself.

Taking them to these doctor visits I got to know their assorted physicians fairly well. Most of them were immensely kind and caring to my Mom and Dad but I also knew that older patients receive more thorough medical attention when a POParent attends the visit with them. I considered my POP job to extend far beyond being the driver. I actively participated, asked probing questions my parents didn't think to ask or felt intimidated about because doctors are "authority figures." I also helped by gently correcting my parents' short-term recall of recent events or even their long-term memory. After the visits, I would follow up with them to see they were adhering to their doctor's requirements and reminding them of the more subtle suggestions they hadn't heard or remembered to do.

Back in the day when it was less common to do so, many of my parents' physicians gave me access to them beyond ordinary office hours via their cell phones. I was delighted to be able to locate such competent and generous people. I knew, from some of my patients and those I've POP Family Coached, that wasn't a usual practice but my family and I were very fortunate in this regard and I will always be very grateful.

How natural it was becoming for me to take care of things for them all the time – to be the parent – instead of the other way around as it used to be! My next step, after seeking to advance their health, was helping with their finances. I set up a meeting at a neighborhood bank branch, introduced them to their new banker and opened a checking account for them. I arranged for their Social Security checks to be deposited directly into their new account, so they'd have their money regularly deposited without any effort on their part. I was listed as a co-signatory on their checking account so I could write checks for them and, should there be a problem, I would be advised. Since I ended up writing all their checks – for caregiver care, medicine, and supplemental insurance – and balanced their accounts, they never met the banker again.

I also took on as my POP "job" when they were newly in town, to arrange for much of my parents' cultural lives. I modeled myself on the way I'd seen them raise me in this regard and felt like I was somehow honoring them when I followed their lead in my POParenting. I was very young when my parents first introduced me to music, comedy and art, sharing their love of these with me. Even when they could barely afford the price of admission, Jack and Lillian felt it important to expose their daughter to theater, museums and even opera, which they didn't particularly like.

I was actually seven when my parents took me to my first Broadway play, "Inherit the Wind." It was an amazing spectacle with brilliant acting, writing and directing. The play reenacted a famous trial from the 1920's when a Southern teacher is banned from teaching the truth of evolution to his students. Seeing on stage how lawyers could play such a meaningful role in bringing about or blocking societal change and being incredibly moved by all I saw, I decided then and there to become an attorney.

Now it had become my turn to take Jack and Lillian to plays, art museums and cultural events in 21st century Los Angeles! What a surprise I had in store for me! Far more important than the entertainment being presented to my folks was their level of physical comfort. They no longer enjoyed walking around museums nor being driven through them in wheelchairs. The effort it took them to get to and exit from the theater, their difficulty hearing the performers and their disliking "missing dinner" at the AL began to be insurmountable barriers to the cultural enrichment I was trying to provide them.

So I realized it was I who would have to adapt. I tried coming up with "fun opportunities" that might be more comfortable for my aging parents. My motivation was good: I didn't want their worlds to become any "smaller." I wanted to keep their brains engaged and heed the dangers of "use it or lose it." But this, like many other things, wasn't up to me.

So after a while, I learned. Mom, Dad and I spent many an afternoon visiting around the radio, like the days of their youth before television. I found the local "time of your life" radio stations that played old show tunes and even standards Jack had written. We'd sing along.

I watched my father relish his peaceful times. He'd borrow a book from the residents' library, settle into a comfortable chair, take off his glasses and be in heaven. I'd smile finding him buried under his book. When Dad's memory starting to fail him, I'd sometimes noticed he was reading the same book more than once. It reminded me of children, endlessly craving their favorite book or DVD. Re-reading never seemed to bother the very young or the very old. I tried to let it not bother me either.

Decades earlier doing the Sunday NY Times crossword puzzles was a family ritual we'd all engaged in and loved. My Mom had been the real puzzle champion, completing the Times' puzzles daily and in pen, a real feat. Especially after her "diagnosis" of Alzheimer's, the fact that she continued to try her hand at them kept me so delighted that I made a "deal" with her: for the rest of her days, as long as she wanted new puzzle books, I'd happily buy them.

Next I checked out their new neighborhood's religious opportunities, something they'd done for me so long ago. Their AL had religious people who held services there on special holidays and other occasions. Even though my Mom and Dad weren't very involved in their religion, the fact that their AL offered a piece of their own cultural tradition right there at home helped to make their transition easier.

Mom and Dad liked dining at the AL and the regularity of their meals and menu offerings there. Nonetheless, they also enjoyed my taking them out to eat and doing so became one of our new rituals, especially after they lost interest in going to plays or concerts. They were particularly snooty about their New York delicatessens. "Jane, you're out in the West. None of these delis can touch the Madison Deli near the apartment or the Stage in midtown," they'd boast with personal pride. Of course, they were right. They knew their New York fare.

On holidays I'd try to take them out somewhere special. My requirements for such during my POPcycle were a restaurant: they'd tried before and already liked; where the acoustics permitted carrying on a conversation; located a short drive from their AL; with a patient wait staff.

My Mom had been a "foodie" and, early on, shared her joy of trying new tastes with me. However at this juncture, her taste buds and sense of smell were likely to have dulled and maybe been dulled a bit by eating the food at the AL three times a day. So, like with kids, my Mother would often "celebrate holidays" by eating too much of a new taste she loved or gorging on a large meal and then a gooey dessert. Getting her home before she got sick in the car was itself a challenge. As with so much of POP, that reality had been long forgotten until writing this. I see how I've often filtered my memories through the mist of time passing and missing my parents.

Neither Jack nor Lillian seemed to be making new friends easily, if at all, at the AL. Dad was content reading, watching his shows on television and spending his time with Mom and with me. He didn't find any men who really interested him as friends and I could understand how his unusual profession and successive life experiences might make it hard to find "peers." One day I approached him and talked about his absence of sociability to which he replied: "Look around, Jane. Think about my interests and the life I've had. I just don't see anyone here I'd really want to spend much time with, aside from you and your Mom, of course. Would you want to be friends with these guys?"

I thought about trying to "fix it." I even went so far as to check out the more sophisticated "New York-looking" couples at their AL when I visited. But I drew the line at setting up play dates for my parents. Talk about over-protecting them! I had no idea how could I be "social" on my folks' behalf.

As Mom and Dad were becoming somewhat familiar faces at their AL, I did come up with one idea that had some socializing overtones. They often staged theme-centered evenings for the residents and, when I approached the administrator with the idea of holding an event – a Frank Sinatra evening with live singing – she was game. The evening turned out to be a huge success. The social director/singer aka Frank crooned out all the favorite Sinatra songs, including a few written by my Dad. Jack didn't say a whole lot about it but looked really pleased. As I'd hoped, this garnered him some brief celebrity status at the facility and Mom and I had a blast, too.

As I was figuring out how to become a better local POParent, I aimed to include some of the POP Family Coaching tools I'd recommended that had proven useful to other families. One such technique involved approaching your own parents "as if" they were complete strangers to you. When we meet new people, we often relate to them with curiosity and much interest rather than assuming we already understand them or their motivations. What I hoped to do with that tool was to develop the facility with people I already know well to hear them "as if" they were new, to take in who they are and what they're saying with a kind of neutral fascination.

I wanted to try that out and act as if these intimates of mine were new to me. In a way, my parents were new people to me. We'd been living apart for over 35 years and each of us had grown and experienced so much during that time. If I could give up the idea (for this exercise) that I knew them well or was supposed to, I might actually be able to "meet" my parents where they were now.

When I became able to offer Jack and Lillian the respect, inquiry and interest I gave to new people, my relationship with them improved dramatically. It wasn't that hard to do since I truly aimed to discover who Lillian and Jack had become as people over these decades, aside from simply being my parents. This required that I ask more questions, listen more fully to their responses and pass fewer judgments. By making just these slight alterations, I noticed my parents began to feel more respected and more at ease with their move, as did I.

Another technique I teach others in POP Family Coaching and thought would be useful for myself at this time was "re framing.[49]" In re-framing, we teach ourselves to not react "automatically" and overly emotionally. By using our intelligence to assign a more uplifting interpretation to events, we can change our moods and expand our head for solutions. When I pictured the scenario of my parents' move as my having dragged my "enfeebled" elderly parents to their last resting place in a senior institution, I felt horrible. But reframed, I could see myself as the gracious hostess welcoming my dear old friends/parents to their new town and new life. Thinking about it that way, I felt less depressed. I wasn't fooling myself but rather adding in another point of view that resulted in my feeling calmer and better able to help them.

Settling my folks into their new life in California -- finding them their AL, their doctors, their local cleaner, banker and delicatessen - was yet another opportunity to see the "role reversal" or the "Circle of Life," as some of us prefer to call it. I favor the term "Circle of Life" to explain my POP experience because it evokes in me a sense of continuity, predictability and an unending connection. The term "role reversal"

---

[49] This is a tool well-recognized and respected in cognitive therapy settings and in many other schools of expanding happiness, self-help and human potential.

suggests something is interfering with the natural order and that things are being forced backwards in the universe. Taking care of an aging Lillian and Jack felt oddly right to me, even orderly.

I had the thought that I wanted to be a better POParent to them than my parents had been to me. I wasn't coming from the position of being competitive but I wanted to become the best me - whether I was being a POParent, a lawyer or a therapist. I loved it when I could exceed my own previous levels of POParental patience or kindness. I felt like I was healing spots in my own heart when I could act even more compassionately when parenting them than they had when parenting me. Jack and Lillian weren't the only ones changing. I was changing too.

The direction of the POPcycle is relentless: my parents became more dependent and I more responsible. Once I'd begun managing certain things for my Mom and Dad, they never asked to regain control of those things. Our roles and functions were in constant flux going one way and that required "dexterity" on my part. The only reliable POP predictor was unpredictability but, at least now, I had my parents settled in and closer to me. Hopefully a long distance phone call wouldn't be all I had to help me diagnose a stroke or prevent a suicide. I could be right there.

Their Story – A Woman Named Vanna

When my beloved husband Xavier died in the late 1970's, I suffered an amazing loss in my life. Fortunately our sons were incredibly supportive and my career as a high-powered magazine editor was still in high gear back then. My children who lived all over the country encouraged me to continue my life even marry another man two years later. And so I did.

My second husband was an advertising executive that Xavier and I had known in business for over twenty years. We too had a fine marriage but after fourteen years, it was cut short when he died in Houston where we'd moved. Dealing with my second widowhood, I returned to New York City shortly thereafter and retired unofficially. I was 79 then.

I traveled to Europe and Asia with women friends whom I had cherished all my life and for a while, that was fascinating. But inevitably age took its toll and travel became more complicated. Eventually even the pleasure of visiting my two older sons who lived far from New York was undermined because of how exhausting the trips had become.

Soon thereafter I also took several falls. One of those required my temporarily living in a home to recuperate fully. My three sons apparently talked together and reached a consensus:

because I already needed some help at my own place and because of my advanced age, their Mom would need to leave the elegant apartment she cherished. She could either move into a secure senior citizen facility – one that would accommodate her and her priceless architecturally designed modern furniture, paintings and sculpture –- or she could move in with one of them.

Live with my children? NO WAY! I adore them and their families but living with them in their homes would be trouble and trauma! But could I live in a senior facility full of old folks whom I believed would be standoffish or suspicious of a newcomer or some hot shot "career lady?" NO WAY! Where did those two "NO WAY" options leave me now, I wondered?

The kids persisted, pressing me for a final decision. As I now like to say, I chose the lesser of two evils. While "screaming and kicking," I opted for a senior facility where I could live in my own apartment with my own things and could eat as many meals as I wished to pay for. In the new facility I could swim, watch movies and invite my boys and their families to the private dining room for holiday dinners with me. The staff here knows to call up to my apartment if I don't show up somewhere in the building by 10:30 in the morning. I am independent *and* my sons feel safe!

To act like the editor I once used to be – and make this long wonderful story shorter – within a month of arriving there, I was asked to manage our facility's library. That job is something I've done and adore doing all these years later. Most importantly within six months of my arrival, I'd met six new women who were the most wonderful people, right here in my own building. They've become my dear friends, museum companions and loving confidantes.

Had I not gone along when my kids insisted on it, I might not have come here or to a place like this until much later in my life if at all. Had I put off facing the inevitable – I wouldn't always be able to care for myself – I feel certain that the best part of my years here, the companionship piece, might never have occurred. Part of the beauty of my sons' timing was that I was still able to make new and deep connections with other people. I've seen with other new residents that if they arrived here "too late" in their lives, it can be really difficult to make new friends and have a good time with other peers.

Now when my family comes to visit, they kid me that I can't find the time in my busy agenda to see them. Well, that's not really true and never will be. I'll always make time for them. I speak my mind and do so loudly and I love my sons most for their not allowing my possible "displeasure" to stop them from saying and doing what they knew was right for me.

I see that my children have indeed become my parents and I toast them and their POParenting ways. They must have had a good role model!

Your Story

Moving is stressful at any age. If you're taking your older parents away from the comforts of their home, the places they're familiar with and things they know, you can plan on having some stressful days. You will need to manage your own as well as your parents' anticipated angst. You will also need to respond to their questions, however many times they may ask. You may find yourself absorbing a lot of emotions and, if your parents are like mine, they will worry before the move, as it's happening and they may even worry after it's over. But sooner or later, they will begin to enjoy their new life. And after a while, hopefully they'll be grateful to you for where they've "landed."

If your parents can comprehend it, your first step will be to explain the whole move from start to finish to your parents. In many ways their understanding the scenario is less important than their confidence that you know what you're doing. It's likely they'll want to know at least the following: when is the move; how will it happen; who will help; what will happen to their valuables; how will the furniture from their three-story house fit into a one bedroom unit.

Do not underestimate the significance of your parents' leaving their home – their place of dominion and control – forever. Even if your parents aren't very talkative and even if it feels odd, it will help if you invite them to sit down and share all their concerns about the move with you, one-by-one. Listen fully. Respond kindly and be as specific in your answers as is appropriate to their level of understanding. Never make fun of any of your parents' worries. You may want to dismiss your folks as "classic worriers" or believe that what they're bothered by isn't very important.

I learned over time to take my parents' expressed concerns seriously. Even many years after my Mom was diagnosed with dementia, any time she expressed a complaint, I found that I needed to carefully check it out. You should honor and respectfully evaluate your parents' apprehensions and complaints.

Their upcoming move may be one where your parents are in less control than at any other time in their adult lives. Under the stress they may become aggressive because of their current lack of control or their inability to remember information you've already told them. For your Dad who will no longer be able to putter around in the garage or have "his" room to watch the games in, leaving home can be depressing. Your parents may be sad at losing the companionship of dear friends or the delights of their old neighborhood. Your Mom may say it wasn't "in her plans" to lose her kitchen, her sewing room or her tub. She too may leave home kicking and screaming, like Vanna or worse yet, balling like a child.

Think of what this move must be like for your parents who often have a limited sense of hearing, sight, smell and may have limited funds as well. They're watching brawny strangers handling their precious, breakable possessions or packing up their undergarments. They're leaving almost everyone they know to go to a place they've never even seen near "their daughter-in-law's house." They can't take all their furniture and beloved art with them because they're going into a small apartment or your house. They're afraid of losing life-long neighborhood friends and that no one will call them on their new long-distance phone number (which they're having trouble remembering). And they're departing from the home where they raised you, recovered from cancer, grieved the death of your sister or whatever life story they lived inside the walls of their home.

Your ability to demonstrate your POP compassion at this significant moment may make a big difference to your relationship with your Mom and Dad. Aim to keep engaging with your parents and attending to their requests with patience even when they repeat themselves. This will help keep them grounded and will add to their confidence in you. During the move your focus will need to be on resolving logistics and on your parents' immediate concerns.

The move may itself bring up some latent fears your parents have been having as it is full of potential trauma. At some later point after they're settled in and, depending on your parents' capabilities to do so, you may wish to address deeper, underlying fears they may be contemplating or even obsessing over, such as their own mortality or concerns about your sibling's future. By being in an ongoing dialogue with them, hopefully you can allay some of these worries or bring them to a professional who can help.

Days before the move you will have asked your parents to select (or you can choose for them, if they can't) some of their treasured items to "hand-carry" to their new home. These things will likely evoke welcoming feelings for them in the new place. Consistency is very calming. Seeing and touching their familiar, loved things in their new residence may mitigate some of the negative feelings your parents have associated with leaving home. The more infirmed your parents have become, the more they may enjoy having a few of their favorite objects around, when they arrive elsewhere.

If you can create familiar smells, tastes and sights in their new place, that could ease some of the challenge to your parents' transition. Doing this may be easiest when your parents are moving into your home (or that of one of a sibling) with people who cook traditional foods, perhaps using your Mom's recipes or, in other ways, reminiscent of their cultural roots. Your decision to "lug" Dad's favorite TV chair and ottoman to his new home, heavy though they were, may make all the difference in his feeling comfortable there. And if you're moving your parents to this country from overseas, bring along some of their favorite regional foods and find a place to refresh your supply: that alone could prove more valuable than you can imagine.

Your kids likely trained you as parents to bring along a beloved stuffed animal, however ragged, wherever you took them. I recommend you apply a similar principle if your parents have to spend time in a lonely hospital room. If you bring along one or two of your parent's favorite objects, even when your senior parents' memories are failing, their handling those things may lower your parents' blood pressure and speed their recovery. Seeing their beloved treasure or trinket can trigger a reminder on a feeling level that they're loved and safe.

Once your parents have arrived at their new home, you can take a series of deep breaths. The first thing you'll want to do is lower your expectations of your parents' immediate appreciation and joy. They may react much less positively than you'd hoped. Even if you're certain their new home is safer, cleaner and now closer to you, don't expect them to share your view that it's necessarily "better." Not yet. Give your parents some time to adjust (remember "old dogs and new tricks..."). Remember that you carefully chose their new place and that major adjustments take some time to absorb.

This is the time to consider how else to make your parents feel settled. If your Mom loves playing canasta, maybe you can find her a game where she's at a similar skill level with her fellow players? If your Dad would still like to putter with tools but doesn't have his garage to do so anymore, maybe you can enroll him in a shop class or ask him to do a small work task at your home?

If your parents are too aged to socialize much or aren't very talkative, you might consider getting them a pet. No, I'm not suggesting you buy your frail parents a 120-pound German shepherd who needs walking four times a day. But being around trained or domesticated animals can provide extraordinary companionship and make a real difference in the quality of your parents' lives.

Since many seniors have limited intimate physical contact and get touched only occasionally, they can suffer from a kind of failure to thrive[50] when left untouched like our youngest infants. Who knows, maybe a cat or a bird could provide your parents a whole new lease on life? I've seen it happen. Even without getting involved in the responsibilities of animal ownership, because of the therapeutic benefits, there are agencies that bring trained animals to visit in nursing homes. If your parents' facility doesn't already do so, you might ask them to consider it.

For their own protection, there may come a time and usually does in every POPcycle when you (or someone on TEAM POP) will need to take over some or all aspects of your folks' business life – their checkbooks, investments, dealings with Medicare, etc. How will you know when that is? Your parents' geriatrician may advise you that "it's time" or your parents may give you clues that your involvement is appropriate. You may discover they've paid someone twice having "forgotten, honey" that they'd already sent the first check. Older parents are

---

[50] See Glossary.

frequent victims of financial fraud schemes so you will want to hear a "wake-up call" to take on their finances before something more dire occurs.

It may be that a small step is all that's needed and that helping your parents with their money involves small incremental changes, like much of POP. You may go from their sharing no information to your being emailed copies of your parents' bank account statements on a monthly basis. The next step may be setting up their accounts as joint with you or someone else they've delegated as a co-signator.

Perhaps even more serious steps may have become appropriate in your family. Doing this in a timely fashion may help shield your parents from real disaster. Based upon your continuing observations of your parents' abilities and shortcomings, the designated person may now be writing all their checks and making all their fiscal and investment decisions. Wherever your parents are on this part of the POPcycle, when you're moving them to a new location, that's often a very good time to make some needed changes.

Taking over many financial responsibilities relieved my parents and me of much anxiety. Although some elderly parents will be relieved, others may be of two minds about your having this type, or extent, of control over their affairs. You may do a better job but your parents may resist especially if you approach it right after their move. At that moment, although your Mom and Dad will appreciate having you there to back them up, they may feel they've lost so much control – over their homes, bodily functions and even their minds – that they'll hesitate to cede more control, especially over their finances. Should this be an issue, you or the banker, broker or accountant should patiently explain to your parents the benefits of having a second person on their account, review their statements, balance their accounts and deal with any delinquency notices.

You will want to scout out your folks' new locale for whatever else they'd need or want nearby. For your family that may mean golf courses, restaurants, churches and shoe repair stores or vegan restaurants and yoga studios. Before signing them up with a pharmacy, you'll want to know which are on your parents' Medicare Plan, deliver prescriptions, are open 24/7, offer flu shots and crosscheck your parents' medications for dangerous drug interactions. Like me, you'll want to help your parents find their physicians, caregivers and maybe even their new friends. You may have to sign them up for phone, Internet or other communication services and then show them, over and over, how to use the remote control or the default settings.

Finally as you aim to bring your parents into the 21st century you may wish to share with them some of the advantages and advances in alternative and complementary medicines. Today many doctors trained in Western medicine agree that there are numerous positive results achieved with practices that might have been considered "out of the box" or untested in your parents' youth. Similarly, many reputable studies have validated a number of techniques that at one time seemed more questionable.

Your parents may find their painful and chronic conditions vastly improved by practices such as yoga, meditation, acupuncture and acupressure, chiropractic adjustments or visualization techniques. Using appropriate supplements for aging bodies, giving more naturopathic substances along with using fewer pharmaceuticals and other alternative treatments may not yet provided by Medicare but things are changing. You may need to advocate for anything outside of the ordinary with their providers and argue with your parents for anything outside "comfort zone." But as good POParents, one of the things you can try to do is to get your aging loved ones better health in their new homes.

Sooner or later, the time will come when your whirlwind of tasks begins to quiet down, your parents find themselves adjusting to their move and you adapting, too. Maybe you'll even hear them say they're enjoying their new home and transplanted lives.

POPlan #10: Settling Our Parents Into Their New Lives After Asking Ourselves: What Age Have Our Parents Been Acting Lately?

The POPcycle reflects the Circle Of Life in all its poignancy with your parents regressing physically and even emotionally in many ways. By this stage of POP your parents often appear less dependent on you than they may be. They're too big to be picked up and carried off to the doctor, even when you may need to do that. Your "charges" have known you your whole life and, in all likelihood, still know how to press your buttons – whether or not they ever formed a successful parental bond and no matter how old they are.   As a result, when you're helping them re-settle into new lives, you'll need to figure out – yes, again – how to be effectively "persuasive" when disagreements arise between you and them and how much you should intervene on their behalf.

Discerning your optimal involvement level will be one of the most challenging parts of settling your parents into their new lives. What should you do for them, how often and how much? How will you know the answer to these complicated questions?

First, observe them and their surroundings more carefully than you usually observe things around you. You can actually "see more" when you set the intention to pay better attention. A great deal of POParenting involves looking, asking and listening to what's being said as well as to what isn't being articulated. POParents often seem to develop that intuitive sense, like parents of children, that alerts them to possible hazards, sometimes to know things that aren't logically knowable. I'd seen that happen myself when, from thousands of miles away, I'd "gotten the message" to call and interrupt Jack's suicide attempt.

Second, you can seek regular and detailed feedback from those who are in frequent contact with your parents, such as their doctors, caregivers, neighbors and the staff at their residence. You can arrive "unbidden" and visit your parents at unexpected times in their new residences now that they're living closer. Although this might seem to be intrusive or rude, were you dropping in on a friend, you should keep in mind that, at this point in the POPcycle, your parents have become "your responsibility." Checking on them when neither they nor their facilities are expecting you can sometimes reveal enlightening information.

If your parents are still able to carry on intelligent conversations, function in their relationships, do volunteer work or go to a job, it's reasonable to expect they'll be making many of their own decisions and need you less at this point than they may later on. If however your parents and you have progressed further along the POPcycle, you can expect to have to do more. And what can you do if your parents refuse to follow any of your suggestions?

By way of example, Jeanne (not her real name) came to my office struggling with her Dad Ed, who at 88, still remained self-sufficient in many ways. He lived in a Board and Care which he'd been enjoying until his feet started hurting him. Ed's foot pain was now so bad that it was getting in the way of his walking, but he refused to go to a podiatrist or anywhere else to get help. Historically "opinionated," Ed now began arguing with Jeanne and her siblings about every idea they gave him. Jeanne told me how frustrated she was. She clearly saw the consequence of Ed's refusal to go to a podiatrist: he wasn't getting out of his room except for meals, had aches and pains from sitting all day and Ed was getting depressed from his isolation. Jeanne was totally at a loss as to how to resolve their dispute.

Before coming to see me, Jeanne had spent many hours trying to understand her Dad's thinking, speculating on why he was refusing her assistance. Maybe Dad didn't want to meet one more doctor? Maybe he was rebelling against any more changes in his life, like having to put orthotics in his shoes or get his toenails cut by a professional? Maybe he was tired of Jeanne and her siblings "helping" him so much?

The significant question for you the POParent is not finding out why your Dad is acting as he is. Instead, the better question is to find out HOW to effectively work with him so he become less defensive and acts more reasonably. I surprised Jeanne when I told her to give up her search for why. She might never know WHY he was so resistant to her efforts. It might remain a mystery to her and even to Ed what was going on in his mind. Your parents' motivations aren't where to place your attention. You're a POParent not a psychoanalyst! I told Jeanne that instead of attempting to analyze Ed, she should focus on how she was going to get him to the foot doctor.

You may be challenged as you're learning how to successfully advocate reasonable positions with increasingly dependent and aging parents. How can you best accomplish that? I suggested to Jeanne that she take the *"HOW OLD ARE YOUR PARENTS ACTING NOW?"* test. You won't find this one in any geriatric textbook but I developed this "test" when I was struggling at this stage of POP with my own parents. When I encountered Jack or Lillian acting "unreasonably," "irresponsibly" or "childishly," I'd ask myself: how old do my parents seem to be acting at this moment? Oddly enough if I asked, I'd always get a number in response.

Of course there's no right or wrong answer to this "test" but thinking of my parents as children who were "acting out" when they were just being oppositional helped me get less aggravated. I noticed I could create more compassion and less annoyance when I used this tool. Even with Ed who wouldn't call for an orthotics appointment, it can be very useful to ask: *"WHAT AGE IS ED/DAD ACTING NOW?"* Jeanne too found it easier to see Ed as a frustrated 11 year-old boy who'd just entered his first debate and was learning the art of "being right" rather than as an irrational old man who "should know better." Jeanne imagined engaging with Ed's intellect and newly learned advocacy skills to "convince" him about the validity of orthotics. By handling Ed that way, Jeanne found she could help him regain his "maturity" and rationality.

Assigning your parents the age they're acting proves to be a surprisingly useful tool. One day when my own Mom was being particularly childish in her ear doctor's office, I was frustrated with her. I asked myself: *"WHAT AGE IS MOM ACTING NOW?"* My answer came back instantly: "six." Having discovered a response, it served as my guide on how to better manage her. When a six year-old is fidgety, telling her how much longer she'll have to wait isn't effective. A better approach is to divert the six year-old's attention by making up a game to play and melting the time away. It worked with Lillian.

When you find yourself at a loss, choosing whether to back off or insert yourself into some situation with your parents, give yourself the benefit of this POP tool: *"WHAT AGE ARE MY PARENTS ACTING NOW?"* Doing a quick inventory of your parents' recent relevant behaviors will not only help you figure out what age your parents have been acting, but more importantly, it will help you know how to change your behavior to be more effective.

Chapter 11

Trying To Make A Permanent Poplan – Do You Want To See God Laugh?

My Story

One evening I picked up my folks to take them out to dinner. I'd last seen them only a couple of days earlier and we'd talked on the phone since then. Dad had been lucid and I'd not ben alerted to any problems. We had an evening of good food and laughter but afterwards, I was troubled by the slowness of Dad's gait as he walked from our table to the door of the restaurant. Although he was moving at "the speed of molasses," my father seemed unaware of anything amiss. When we got outside, I watched as he slowly and deliberately inched his way onto my car seat.

I asked him specific questions about any recent events that might have triggered this particular change. He demurred and seemed confused. I wasn't sure how reliable his memory might be so I continued inquiring of him when he volunteered: "Maybe this has something to do with the fall I took in our bathroom a while back."

"What fall? You took a fall in the bathroom? How long ago? How come this is the first I'm hearing of it?" I sputtered out, trying to ask four questions at once and sound patient all at the same time. "You know. When I fell and hit my head the other day," he answered.

Apparently Jack had slipped and fallen in their bathroom and then neglected to mention it to me or to anyone else on the AL staff. It looked like Dad's fall had occurred nearly a month before! Upon questioning, he recalled hitting his head on the way down as he tried unsuccessfully to break his fall. He said he'd told Mom right after he'd pulled himself up from the floor in the bathroom. Likely she'd forgotten about the event soon thereafter. Generally speaking, she was no longer a reliable person to prompt Dad to remember things since Lillian didn't recall that much herself.

I tried to under-react, that technique I've described that worked for me repeatedly. I didn't want to chide my Father, like he was a bad child, for not informing somebody more appropriate, someone with a better memory than Mom about his fall and head injury! But I would have appreciated not having to wait a month to hear about and then respond to the potential repercussions of this fall. My being able to react quickly to things like the fall he'd taken was much of why I'd brought my parents closer in the first place. Hadn't I planned on being able to keep more current with their lives here?

What happened to that portion of our POPlan? Now, even with my parents living closer, I still felt out of the information loop. I was beginning to see that neither the short distance between their home and mine nor the small amount of time between visits would ensure I'd always be timely informed about everything POP. What were the implications of that, I wondered?

In the morning I arranged for the earliest possible visit with Dad's geriatric physician since I recognized that a blow to the head of an elderly man could be highly problematic. After a brief exam, his doctor had me take Dad directly to the ER to undergo brain scans. Those revealed a cerebral aneurysm, a weak or thin spot on a blood vessel in Dad's 89 year-old brain. An aneurysm can put pressure on a nerve or brain tissue and even rupture, spilling blood into the surrounding tissue. This one was growing so rapidly that it now threatened to pressure his brain and push it through the skull. Dad might have had the aneurysm since birth, I was told, but the more likely scenario was that this head trauma occurred during the recent fall. It all sounded unbelievably scary.

Dad's doctor and I quickly consulted several brain surgeons. They advised that unless we allowed him brain surgery, Dad's aneurysm would continue to protrude into the skull and end his life. I was told there were the three risks associated with Dad's having brain surgery. The first involved the anesthesia, the second was related to whatever injuries he might suffer from the invasive procedure and the third involved the challenges of brain surgery and recovery on a man his age. I was told to bring a copy of his DNR orders.[51] "Just in case," the doctors said.

I was told that Jack would also need extensive post-operative rehabilitation so he could relearn how to speak, eat, swallow and otherwise function. Unfortunately, their post-surgical prognosis wasn't much brighter. The doctors weren't certain he could recover successfully as no one yet knew how profound were his aging brain's limitations to learn "new things," how long it might take him to recover functioning or if he would he ever "come back."

I was filled with questions and there were few definitive answers. No one really knew. There were simply too many unknown factors. What I did know was I had no other viable choices since my father needed the surgery to survive and he needed it now. So, with a heavy heart, I authorized the doctors to shave his head in preparation for brain surgery and saw him instantly become my favorite bald-headed guy.

I wanted to concentrate completely on my Dad at this time but couldn't because, as any parent with more than one child knows, part of us needs to attend to the "other kids," even during an emergency. In my case, Mom also desperately needed me to be there for her. As might be expected Lillian too was suffering from shock and filled with her own fears and confusion while we were hearing about Dad's condition and proposed treatment.

Mom's dependence on my Dad had been part of their ongoing dynamic. Since his retirement, they'd done just about everything together. And by this point, my parents were spending most of their waking hours in the same room. They expected to eat together, take walks together, watch the same television programs and be with each other all the time. If my Mom needed something opened, Dad was there to open it for her. Even if Dad were hungry for lunch, he'd wait until she was ready to go with him.

During our endless wait for the surgeon to re-emerge with his crucial news, the woman who'd loved her husband for over sixty years and their only child agonized, sitting in limbo. Anyone who has had to sit in a hospital while a loved one is undergoes a complicated and dangerous procedure can identify with the agony and the fearful imaginings of what's ahead.

---

[51] See Glossary.

I thought of every possible concern. How would Dad's fall impact "the rhythm" my parents had created in their marriage and now at their facility? What would it be like for Jack to be staying alone in some rehabilitation center after his surgery? Would be lonely? Disoriented? Would Dad miss his wife and be unable to sleep? Would he ever learn to walk and talk again or spend his remaining days without Mom in continuing decline?

I further worried how Mom would survive her time without him. Would she continue to attend the activities she enjoyed -- her chair yoga classes and the bingo games? If Dad remained away long or didn't live beyond the surgery, how badly would Lillian's anxiety interfere with her functioning? Would she make new friends? How much additional attention would Mom need during Dad's rehabilitation? And on and on ...

When the surgeon finally emerged hours later, his demeanor was measured and calm. His tone reminded me of Sgt. Friday from Dragnet, "just the facts ma'am." I listened to him say he'd successfully removed as much as he safely could and that Dad should make a "decent recovery." I had just begun to breathe more freely when he added: "You know Jack's brain has been reduced to the size of a walnut from all his dementia." This was news and really shocked me.

None of Dad's physicians had ever alluded to his having this dreaded affliction. I tried to process both the cruel visual and the long-term consequences of this news when he dealt a second blow. The surgeon actually took a plastic soda bottle out of my mother's hand, pointed to the remains of her drink and said: "I had to take that much fluid out of his head." Unbelievable!! What insensitivity!! Thankfully, I don't think my Mom fully understood. She'd only heard the part that her man would be okay and returning to her and that made her very happy.

We were permitted a brief visit with him and Dad looked even smaller and frailer lying there attached to monitoring machines than I'd ever seen him. I could see that his would be an arduous recovery. Dad would need rest and then extensive rehabilitation in order to learn to walk and talk again. And I didn't know what, if anything, could be done at this point for Dad's newly reported dementia. I did know that Mom would need me to manage more things for her now that Dad would be unavailable and I wondered where I'd find the additional time.

According to his surgeon, Dad had a very limited brain but, according to the hospital's physical therapy staff, it was a teachable brain. Jack remained remarkably cheerful throughout. He developed this habit of thanking everyone who took care of him, often three times. People at the rehab facility often stopped me in the hall to share their appreciation of Dad's inspiring results and his attitude. He was willing to allow the doctors to probe and push him without complaint. He took his medicines, food and water voluntarily and as prescribed. He did his rehab as regularly as he'd done his exercising every morning when I'd been a girl. Dad went through the process with the same resolve I'd seen in him in his younger days. Through rehabilitation he was able to regain most of his strength and all of his speech.

My Mom did as well as she could without having him by her side to help her stay organized and calm. I saw her more often during the weeks Dad was away recovering. She continued going to meals of course, to the activities she liked and she even started making some new friends. She never complained to me and, only once during Dad's absence was I called in to see the AL administrator about Lillian's questionable behaviors. Then Jack came back, they were together again and things went along pretty ordinarily for a little while.

Your Story

Frankly there are limitations on how much permanence you will get or can expect from any of your POPlans, no matter how well thought out they are. And there are limitations on how much you can protect any other human being, especially another adult, something you've undoubtedly seen. Even with many sets of eyes watching, a frail elderly person can easily take a fall, forget to take the right medication at the right time or lose a hearing aid in the sheets. Nearly one in three women who are 65 years old today will take a fall. One half of those over age 85 will fall whether they live at home or in a senior facility.[52]

The consequences of falling can be potentially life changing. Certainly they'll require you to alter your POPlan. Eighty percent (80%) of those in California rehabilitation facilities are there because they took a fall. Of those, sixty-five (65%) will never return home. Falls are the most common cause of traumatic brain injuries (TBI).

In 2000 TBI accounted for 46% of fatal falls among older adults.[53] People who are 75 and older who fall are four to five times more likely than those aged 65 to 74 to be admitted to a LTC facility for a year or more[54] as a result. Hip fractures are particular concerning because older people often can't learn to walk again. Thereafter, their prolonged immobility and functional disability put these seniors at even greater risk for additional diseases.

---

[52] See, http://www.netwellness.org/healthtopics/aging/faq9.cfm.

[53] Stevens, J. A. Fatalities and Injuries From Falls Among Older Adults – United States, 1993–2003 and 2001–2005. MMWR 2006a; 55(45).

[54] Donald, I.P., Bulpitt, C. J. The Prognosis of Falls in Elderly People Living at Home. Age and Ageing 1999;28:121–5.

No matter how watchful everyone's eyes and how attentive you are, it seems impossible to prevent all falls and accidents. One of the dangerous and limiting "side effects" for people who've fallen is developing the fear of falling. That concern may cause your parents to "unduly" limit their activities. Ironically, by reducing their mobility, your parents will lose some physical fitness and actually increase their risk of falling.[55] In a moment, on the way back from the bathroom even with a caregiver holding on, your parent can take a fall. No one is immune.

Since I never recommend more oversight of your parents than is necessary, your POP task here, as elsewhere, is determining "the right amount" of care and oversight. Would more caregiver help have prevented my Dad from falling in the bathroom? Probably not, but maybe the caregiver would have walked him to the john? How much oversight might I have needed when Dad's "silent" aneurysm was growing? Hard to say and maybe no amount of prevention is perfect.

To do more for your aging parents than they need can infantilize and weaken them. If you hire too much caregiving too early or hover over your parents day and night, you may encourage a premature loss of confidence that may lead to many unwanted outcomes, including falling. While some parents do need substantial help, others do not. Anyone can get "lazy" when there's someone around to do all the "lifting." When your aging parents rely on others unnecessarily, their results may include: loss of muscle mass; weight gain; diminution of cognitive ability and of the joy of feeling independent.

How will you know the right amount of attention that your parents need? You won't always know. But to get the best estimate, watch your parents carefully and ask as many of the "right" questions as possible. Evaluate your parents for something called the "frailty syndrome," a condition primarily due to the age-related loss and dysfunction of skeletal muscles and bone. Stay alert to the five most common elements of "frailty syndrome": unintentional weight loss; muscle weakness; unexplained exhaustion; low physical activity level and a slowed walking speed. Those seniors rated most frail on this scale have the greatest potential for harm and need the most attention.

Another thing to do *before* your parents have accidents or take the kinds of falls mine did is to look at whether there are better ways to prevent such events. There are some simple things you can do to lessen the probability of serious falls, like putting down non-stick mats under area rugs, eliminating unnecessary electrical cords and wires and ridding their halls of the attractive nuisance of clutter.

---

[55] Vellas, B. J., Wayne, S.J., Romero, L.J., Baumgartner, R. N., Garry, P.J. Fear of Falling and Restriction of Mobility in Elderly Fallers. Age and Aging 1997; vol. 26:189–193.

If you've been carefully watching your parents' decline, it's likely you've seen erratic changes. Part of your difficulty in knowing the correct degree of protection your parent need is that it may vary from day to day, even change for the worse after sunset or over the course of a single day.   Even if they've been diagnosed with some form of dementia or delirium, parts of your parents' brain may still be working fairly well, especially at certain times of day. It can be eerie to have a parent forget your name one day and, the next day, to have them recall the most embarrassing stories from your past.   Your parents may sometimes "dissemble" which can confuse you or they may be "very needy" on a Wednesday night but, by Friday morning after a refreshing night's sleep, their appearance and needs have changed substantially. Even as you aim to protect them, you'll need to avoid underestimating your parents' abilities.

Each parent has his or her own disabilities and declines at a unique pace. That is part of why your seemingly perfect POPlan may fail. Inequitable aging patterns alter the dynamics of your parents' lives together. Not only can be stressful in a long marriage with its well-established habits, but it may require you to come up with alternative plans you'd never considered.

When one of your parent's limitations exceeds the other's, everyone involved may feel unsettled. Sometimes one of your parents becomes the caregiver to a more disabled or substantially older spouse. Other times, their divergent conditions require placement in different facilities. You, like me, may have several of these happen over the course of your POPcycle. You will want to be aware that intense feelings – such as abandonment, "survivor guilt," shock, betrayal and even rage – may arise for the spouse left behind by one who no longer functions well or remembers the other. Ironically it may be a relief as well.

Now that you've come to the point in your POPcycle where you've put in place as many "safety measures" for your parents' lives, homes and property as you can manage and they will tolerate, many of your remaining tasks will simply involve maintenance. You may even have a lot of time on your hands to watch and wait. Ironically, much of your challenge may involve the fact that there's little to fix or do.

Sometimes when you're "frustrated" because you have nothing POParental to do, you may decide to do something, anything, to "be helpful." You might even find yourself making up things to do for your parents. You may have their swallowing re-tested to see if they can eat more interesting foods. You may suggest more physical therapy to see if it will lighten your parents' depression or give them more physical challenges through exercise. There may be times when your efforts are relatively fruitless but you may just want to feel you're doing something useful.   To be candid, I did all of those.

When you feel sad that your loved ones are failing in front of your eyes, you may even try to "fix" those things that are already working. You may try to micro-manage your parents' care, unconsciously hoping you can regain control over things that feel uncontrollable. Don't change things in your POPlan unless they're not working and you have to. What can you do instead of messing with what's working? You can focus on your gratitude for their health and longevity.

Often there isn't a lot you can do but sit by patiently, be grateful for their aliveness and enjoy your parents as much as possible in the time you have left with them. There are times when listening to your parents may be the most kind and POParental thing to do. Listen to them respectfully. Pay attention to what your parents say they want or need and what they don't say. Some days it just plain hurts when the people you looked up to and loved become diminished. But it *is* all part of the Circle of Life. Does that make it hurt any less? Watching and waiting can be oppressive or joy-filled. It's up to you.

POPlan #11: Discovering If Your Parents Are Better Off With You Watching Carefully Or Taking More Action?

Knowing "when to hold 'em and when to fold 'em" can be another very useful skill when you're doing POP. For a variety of reasons that probably becoming apparent to you, POParents are often concerned that we're not "doing enough." When you're in that "place," you don't necessarily know what else to accomplish and there really may be nothing more to do. Nonetheless you may find yourself "tinkering," maybe even unsettling some POP things that are actually working just fine. How do you figure out which course of action – or inaction – would be your best version of POParenting now? This plan will help you.

If you're feeling "the need" to try some new POP approach but don't really have the time, money or any assurances of "success," ask yourself:

Do my parents really need this to be done?

How do I know that to be true?

What would happen if it weren't done?

What supports my idea that this "must" get done since I lack the time, money or assurances that it will succeed?

Would it be better for all concerned to wait until I had the time, money or better assurances of success?

If I still insist this must be done and done now, who would be best to do it?

Do others on TEAM POP agree this needs doing and the person picked is the best choice to accomplish the goal?

Is that person available and willing to do this?

Who on TEAM POP is best to contact that person for a successful result?

If you're feeling flooded with emotions and unsure whether it's better to act now or wait, ask yourself:

What POP change do I hope will come from my taking this action?

What evidence do I have that it will succeed?

When I think about taking this action, what emotions do I feel?

When I think about not taking the action, what emotions do I feel then?

What standards do I ordinarily use to decide whether to make a change to my POPlan?

What have I told myself taking this action will do and for whom? Is that accurate?

If my proposed action won't enhance my parents' lives but will make me feel better, is that a good enough reason to do it?

If I waited until I felt less flooded with emotion, would I still believe this worth doing?

Wouldn't it be better to decide when I'm feeling calmer and maybe more rational?

If you're "itching" to fix some POP thing but find yourself hesitating, ask yourself:

Am I about to "fix" something that's already working well?

Do I want to do something, anything because I'm frustrated I can't "fix" my parents?

Will my proposed solution solve what I'm trying to fix?

Is there a better way to fix what's "broken?"

If this doesn't need to be fixed, could scratching my itch make my parents' situation even worse?

How might I use my creativity to fix something POP that does need fixing?

If you think you might be obsessing ("the mental treadmill to nowhere") over every little POP thing, not accomplishing much that's useful and don't know if you should stop, ask yourself:

Am I obsessing over every little thing without accomplishing much that's useful?

Is my micro managing by trying to oversee everyone else's POP tasks just another way to obsess or am I really the best person to tell everyone else how to do his job?

Does my obsessing or micro managing POP seem useful? If so, how so? If no, why not? Could these behaviors actually be disadvantageous?

Am I micro managing because I feel out of control about my parents?

Am I micro managing because I really want to manage my feelings of helplessness and hopelessness?

If you're wondering how you might help when your parents are not acting constructively or are even being self-destructive, ask yourself:

Am I sitting by and just watching while my parents are doing things that are harmful to themselves?

If I see my parents alienating people who've come to help them, should I intervene to change the situation to be more favorable for my parents? How would I do that?

If my parents' behavior reminds me of patterns from my childhood but, given I'm now the "grownup" and doing POP and those old patterns need changing because they're no longer appropriate, should I intervene to change the situation to be more favorable for my parents? How would I do that?

How might I avoid having my parents' be self-destructive in the future?

Chapter 12

Expecting The Unexpected
When We're Doing Pop

My Story

It was early one morning when I got another significant POP phone call. This time it was from a concerned employee at my parents' AL. Mom had taken a bad fall. She tripped while making the bed I'd erroneously believed was being made for my parents by the staff. Lillian had turned away the first set of medics, refusing their help or to go to with them to the hospital. Clearly a "disciplinarian" POParent was needed on site. I reassured the staff member that I would come and things would be taken care of. "Please call her another ambulance. I'll be right over and make sure she gets to the hospital."

By the time I arrived, the paramedics had already returned. One was in the bathroom where Mom apparently had "landed" after her fall. Now she was in much pain and "acting out," as therapists say of teenagers. I overheard the brawny professional warning her: "Look lady, I don't care if you are 90 years old, if you don't stop fighting me and let me do my job, I will call the police." He came out to the living room where Dad, the head of the facility and I all sat demurely. "Is she always this difficult?" he asked. Three heads shook up and down simultaneously.

As it turned out, my osteoporotic Mother had taken a serious fall and damaged her hip. The hip is the body's second largest bone and is central to all lower body movement. Within minutes, Lillian was transported to the hospital where her frail body was soon clothed in the now-familiar patient gown. The details and sequencing of events in the ER blur for me. The combination of stress, super bright lighting, the list of endless unknowns and just plain fear generated my feeling of timeless and space-y.

Hence the next thing I recall was coming back to "consciousness" and watching my Mom being wheeled away a gurney, apparently headed for major surgery. I jumped up and started running after them, realizing no one had spoken with me nor gotten my signature on her consent forms. The confused-looking nurse told me: "Lillian said it was fine and told us she had no family." Uh oh.

Mom's post-surgical experience evolved into a far bigger nightmare than the early morning. Never a "shrinking violet," my Mother had seemingly morphed into the patient from hell. In the days following the procedure, Mom's surgeon actually refused to visit her in the hospital, claiming he wouldn't attend a patient who was spitting and biting him and the hospital staff.

Subsequent to those episodes my mother mysteriously began refusing both food and water. As a result, she couldn't take her medications or food and soon would become malnourished, should that continue. Her decision put the hospital in a legally compromised situation. Since they lacked the legal authority to force her to ingest anything and feared for their liability, the hospital personnel spent hours and hours trying to place Mom in a psychiatric ward, even in a rehabilitation facility – anywhere to get her off their wards.

As that long Saturday afternoon dragged on and no one could locate a single facility in Ventura County willing to accept Lillian Wolf, things began to get desperate. Mom's health was being compromised by her actions and attitudes and it would only get worse with more time.

With the clock ticking away and frustration increasing from all quarters, only one viable option remained. I had to leave the hospital and bring in "the Big

Guns " – Dad! I raced back to the AL and briefed Dad about our situation in the car as we drove back to the hospital. As he approached his wife, Dad put on his grimmest, most authoritative face and announced that, until she took food, water and her meds, he would neither talk with nor listen to Mom. That put an immediate end to her boycott. I knew it – Jack still had the power with his wife!

In the long run however, Mom never did really recover from the fall. She never learned to walk on her own again, despite valiant efforts by the "oft-abused" physical therapists. Even I tried to work with them by holding out my open arms to her, quite literally, during her Physical Therapy ("PT") sessions. Her fear of falling again, the cognitive limitations that made it too hard to learn "new things" or follow directions, her physical weakness and whatever unknowns all conspired together.

With her life confined to chairs and beds, not surprisingly, my Mom gained weight, became less mentally alert and more depressed. Unable to follow through with the demands of PT, Medicare soon cut off that option and Mom's once graceful body became forever limp. Several people would be needed thereafter to lift and then transfer her "dead weight."

Clearly Mom's returning to the AL would not be possible. From a financial point of view, we couldn't afford the monthly expense of two full-time caregivers on top of paying for AL for both of them. Nor was the AL was viable from the point of view of the level of care she was beginning to require, which was readily provided in a SNF.

Jack's physical, cognitive and emotional needs didn't require the same level of care that Mom's did. He chose to stay at their AL where he was comfortable and created a life there by himself. Although his world had become smaller in a way, Dad seemed to thrive, reading his books - sometimes over and again - watching his TV shows and sharing himself with only a few. I saw that he craved the peace and quiet he'd not had living with Mom, for a long time - perhaps since their beginning together.

Frankly, he seemed somewhat relieved. Dad enjoyed the role of being "called in" to rescue Mom, comfort her and visit with her. Without having to share space with anyone, Jack took the opportunity to create his "man cave" of books, television, Mom and me and, occasionally, some music.

My Mom's life would now be spent alone, too, but differently than Dad's. After her fall, like so many older people, Mom lacked what she needed to regain most of her old life. My parents' married life together as they'd known it for over 60 years was over and I witnessed her life becoming very limited.

Your Story

One of the most challenging jobs as a POParent is to get proficient at managing the "unexpected," whatever its source. What caused my family's POPlans to be dismantled, like Mom breaking her hip and Dad not using his thickener, won't be the same things that disrupt your POPlans. Your family will need to use its available resources to address your parents' "unplanned for" happenings and the further consequences of those events and then craft its own unique solutions. Nonetheless a common theme emerges for all POParents: how can you "plan" for the unexpected when you're doing POP?

The expression "snafu" is attributed to the American military from the Second World War. The initial letters spell out a word whose meaning is: "systems normal, all fouled up." If you're doing POP, snafus are probably an everyday occurrence. Your ability to remain flexible and resilient, to not "crumble" when things don't go as expected is – and will remain – one of your most important qualifications for doing this job satisfyingly. Like all POParents you'll do a better job when you're willing – and able – to face what's ahead with candor and objectivity rather than fantasy and wishful thinking.

Even if you can't predict exactly when or why snafu's will occur, you can: predict they will; have some "fall-back" POPlans and work on how to regain your equilibrium as quickly as possible after they descend. You also can get better at managing your emotions and yourself when unexpected events do occur (see POPlan #12, below for details). Finally, you can learn to get better at re-setting POP back on a useful course as quickly as possible when your POPlans do get interrupted.

Tragically your aging parents may have been let down by one (or more) of the many institutions originally set up to protect them – Medicare, Social Security, their insurers, their Assisted Living facility, etc. In some cases you may find yourself "sailing" solo in seas where there are three "Goliaths." Each of these behemoths may be staffed with lots of experienced people who have time to get things done whereas you, "David" here, may be extremely limited in terms of your experience, "staffing," time and energy.

You may also be frustrated by "fussy" aging parents who may be confused by these entities, want something "special" or don't want to go where you've found them the "perfect" place. It's insulting and disappointing that the profit motive has so often trumped private institutional caring and how often governmental agencies have disappointed your elderly and disabled. You may find yourself seeking solutions to complex situations where it feels like you're navigating a course between one institution, say the Medicare "rock," and another institution, your parents' insurer's "hard place."

You and your siblings may be scratching your heads, figuring out how to keep your own paying jobs, health and marriages while also performing your POP "miracles." Hopefully you won't need to get your Dad a timely admission to an appropriate placement (one corporation and its rules) before the hospital (a second giant institution) sends him home, having been pressured financially by Medicare (a third institution) to release the patient quickly. Nonetheless you will likely encounter your own challenges with "rocks" and "hard places."

POParents can no longer expect these "Goliaths" to be viable advocates for your "underdog" parents. You'll have to discover what you need to know about these organizations and how they work (or don't work). Doing so will be imperative for helping your parents through this part of their lives. You will need to recognize that this arena is of one of shifting sands legislatively and administratively.

As a result, you can rarely learn all you'll need to know in advance of needing to know it. You must jump in and immerse yourself whenever a POP problem needs solving but that's considerably easier now than it was in years past because of the Internet, social networking and POP's home website: www.ParentingOurParents.org, as we'll talk more about in this book's final chapter.

It is useful for POParents to be conversant with the most common ways those seniors "in our charge" may become weakened or even die unexpectedly. You'll want to be conversant with the diseases your parents may be particularly vulnerable to. But at the same time, you need not become familiar with every geriatric disorder nor obsess that your parents will come down with any particular disorder just because they're advanced in age.

To pay proper POP attention to a disease or disorder, you'll need to be aware of its most common symptoms. So, for example, if your parents have had pneumonias and you hear them coughing persistently for five to ten days, you'll want to stop and take them to the doctor's. Pneumonia is one of the leading causes of death among seniors and the leading cause of morbidity and mortality amongst those seniors who live in long-term care facilities.

Over the course of our POPcycle, my parents came down with pneumonia so frequently that I lost count. During their California years pneumonia was the cause of every hospitalization for both my parents, except for the consequences of their taking falls. I'd expected to be able to better protect Mom and Dad from the ravages of pneumonia in balmy southern California but that didn't prove to be the case. Pneumonia also is the primary reason that Long Term Care facilities transfer their residents to more acute locations, like SNF's and hospitals. Other symptoms of pneumonia include fever, fatigue, loss of appetite, discomfort in the chest, lungs or upper abdomen, discolored sputum (green or bloody phlegm), and disorientation. Take your parents to competent professionals for diagnosis and treatment, especially if their coughs or runny nose appear to be chronic.

Physicians often rely on reported clinical changes (physical, functional or mental) in an older patient's status to signal that something may be wrong since pneumonia can be difficult to diagnose and x-rays are not always helpful. But because your elderly parents often lack good memories, they aren't always useful as their own "historians." They may lose track of how long they've had their symptoms. Your aging parents may also wish to avoid yet another trip to the doctor for "just a cough." When asked about their cough or runny nose, your parents might say: "I don't like to complain, honey." Therefore it will become even more your POP responsibility to pay attention to symptoms that persist.

There are two distinct types of pneumonia: community acquired and aspiration pneumonia. Community acquired pneumonia is airborne and easily communicable, thus presenting major challenges both during cold winters and in senior facilities where the large number of people present may support quick contagion. Seniors often arrive at facilities with their immune systems and swallowing functions already compromised due to age and preexisting medical conditions (such as a stroke, congestive heart failure or other disorders).

There are some steps you can take to prevent the spread of community acquired pneumonia, influenza and colds. You can remind your parents to wash their hands frequently with sanitizers or other substances that stop the spread of bacteria. You can easily and economically sanitize handles on their shopping carts at the market and on their light switches, door handles and window handles at home. You can ascertain if your parents' phones and any community computers they touch are sanitized. Similarly if your parents use keyboards in public places like the library, you can recommend ways to clean them thoroughly beforehand. You and your parents can avoid using public telephones especially in emergency rooms. You might also urge your parents to forgo reading magazines in doctors' offices where many sick people may have fingered them. Instead, bring along your own periodicals, tablets, iPads and the like to amuse your folks, show them your photos and play games with them while you wait.

The second type is aspiration pneumonia. It develops from a combination of factors that may include fairly common things such as impaired swallowing, fluids draining into their lungs and inhaling bacteria from the back of their throats, mouths or noses into the lungs. Preventing your parents from getting aspiration pneumonia is possible but it will require your parents to change some of their habitual ways. That is not easy and it's far from foolproof. You can begin by altering your parents' diet so it consists primarily of softer foods that are easier to swallow. You can also give them thickener to add into their liquids and perhaps you (or an occupational therapist) can teach your parents new swallowing maneuvers.

The treatment for pneumonia is generally straightforward, typically lasts 10-14 days and doesn't depend on how the disease was contracted. Initially antibiotics are administered to kill the bacteria. With this illness, as with others, you will want to check that your parents are receiving the correct geriatric dosages of medications. Seniors' bodies often require or can handle only smaller amounts of prescription drugs than younger adults. Breathing treatments and expectorants are also frequently introduced to open up their airways, loosen phlegm and cough out the mucus that accompanies pneumonia. Some of the most serious hazards are caused when your parents lie flat in bed all day because fluids tend to settle into their lungs.

Seniors with pneumonia in just one part of their lungs have a good chance of full recovery. The presence of pneumonia in several parts of the lungs is more severe and makes recovery more difficult. With advancing age the lung tissue becomes less elastic decreasing the lung's ability to expand and contract. Even osteoporosis, another common geriatric disorder, with its resulting deformity and curvature of the spine can affect breathing by impairing lung expansion.

Your POP responsibility includes helping your parents avoid all predictable health risks. You'll need to research the advantages and disadvantages of having your parents receive pneumococcal and influenza vaccines. Many geriatric professionals believe that because seniors' bodies are more vulnerable than other adults, everyone over 65 should be inoculated against such diseases. Others hold differing views. If you've hired professionals you trust and they think a course of treatment is best for your parents, you'll want to follow much of their advice. If you find you are consistently not aligned with your parents' physicians' point of view or you aren't taking their advice, find other doctors with whom you can work in better accord.

One health hazard for your senior parents that may surprise you is being admitted to a hospital. Hospitals concentrate lots of people with serious health problems into small spaces. Many POParents attempt to keep their parents out of the hospital unless it's absolutely necessary. Even when I'd visit one sick parent in the hospital, I'd try to keep the other parent at home, rather than exposing my healthy parent to a lot of sick patients.

Some of their hospitalizations caused my parents unforeseen complications. I was told that my Mom contracted a case of MRSA[56] during one such hospitalization. MRSA is a highly contagious predatory infection that weakens the immune system of those already vulnerable physically and it's rampant in some hospitals. When I would visit my Mom in the hospital after she got MRSA, I had to wear a mask, a gown and other protective clothing. Later on when I would need to place my Mother again in other SNF's, some refused to admit her because she carried the contagious disorder.

Generally speaking, parents who reside in LTC facilities have higher levels of functional disability and underlying medical illness than their peers who live out in the community. I was unaware of that fact when I placed my parents in such residences. I also didn't consider that some contagious diseases would spread more easily in these facilities. However, as I like to tell my patients, we must make all decisions with "inadequate information" and nonetheless,

---

[56] Methicillin-resistant Staphylococcus aureus (MRSA) is a bacterium that can be fatal. Sometimes MRSA is called the "superbug" because it is resistant to many commonly used antibiotics.

we must decide. I probably wouldn't have changed many of my POP choices since they seemed wise when I made them but I see now that I based those choices on "inadequate information."

Some estimate that, in the near future, as many as 40 percent of Americans will spend some time living in a long-term care facility. Given our Baby Boomer demographics, it's foreseeable that the number of frail older adults living in these facilities (including ALs, SNF's and B & C's) will increase dramatically over the next 30 years. Some POP families may find community-based options preferable to LTC facilities.   But as responsible POParents it's important that you not overreact to every potential danger nor "jump" to hasty and unwarranted generalizations. Whether or not the results turn out as you expected, as good POParents you must decide things sanely and thoughtfully, considering all the elements available to you at the time.

POPlan #12: Expanding Your POP Confidence To Deal With The Unexpected

Even though you may feel inundated by the number of unexpected and unplanned-for changes that occur during your POPcycle, for most people the most challenging part of is not dealing with the unexpected.   What's even harder is facing up to what IS expected: the "biggie," our parents' deaths.

Helplessness and hopelessness, feeling out of control as well as sadness and anxiety are some of the symptoms that characterize depression. They also represent many of reactions POParents feel, passively watching as our loved ones head towards their last days and our well-laid POPlans disappear into dust.

Focus your thinking on how to stop feeling out of control and helpless since you're neither and, in fact, have responsibilities here.   Remind yourself that the true location of your control is in your own mind. Use your intelligence to calm you and to find out what it is that you can control. Armed with only that piece of information, you can begin to prepare for that.

It also helps to know what you can't control – other people, including your parents. The giants (or to some POParents, villains) of your youth are mortal and they are going to die. So are you and I. You cannot stop that, control that or ever fully prepare for it in advance.

If you're concerned that you're the one POParent who will be helpless, who can't regain enough equilibrium to keep on doing POP when events "kick you in the teeth," that's not so. You've frequently needed to develop resilience and flexibility already in your life, just to have lived this long. If you've raised children, been through a life-threatening event or just survived on the planet for decades, you've undoubtedly found you had more stamina than you'd thought was possible. If so, you already possess much of the skill set to succeed in this part of the POPcycle.

You will want to hone your skills further for what's ahead and POPlan #12 will help you do that. You'll learn how to tune up both your "defense," to better protect yourself internally from unnecessary disappointment, as well as your "offense," to assert yourself more confidently when making POP changes in the external world. So, how can you and your family "prepare" for the unexpected?

Would it be useful to sit down and write out a list of every undesirable thing that could befall your parents? If looking at "worst case scenarios" makes you feel in better control, do that. Looking at my story, you'll appreciate that you probably can't write a definitive list of fears: you don't even know them all. If you try that and discover that writing your list adds to your fears, it's probably not a very productive approach for you. Nonetheless some people do feel calmed looking down the barrel of the unknown possibilities.

Another approach you might try is to get "totally informed" by learning everything there is to know about Medicare, Social Security, Long Term Care and good placement professionals. Would that make you feel like you have a good handle on POP? Maybe. If you could ever find the time and patience to do that, it might prove informative but regulations, policies and benefits may well change again, as they have in the past, before you could ever apply your vast learning to your parents' benefit.

These theoretically "logical" suggestions are not likely to be of too much help. I've learned that a more successful route to becoming more resilient and feeling in greater control – both offensively and defensively – is oddly counter-intuitive. How? You can actually decide to operate like a more confident POParent! Huh? More confident than whom? At the least, you can become a more confident POParent than you've been until now.

As you'll see, you can actually learn to act with more self-assurance than you've yet been able to during your POPcycle!

Ask yourself these questions:

- *What are the characteristics of the people you know who are confident and self-assured?*

- *Do they have something special that you don't have or can't get?*

- *How might you become more like the secure people you know?*

- *Why can't you become more confident even if you don't know what will happen next, after all no one does?*

No matter how much you and I may pretend we know what lies ahead, the truth is: none of us ever knows what will happen next. But consider how secure people seem to manifest their desired results. Confident people share a core belief that when something demanding presents itself, they know they'll do their best to solve it but they know they can't do the impossible. They act in an assured manner but not because they believe they can control every outcome. In fact, they are realistic in appreciating their own limitations and know when to enlist help.

People who are self-assured don't necessarily expect miracles but they seem particularly available to find favorable solutions out of nowhere. You may have noticed that answers to your most perplexing questions appear most often when you're feeling serene rather than anxious and helpless. Confident people begin becoming more assured and calmer because they've come to know and trust themselves and have learned to accurately evaluate others. They can distinguish which people to place their trust in versus those they shouldn't.

Many of you may have decided that certain people in your life "cannot be trusted." You may have reached that erroneous conclusion because you often put your reliance on the wrong people. Secure people have developed a good relationship with their intuitive right brain and as a result can more accurately evaluate what's needed in the moment.

As a confident person you'll want to be realistic about trusting others to protect your POP family, be they institutions or individuals. By way of example, let's say you want to believe that your nephew Bob, was "trustworthy" so you can feel comfortable with his driving your Mom to her doctor appointments.

How would confident POParents know they could trust Bob with that POP task? They would examine their past experiences with him candidly in order to "learn" if Bob is "trustworthy" in the present (and the future) to accomplish this important POP job. They'd have considered both his past habitual behavior and the nature of this particular job in order to ascertain his suitability now. They'd want to know: Is Bob customarily a later arriver to events, suggesting he might not get your Mom to the doctor on time? If you've relied on Bob in the past to be on time for something special, has he been? Does Bob frequently run out of gas and need a tow or does he keep his car in good working order? Is Bob the one who usually drives you to the airport because he and his car run efficiently and on time?

When you're overwhelmed by the unexpected during POP and disturbed by your reactions to it, think about those people you've been able to depend on up in the past. That will inform you in significant ways whom you can depend upon now. If someone's proven himself trustworthy over time, there's a good chance that your POP reliance can continue into the future.   Remember to ask yourself the second half of the question: what is it you're wanting to trust somebody to do or not do? You might trust someone to pick you on time from the airport but not trust that same person to look over your financial accounts because they're not qualified – and therefore not "trustworthy" to do the second of those jobs. You may also discover that not relying on some people is a wise POParenting move!

By asking these questions and listening honestly to your own answers, you may find, much to your delight, that you can delegate a number of POP tasks; you *can* trust certain people because you've "vetted" them from the point of view of trusting them to help you with specific POP work. These folks may be from your church, local community, your parent's neighborhood or may be your partner, a close friend or even Bob.

When you do depend on people and institutions you've decided you can trust for POP and they prove you right, you're building more faith in your ability to make good POP decisions. As that unfolds, your confidence will increase and you'll feel more comfortable and secure in your POP skills. Self-assured people recognize it's their job to sponge out lessons from all their experiences, even the ones they don't seek out or enjoy.

Confident people also have healthy skepticism and don't rely exclusively on what others have told them. Good POParenting includes doing your own research and finding additional sources of information to corroborate or dispute what you've been told. You may discover, hopefully not too late, that even some doctors who've been helpful in your parents' past may currently be uninformed or unaware of cutting-edge research. Information is a powerful tool to grow your confidence and the vast amount of data available online makes getting informed a simpler matter than in earlier days. Now more than ever, you're not at the "mercy" of individuals who can withhold valuable data you'd like to have. Living in the 21st century you have extraordinary access to information about health, money, people, and programs.

As someone aspiring to be a confident POParent, when your parent receives a new diagnosis, you'll want to face that squarely and then get better informed by doing research about that condition. You may go to various well-respected medical websites and you may have your favorites. You can also check in at www.ParentingOurParents.org where you can talk to other POParents who've dealt with that disorder, learn more about how it may affect your family and see how others have formulated helpful solutions. As you become better informed, you will feel in greater control and more grounded.

Another way many POParents have more confidence is by relying on "faith," having a notion that there's something bigger than yourself or what you can see. When life seems to be spinning out of control, your beliefs can be the source of relief and strength. Many research studies validate the positive effects of prayer, affirmations and meditation in how people fare after illnesses, surgeries and other trauma. Experiencing a beneficent force, a caring God or a kind universe may offer you a great deal of comfort and even some confidence during the most challenging POP days and nights. Whether or not your faith can change the outcome, you'll certainly function more effectively and feel better as POParents when you allow your positiveness to keep you and your parents stronger.

You can specifically grow your own internal POP confidence by spending time alone with yourself, reviewing aspects of your personal history:

1.) As you've lived your POP life, even without noticing it, you've been expanding your ability to be flexible, balanced and confident. How have you allowed your life experiences to support you in trusting yourself? If you haven't, could you start now?

2.) Haven't you been able to make lemonade when you were handed lemons, sooner or later? If you weren't, what do you think stopped you – were you unwilling or did you not know how? Wouldn't your life now be simpler if you adopted a "lemonade" point of view?

3.) Haven't you re-invigorated yourself in the past after you felt exhausted and out of control? How did you do that? When you were able to get calm and bring yourself back to "center," didn't you notice you could repeat that process over and again, as you needed it? Did that help grow your confidence in you? It could have, had you let it.

A theme that emerges from POP is that you can learn during your POPcycle to develop more self-confidence and, when you do, you'll actually succeed in getting better at your POP job. Sometimes this just comes with time because surviving the stages of the POPcycle, like surviving your kids' childhoods, makes you more resilient. Some families may want to ask for some POP Family Coaching to help gain more self-assurance and cohesion.

After you've done POP for a while and gotten this far, you really *are* better able to trust yourself, so believe it! You've faced a lot of hard truths and gained a more profound sense of controlling the things you can control while becoming more peaceful about the things you can't possibly control. Taking some time to remind yourself of all you've accomplished thus far in life and POParenting will bring you more confidence, helping you to access your inner resources and better prepare you what's inevitable – more unexpected change. Don't worry. Confident POParents understand that we can only do the best we can and your best *will* be good enough.

Chapter 13

Turning Pop Into Our Giant "Do-Over" – Forgiveness, Compassion And Gratitude Fill The Space

My Story

I fondly recall "do-over's" from my childhood. In the day my aunts, uncles, cousins and a myriad of kids would regularly congregate at the midtown "penthouse playground" where my cousin Rick and his parents lived. It was a New York City child's Disneyland. Spanning over all the apartments in the building, their penthouse had endless rooms and space outdoors for us to play in. Their roof patio was so vast that we could even "lose" our parents there and I think they got the chance to lose us kids, too.

A ping-pong table dominated the entryway and always a major attraction for me. Often the adults and children would play "round-robin" ping-pong where each team would race around the table trying to score points. In my family and maybe in yours, if one of the children shouted "do-over!" while playing a game, she or he would be allowed to take a second turn.

A rule that permitted "do-over's" seemed ironic, offering my young mind food for thought. I remember contemplating that the world would be a less harsh and more magnanimous place if we could all try again when our first attempts weren't all we'd hoped they would be. The rule was grounded in an underlying optimism – if we were given another chance, we'd play better the second time than we'd done the first. The "do-over" rule seemed a beacon of hope, suggesting a universe where there was fairness and flexibility for those less able – in that case, small children.

I began to wonder: could there be "do-over's" in life? And, why should only to young people get them? Weren't there disabled people or very short people or others who could benefit from getting a "leg up," a "do-over?" Why couldn't everyone be afforded such a compassionate opportunity to perform better or get a more desirable result? As I continued to ponder these ideas, I also warmed to the rule when I saw that it actually allowed for and encouraged forgiveness. If my first time didn't have to count and I were able to try again, I might be "forgiven" my bumbling first attempts at certain things. Surely that kind of forgiveness would moderate some of life's harsher moments.

What if anyone could re-visit parts of their life and call for a "do-over" to produce more desirable outcomes? What if we were given the option for "do-overs" in our relationships with our spouses, parents, children and siblings? Wouldn't we all want a few "do-overs" now and again? Would such a rule discourage people from doing their best the first time out? Wouldn't it supply a handy excuse for people's "bad behaviors?"

I mulled over these questions and then asked myself an important philosophical question. What if we could all have a greater chance for happiness "the second time around" with some life "do-overs?" Wouldn't that be more humane?

Years later when I became a psychotherapist, I again considered the possible implications for healing: would we be more

healthy and perhaps more peaceful, were we able to invoke a "do-over" consciousness but also do that responsibly and thoughtfully. What if we were given something like a second chance to "do over" parts of the past and, this time, we could possess the understanding, knowledge, sensibilities and skills we have now? Who among us wouldn't want the chance to be a better parent to our kids? Or a better friend to someone we may have let down? Maybe even those people who've treated us unkindly would want a "do-over" too?

Periodically I have asked my patients a question that, at this point in the POPcycle, I asked myself as well: if you could wave a magic wand and improve something from your past, what "do-over" might you choose? My purpose in accessing regrets, as the question does, is in order to inform ourselves about our current values. What are things we hold dear today that we may not have demonstrated as much in the past? What might we have done "better," with a "do-over?"

One answer that came to mind was: could I be a more loving as daughter, step-mother or more devoted POParent with a second chance? What if there were a way to "reverse time" so I could get to try parenting again, now as a more mature and compassionate person? What if POP could give me that chance?

As I'd matured, I often found myself admiring and even emulating many of my parents' qualities. And as I began taking on the challenges of raising young stepchildren, I often tried to borrow these parental qualities. Now I had even gotten the chance to become the "mother" that Lillian had said I was.

One of the qualities I emulated was my parents' determination to get results. Even those first days of POP, I'd insisted upon taking Mom to not one but two doctors and thereafter to the hospital to get answers and treatment for them. My mother and father had done the same for me when I'd been the child.

Dogged pursuit was a parental quality I'd learned, perhaps copied, from my parents. I remembered their tireless quests for whatever I needed. They vigorously searched for those things, whether it was a book for a class assignment, a doctor with the answers to some mysterious condition or the right matching blouse for my camp uniform. Sometimes I wouldn't even ask my parents for something to avoid their intensity. Maybe this makes sense solely to an only child but two tall parents with their intense pursuit can be overwhelming to a youngster and that hadn't always been easy for me.

When raising me, they'd encouraged my young brain to keep learning and expanding: another of their parental qualities I valued and sought to emulate as my way to "pay them back." With my "do-over" and me as the POP Mom, I aimed to discover how to similarly promote their aging brains and bodies' continued development.

They'd also been generous as parents, Lillian and Jack, sharing all they had: their time, their love and themselves with me. Now with this "do-over," I asked myself if I could show my parents even more generosity and benevolence in my POParent role than I'd yet shown them or even my kids? The second time around, now as the POParent, could I do even better?

If I could parent my Mom and Dad with the best of what I was today (the more mature, spiritual woman I'd tried to become) maybe my Mom and Dad would receive better POParenting from me now than the parenting my step-kids had gotten decades before? Now I possessed more patience, compassion and even more humor than years before. Maybe at this point on my journey, I could do an even better job POParenting Lillian and Jack than they'd done parenting me. What a crazy thought that was!

I'd long felt POP held the potential to be transformative, both to the POParents and to the aging generation as well. As I more immediately anticipated my parents' mortal end and my own, I saw even more clearly that doing POP could absolutely change the participants' lives!

To act as lovingly and generously as I wanted meant discovering the place in my heart where I was whole and unconditionally accepting of these two people I'd chosen to POParent. My years of counseling and spiritual work had shown me that to know that kind of love I'd need to place forgiveness at the entryway to my heart.

To become a non-judgmental and consistently generous POParent, I would need to repair whatever wounds still remained unhealed from my own childhood. I began to envision how to do that, create a clean slate. I wished to discover if and how I could use all my thoughts and feelings, even the "unwanted" ones like sadness, anger and abandonment, in support of my goals. I understood that the road to the kind of loving state I hoped to offer them and myself was through forgiveness.

As odd as it sounds, I saw that I would need to forgive my parents – for just being human and making those "mistakes" that parents often make. At some time all parents neglect, scold, embarrass or even reject their offspring. My parents had and when I was parenting, I too did some of those things. To be able to lovingly and fully POParent them now, I saw I'd need to forgive my parents for doing whatever "unfortunate things" they'd done all those years ago.

It wasn't long before I saw that there was someone else I'd need to forgive first. I would need to forgive myself even before my Mom and Dad. I had learned over time that, when doing work on forgiveness, the first party to be forgiven is ourselves. Forgiveness has been called "an inside job" because, after taking inventory of all our acts of commission and omission, it's ourselves we must forgive first before we can truly forgive anyone else. Why? I have my theories but can't say for sure. What I can say is that witnessing this happen hundreds of times has warranted the conclusion: forgiveness starts with ourselves.

I knew that to become the POParent I aspired to be I'd need to discover how to forgive myself – and thereafter my folks. How would I go about this process of forgiving myself? Taking an inventory, as people do in their Twelve Step recovery programs,[57] was a helpful beginning. I focused on revisiting the ways I'd disappointed myself, the times I'd lost my way. It wasn't a comfortable activity, looking my personal history straight in the eye, the parts I liked and those I didn't. Nonetheless, I aimed to stay with it. I also asked myself if there were parts I could mend? I considered: were there people I could apologize to? Things I could now fix? When the answer was yes, most of the time I would go off and do those things.

At other times it was more difficult to forgive myself. Maybe I'd see a pattern that was self-destructive or hurt others and want to judge myself harshly for it or "defend" myself by denying it or attributing the responsibility to someone else. After more work, I had a refreshing and energizing revelation: all my acts of commission and all my omissions, the "good" and the "bad," all I'd ever experienced had led me to today. I'd become who I was today as a result of all my experiences and how I'd interpreted them. Rather than cursing the "bad parts" I regretted or resented, I could try to bless them for how they'd served me. I really could forgive myself.

When I finally got that, I found I was able to magnanimously forgive myself. Thereafter I was able to forgive Lillian and Jack of any residual blame for my past hurts. I was able to "absolve" my parents for things they'd done or not done to me. When I could do that, it became unnecessary to hold on to any historic faultfinding. After going through all of that, forgiving anyone else became much easier.

To be a good POParent, it was love I wanted to feel for them, not long-cold resentment. I wanted to feel and act compassionately towards those who'd given me life. Holding on to those past "wrongs" really made little sense. Not only did it get in the way of my being the loving person and POParent I wanted to be but, in all candor, Lillian and Jack could hardly remember breakfast, let alone any harm they may have caused me fifty years ago. Retaining unresolved thoughts and feelings from the past interfered with my ability to love my folks – and myself – in the present.

When I was able to invoke my compassion through my intention to be lovingly POParental and my process of forgiveness, I'd notice I was filled up with gratitude. I would experience being grateful for having my two parents alive. I was grateful I could provide them loving attention. When I could sit long enough to bask in the gratitude, my mind would often reward me with positive recollections. Triggering happy

---

[57] These are programs aiming to help people recover from their addictive and compulsive behaviors. Based upon spiritual principles, the programs involve a series of steps, including making an inventory of troubling past behaviors and seeking amends. They were originally proposed by Bill W, and Alcoholics Anonymous (AA)

memories gave me the chance to consciously savor the good times, past and present, I'd shared with my family and reminded me there could be more of those in the future.

Scientists have reported that focusing our attention on three activities can provide a good basis for expanding human happiness.[58] They are forgiveness, gratitude and savoring the good in life. Being able to do each of these while facing the challenges of POParenting can be hard work. But I was also observing that such efforts could bring much joy to me and my family!

Because I was doing my own work with these activities, it had become easier to recognize that POP was a remarkable opportunity for transformation and healing as well as responsibility and worry. When I saw I could use the whole POPcycle as my own giant "do-over," I realized how much participating in it could boost for my personal growth. The unexpected result of parenting my own parents could turn out to be my own personal expansion. And once I saw that so clearly, I knew I'd need to share my realization with others. Then others who were still feeling as alone and burdened as I once had doing POP could also feel the freedom, love and joy – the extraordinary transformative potential of POParenting.

Thereafter I began to act more patiently, more compassionately than I ever had previously. My heart was open to feeling things in new ways. I was finally able to put myself in the shoes of my parents. I felt more deeply what each of them was going through as they headed toward their end. Could I "play it forward," I wondered? Could I become the unconditionally loving parent to Lillian and Jack that I'd always wanted to them to be?

In spite of all this work I did on myself, some days the emotional and practical demands of doing POP alone, without any siblings to support me or help make decisions, seemed too vast to manage. If it took a village to raise a child, I thought, how many does it take to raise a parent? Especially during this part of the POPcycle when I felt so unable to control aspects of my parents' lives I revived an old childhood daydream about having a sibling.

As an only child I'd often found myself wanting a sibling, someone else to help me with perspective on our parents. None arrived. My most recurring fantasy was of having an older brother, someone to protect me – although I wasn't entirely sure from what – and someone to "hang out" with me although, in truth, older brothers rarely wanted that. I'd imagined that having a brother I'd have someone "on my side" of the child-parent dynamic and life would feel less lonely even when I also saw siblings mistreat one another, act jealously or unprotectively and not want to hang out together.

---

[58] Authentic Happiness, op cit.

At this time in our POPcycle, I found myself having similar daydreams that a sibling would appear and make my POP life easier: we'd co-POParent. I would have more help. I could share the burdens of decision-making. I'd have a brother or sister to hang out with me while we did POP together ... they'd protect me – from what, I again wondered?

Then my logical left-brain returned to poke some holes in my fantasy of co-POParenting. No one could protect me from the hardest part – my parents' inevitable deaths that lay ahead. No sibling, friend or lover could do my healing work for me. Whether or not I had siblings, it was only I who could practice forgiveness, bring more gratitude for all I'd been given and savor the wonders of my life. Only I could do these things for myself.

I further considered that there could be a "downside" to having sisters or brothers. I'd have to consult with them on POP, or they with me. We'd need to reach a consensus on every important POP decision. What if we didn't? That could present its own challenges ...

I also knew from doing POP Family Coaching that co-POParenting with some siblings is far from stress-free. I've seen first-hand how having siblings co-POParenting can sometimes be far harder than those doing it solo. By their nature, siblings always contribute divergent amounts of time, money, attention different skills and other resources. The most positive way to see that is that everyone brings different things to POParenting, enriching the collective effort with their unique contributions. But different ways of contributing can be a source of family feuds especially when some family members ascribe a negative meaning to those inequities.

The most common form of feuding occurs after POParenting is over when siblings fight over their parents' possessions. I've witnessed feelings that had lay dormant, unresolved possibly for decades, get stirred up in this process. As a result, hurtful protracted litigation and further family divisions have sometimes ensued.

When I weighed some of the advantages of being a sole POParent versus one with siblings, I realized that, despite looking good from the "outside," co-POParenting carries its own burdens. There is no ideal formula for POP satisfaction.

Nonetheless I still felt an emotional longing to have a sibling. I decided that I didn't want to live the remainder of my POPcycle or my own senior years without someone in the role of my sibling. I told those I counseled that if you want something enough in this lifetime, go out and get it rather than wishing you had later on – so long as you don't hurt others along the way. Why couldn't that apply to me about having a sibling? What did it matter that my parents were 90 years old and had long lost their reproductive capabilites? Why couldn't I adopt a brother or a sister because I wanted one?

Presumably any sibling I'd want would already have a strong affiliation with me, probably would have shared my childhood memories and known me "in the day." I hoped that someone would also share my spiritual point of view, live in the same state and be intrigued to have a new sibling of their own.

Immediately I thought of Rick, my first cousin, whose amazing "penthouse playground" had been my second home when we were growing up. Of all the cousins and friends I'd been close with, he and I, two only children, had always been closest to each other. We'd always stayed involved in each other's lives as we grew into adults, parents and then POParents. Rick had moved his family from Texas to California in order to POParent my aunt Molla, when she'd needed his loving attention a while back.

I sat down and wrote to Rick, proposing that we adopt each other as brother and sister and then awaited his reply to my unique request with some apprehension. Rick, of course, thought it a great idea, but we did kind of think alike!

Once onboard, Rick and I collaborated on what language our sibling agreement would contain and how we'd "formalize it." We decided to perform a little reciprocal adoption ritual we designed, where we made pledges of sibling love and caring and invited a friend to bear witness. The ceremony was officiated by Rick and me on his patio at sunset under trees where we'd said our few lovely words of commitment to each other. Afterward, we three drank a glass of bubbly in celebration.

Although we did nothing to give it any official recognition, our sibling relationship has been recognized in our hearts since that day. The "adoption" was never about expecting the other to take on any financial or other responsibilites for each other. Rather it was a sweet statement about our being family. It added a new level of affection between Rick and me.

As I observed my parents becoming less and less present at this point in their POPcycle, adopting Rick gave me a sense of being less alone on the planet. Having this new brother added to my feeling rooted at the very time when my original family roots would soon be pulled up from the earth. The ceremony had also been my way of becoming a more loving parent to the Jane whose parents weren't going to be able to "protect" her or themselves much longer.

I'd spent much of my time and energy at work supporting others to have what they wanted – whether it was to be some way, to do something or to have something. I loved that my work afforded me so many opportunities to do that and considered it a real privilege. Acquiring a long-sought older brother in my 50's did seem like an unusual accomplishment. Effectuating this adoption gave me the chance to feel good about supporting myself and added to my optimism that we all can "create" solutions for what's wanted and needed, however unconventional those might be.

It was during this part of our POPcycle when Lillian was having a particularly lucid day that I decided to tell her I'd started writing this book. It is an odd thing about people who suffer from dementia, as any POParent with a Mom or Dad who has it knows, occasionally they act like their "old selves" but, within a few hours or sometimes even within the same conversation, they disappear into some netherworld all their own. Even though we understood that phenomenon, the speed of those transitions and inconsistencies in behavior and comprehension were confusing to those of us who loved Lillian and sometimes, it was downright painful.

I felt apprehensive telling my Mom about this book. I wondered if she'd be able to understand the concept of POP. Would she be able to relate to the irony of our roles having changed or grasp the potential for how others could be helped others through a book about POP? However silly or "retro" it may have seemed, I really wanted my Mom to know about the book and what I'd been doing. We probably never get over wanting our parents to feel proud of us. And, after all, it was Lillian who had been the first to see it and name POP, in a way – calling me her Mom at the ER that night so long ago.

A part of me wondered if Lillian might berate me, when she heard I was writing a book about our life: I imagined she might say: "You're parenting ME? How dare you say such a thing? I knew you before you were in diapers …" But that wasn't at all how she reacted.

I was both relieved and inspired by her response: "Why, honey, that's so wonderful! You're writing a book about parenting parents. I always said I loved how you wrote. And you know, Jane, parents are always working in their children's best interest. Now that I can see you're parenting your Dad and me – and helping others to better parent their parents – I feel reassured. I know you'll always do your best for Daddy and me. And reaching out to help other families, that's my girl!"

The day I told Mom about POP and this book, she'd seemed alert and asked me lots of questions. After a while, she looked up and very genuinely, even innocently, asked: "Where did you ever come up with the wonderful idea that you're parenting your parents?" I gulped, not really knowing what to say and through newly forming tears, I told her: "I got the idea from you, Mom and I thank you for it." But by then she seemed to have drifted away.

Your Story

No one gets out of childhood unscathed. At one time or another anyone who's parented a youngster has been too busy or tired to listen, has reacted too quickly or over-reacted to events. No parent raises each child "exactly right" every day of the year. Put another way, all parents including POParents make mistakes.

And all children feel let down in some way or at some time by their parents, no matter how well treated they are. Each of you, like I, had times during your youth when you felt disappointed, abandoned, neglected or rejected by your parents, even if their view of those incidents differs dramatically from your own. And since feelings are subjective and personal to each one, you can feel abandoned, neglected and rejected even when the facts don't necessarily say you were.

As you've looked back over your growing up, it's likely you created a narrative, whether or not you're aware of it. The narrative was a shorthand way to explain to yourself and others "what's happened to me," from your point of view. To compose it, you picked out some key examples that illustrated and then confirmed your viewpoint from among the hundreds of possible memories you have of your childhood.

One way to "see" your own narrative is that it might be the story you traditionally tell someone new, maybe on your second or third date, about your past dating history. It might be something you share with a seatmate on a long plane ride. Most people, perhaps you too, further solidify the "truth" of their narratives by retelling it until, after a while, you may have begun to believe your version is the truth, forgetting that others who lived through the same situations construe them differently.

If your personal narrative includes the fact that your childhood was damaged because of self-centered parents who didn't care about your needs, the memories you'll find will bear witness to that. You'll easily recall incidents when your Mom and Dad disregarded you while lavishing gifts and attention on themselves. By contrast, if you viewed your parents as self-sacrificing people, your narrative is likely to be filled with incidents that corroborate those parental qualities.

It's not pathological and, in fact, it's quite natural to consider and remember your experiences from your own perspective. However you'll want to remember that your narrative is self-constructed and, most importantly, that you can always publish a different, more positive version of your narrative. That is so because you wrote it in the first place, so you can write a better one. It turns out that the way you "organize" your narrative proves to be being quite important because it reflects how you see yourself and, in turn, how you're likely to interpret events that occur in your life.

Some of you were given a bushel full of "lemons" during childhood. If your early years were harsh, hopefully you've taken away many life lessons and been able to "make lots of lemonade." You might have seen that time as victimizing you, leaving you "damaged goods." Or you might interpret those years as "strength building," explaining why and how you became the competent and powerful adult you are today. Those who suffered because of difficult parents or childhoods also had the "benefits" of having to learn much needed survival and resiliency skills early on rather than later in life.

Sometimes your version of you may not reflect how others see you or may be outdated. For example, your narrative may still portray you as a victim of numerous abusive relationships since childhood. But since then, you may have worked on yourself and now see those experiences as lessons and training tools. Because you and others perceive you now very differently from that old story, your narrative needs to be updated. Your self- esteem and the perceptions of others have changed your viewpoint so that your new narrative should focus on you as a strong and resilient person who's learned to survive, even thrive, despite difficult odds not the weak child.

Your narrative has the potential to either expand or limit you. It can restrict you if, no matter what occurs, you "automatically" reach all the same life conclusions and don't allow yourself to see yourself and the present as different from the past. Your narrative can also expand you when you use it to guide you to more positively interpret what's happened to you or more accurately attribute meaning to your experiences.

As a way to look at recomposing your old narrative, I encourage you, as I do my patients, to examine what you'd like said about you at your funeral, what epitaph you might like on your tombstone. When you try on that view of your life, you often see that your older narrative no longer suits who you've become and how you'd like to live out the remainder of your days.

It may be that the very act of composing a new narrative will support your having a more positive view and therefore making wiser choices. For example, rather than belaboring the pain, drama and blame of years ago when people "done you wrong," your new narrative can reflect your forgiveness and strengths in the face of adversity.

You can choose to forgive your parents and let the past just be complete and over because you are. How can you do that? Each of you will find your own way to achieve that highly desirable goal. You may seek counsel from your faith, a spiritual guide you trust or from the many books that concentrate on achieving forgiveness. You may do your work by attending workshops, going on retreats alone or with your POP family or sitting at home with your computers and phones unplugged. Whatever it takes, find your particular route to more emotional freedom! It will be worth the effort. I've shared my techniques in MY STORY and, in

POPlan #13, offer you additional tools intended to help you become more forgiving and loving in your POP role (and wherever else you'd like to apply it).

If you choose the path of forgiveness you'll be heading away from many destructive and frankly, self-destructive feelings. By releasing undesired grudges, hurts, memories and misunderstandings from the past, you'll be headed yourself towards more productive and satisfying times ahead. But be aware that everyone in your environment may not be as forgiving as you and, when you opt to release old negativity about yourself and others, you may fighting an uphill battle in the highly litigious society 21st century America you live in.

If you buy the original premise of this section that all parenting is flawed, maybe those of you who've had difficulty up until now, can also forgive and let go of the pain you believe your parents "inflicted" on you. If you can, let go of your residual blame, faultfinding and judging of your family and yourself. If so, it's likely you'll be able to experience POP with a new lightness of being. Perhaps you'll have emptied out enough emotional toxicity to create the space for a new kind of reconciliation and authentic happiness in your POP family.

Releasing your past hurts means living with more peacefulness, cooperation and joy in the present. That is a truth many can embrace, even if as only as a wise thought. The aim here, after you've released your past wounds about your folks, is to have that peace become your experience during POP. Practicing forgiveness can disappear your sense of obligation and help your joy and compassion emerge more fully.

The POParents I've coached consistently report empowering reactions to doing this type of emotional "house-cleaning." They have far more energy. They say they feel less worn down and more available to do POP in the present moment, as it's occurring. Maybe even more significantly, they experience a kind of "softening," feeling a new capability to do POP in a more positive and life-affirming way. With what you're learning here, you too will hopefully be freed up to focus loving attention on your parents rather than on your unresolved issues.

If you have siblings, consider how your POP family can avoid the predictable pitfalls that have divided others. During the stresses of a POPcycle, unresolved issues from childhood may often re-appear, even ones you'd thought were resolved long ago. If they do resurface, one or more siblings may aggravate the old wound. A common way you may see that is someone assigns a false meaning to something in the present although what's really going on is that something still hurts from the past. Your unresolved family dynamics may sound like a lot of things and perhaps like this: "No wonder you don't want Mom living in the nursing home I chose for her, right down the street from me. You were her favorite child and were always jealous when Mom paid any attention to me. Now you think I'll get to see her more and that's why you don't like the home I chose ..."

Sibling rivalry takes many forms and, unfortunately, has no age limit. In one family a POP daughter may carry residual resentment that her brother always got the "fun" jobs at home during childhood while she got to do more "domestic" chores. Now co-POParenting with her brother, she may insist on keeping all the "fun" POP tasks, leaving her brother to change diapers and empty bedpans. In another POP family two sons might compete for who will take their mother to the doctor's office, each bearing the unconscious notion of "one-upping" the other with superior information.

Speaking of old programming, some of your family may have the belief that caring for old parents is "women's work." That is belied by current statistics. In many families and that may include yours, POParenting is regularly being done by sons and son-in-laws as well as daughters and daughters-in-law.[59] In some families, the POP work done by siblings is not based along gender lines whereas, in others, there may be a division of roles based on sex. In the latter, sons and sons-in-law may primarily be involved in POP banking, financial management and legal matters while females are making meals, washing dishes and changing diapers. In other POP families where there may be no daughters to do the more personal tasks, there may be daughters-in-law who attend to those, paid help or even the sons may take on such intimate tasks.

POP work divisions among siblings may find their roots either in your culture's expectations of men and women or in early family roles seen in your home. If you and your siblings aim to "equalize" POP tasks and "democratize" POP decision-making, it's likely you'll find it easier to deal with each other unless your traditions strongly dictate otherwise. That type of equalization and demonstration of respect can heal siblings' lifelong resentments and inequities, as well as serve your aging parents more appropriately in today's world.

After you've become aware of your issues and done your forgiveness work, a part of healing involves creating the new life or changes you want to have and then savoring that. By way of example, you too can choose a sibling at any age. Any of you who were raised as only children and still yearn for one as I did or if your siblings have died and you don't wish to go through your POP days, your older days or any more days without a brother or sister, you can do something about that. Although my qualifications for a sibling included someone remembered me from childhood, which need not be one of your criteria. Anyone can be an eligible candidate so long as each of you desires to make the other a part of your family.

---

[59] A new survey from the National Family Caregivers Association shows a much more even split than the historical numbers of seventy-five percent or more who were women. Today: 56 percent female, 44 percent male. Fifty-two (52%) percent of the survey's respondents, 39 percent of whom were men, stated they provided physical care including help with dressing, bathing, toileting, eating and mobility. Forty-six (46%) percent of respondents, 41 percent of them men, reported being involved in performing nursing activity such as managing medications, changing dressings, or monitoring vital signs. Reported at: http://www.celebratelove.com/caregivers.htm.

The sibling adoption between Rick and me was not a legal adoption in the sense that we filed no papers and ultimately there were no legal consequences. Others of you who choose this "feeling" step may wish to draw up legal wills to leave your "sibling" a portion of your property at death. You may find it comforting to exchange other legal documents or responsibilities with your new sibling, such as giving them your durable health care proxy or your power of attorney. This may be especially helpful if you're single and feeling scared of being "alone" when your parents die.

When I heard my Mom tell me that I was "doing good" as her POP Mom and that she could now "rest comfortably," I loved it. It didn't matter that she had cognitive issues or that I was way over 21, it just felt good. Some of your parents may not express their approval or gratitude all that often – and some maybe continue to grumble – but you should know that they really are grateful. You may need to remind yourself periodically that in spite of your uncertainties and challenges, your aging parents are truly relieved that you noticed they needed help and stepped up to make their lives better by doing POP.

You may feel that you're motivated to POParent primarily by guilt or obligation. From where I stand, however, I see how many of you are doing POP lovingly, generously and competently. And after you do some more "forgiveness work," as is set forth below in POPlan #13, you may come to the unexpected recognition that you're actually motivated more often by compassion and love than anything else. At the sunset of their lives, is there anything more you want from your parents than giving them greater comfort and receiving their pride in you? Perhaps the one who gets the most from the giant "do-over" called POP, may actually be you!

POPlan #13: Becoming The Parent You Always Wanted – To Have And To Be!!

POP VISIONING

What you have in POP Visioning is a healing tool designed to expand your ability to forgive, understand and accept yourself and your parents. Fill in the details of the vision you probably had back when you were growing up (and may still have) of how you always wanted your parents to be, when they were parenting you. If you never had such a vision, make it up now. If you allow some free reign to your imagination, that will help you access your creative right brain. Even if you didn't raise children, try answering the questions. Most of us retain a part that would still like to have those idealized parents. Maybe, if you're fortunate, your parents have become that way over the years. If that's the case, you can move on to the next part of this POPlan. Or maybe you were visionary enough to become the parent to your children that you always wanted, in which case, this will be easy.

Should answering these questions incline you to want to make your parents wrong for their inadequacies or for hurts they may have caused during your childhood, don't "hang out" there for long. This technique is not about that. It is about moving through old hurts to arrive at a place of serenity and wholeness.

Seat yourself in a quiet and restful environment, detach from your phones, computers and other distractions. Allow yourself time and space to remember, dream and heal. Then ask yourself:

- *What is it that I didn't get from my parents that I believe would have made a difference? If I'd had those, would I have felt more loved, done better in school, stayed married to my first spouse? (This is the time to get very specific about what you craved and didn't receive enough of from your Mom and/or Dad and what you decided when you didn't' get those things from them.)*

- *Did I want my parents to be more affectionate with me? Did I wish for more attention or personal acknowledgement for my accomplishments? Did I feel I was competing with my parents' work, television, friends or hobbies just to get noticed? Or was I competing with my siblings for my parents' time or appreciation? Did I feel I was never enough for them no matter what I did? When I asked them for something, did my parents tell me how many sacrifices they'd already made for me?*

- *Did I yearn for my parents' acceptance but feel I never belonged in my family? (Allow yourself full reign to feel the emotions that you trigger when asking yourself these questions.)*

- *Do I have regrets about my relationship with my parents and wish they'd treated me differently? If so, what can I think, do or say that will allow me to release those feelings today or soon? How can I turn those memories and emotions into more positive ones so I can forgive them and embrace my compassionate nature? If I can do that, will doing POP become more manageable for me and will I be more loving? What if anything is standing in my way?*

- *How can I become the kindest and most compassionate POParent I'm able to be? What if anything can I think, say or do to enable me to show those feelings to my parents now? What if anything is standing in my way?*

- *When I was a child, what actions, words or feelings did I miss and most want to receive more of from my parents? Is there any way that my parents may also be yearning for those things now? Could I "pay it backwards" – rather than pay it for-wards – and give, do or say to my parents the very things I missed the most during my childhood? What if anything is standing in my way?*

- *When I was a child, what did I get too much of from my parents and what did I want less of from them? Is there any way that my parents may also be overwhelmed with too much of some things I'm doing now? Could I "pay it backwards" – rather than pay it forwards – and avoid doing those things to my parents now? What if anything is standing in my way?*

- *When I was a child, what activities and joyous times did my parents and I get the most pleasure from doing together? Is there a way to recreate some of those with them now? What if anything is standing in my way?*

- *What would I like to have done better when I was parenting my children or step-children? How can I use that information now to "do better" as a POParent to my aging loved ones? What if anything is standing my way?*

- *How distraught am I today, as a result of missing whatever I wanted and didn't get, back then? Look at yourself. Do you feel you're productive? Do you have long-standing friendships and other relationships where you feel loved and loving? Do you live a decent life and feel good about yourself?*

It may be that, in spite of your childhood, you've learned to become pretty functional and feel fairly good about yourself and your life. You did, after all, survive your childhood with your imperfect parents and without whatever it may have been that you pined for made it into adulthood. You probably no longer need to haul around the wounds of lost opportunities or early parental detachment.

It may be that what you missed in your childhood hasn't really deterred you from living a good life. And what if what you'd previously thought was "unforgivable" or "harsh" parental treatment actually served or benefited you? It could have seeded the resilience you're so proud of and other qualities you've come to respect in yourself. What if you could "reframe" your early life and "extract" all the benefits you derived from events you'd previously seen as the "downside" of your narrative? After all, didn't those all bring you to here on your life journey? Couldn't those experiences be ones you could appreciate because of what you've learned?

Finally, perhaps since starting POP, you've also come to learn things about your parents' childhoods that make their ways of parenting you more understandable now? Maybe you can learn to forgive the past and have a better, more fulfilling present and future!

188

POP Music: Let The Good Times Roll

Pretend you can make your own YouTube in your mind of the best "do-over" opportunity you ever had during your POPcycle. Find a song of your own that reflects the joy of your great "do-over." Bookmark that music video so that at some later points when you're having a rough day or heavily feeling the burdens of your POP job, you can access it at will. Then play it loud and let your heart sing your song of inspiration!

When you join our website, www.ParentingOurParents.org, you'll be invited to share your postings of POP music, any tunes that have helped you or you think can support your fellow POParents while doing POP! Jack would have loved this part...

Chapter 14

Waiting As Our Parents Become Frailer, Weaker, Smaller And Maybe Worse

My Story:

    My folks had resisted moving so hard and I'd had to tolerate long-distance POParenting for so long that when I finally did move them close to me and found such a suitable place for them to live, I fully intended them to remain there indefinitely, maybe with some additional caregiving support. That was a real comfort to me, knowing they were finally settled.

When I considered how much harder a second move might be for progressively aging parents, should that ever occur, I feared that the next move might claim more from my Mother's aging mind and spirit than she had to give. Nor did I anticipate that Dad would fare well either, were there unnecessary or repeated transitions.

The reason I felt so secure about Mom and Dad's staying "forever" at their AL was because, prior to my signing the rental contract, the administrator had verbally agreed to that. I'm a careful listener and pride myself on paying close attention, especially if I'm having an important conversation about the "requirements" and "advantages" of my parents' last home.

But as events began to unfold, I found myself uncharacteristically questioning my memory. I recalled being told there might be changes to the AL contract in the future. But as I remembered it, those changes would be as to pricing. There might be increases to the rent, perhaps annually. It was also stated by the administrator that Lillian and/or Jack might need more help in the future and if so, those fees would be added to the initial charges.

No other changes to the contract we had with the AL were spelled out. Events such as a corporate buy-out of the AL's ownership, changes in the AL's policies and my parental potential behavioral problems were never mentioned as factors that could lead to termination of their lease. As it turned out, as careful as I'd been and as clear as I thought I was, I hadn't asked about those kinds of contingencies, all of which occurred. Who knew? As I would soon see, not thinking to ask would have serious family consequences.

Upon their arrival new residents were invited to eat a few meals with their more "veteran" peers at the AL. It was the facility's way to hospitably offer recently trans-planted residents a welcome. I noticed that even that simple a socializing experience seemed stressful for my parents: Jack was uninterested but trying to please Lillian and Lillian was concerned that she couldn't hold up her end of the conversation.

Jack was no longer predisposed to meeting new people at this point in his life. Although he was pleasant with others, my Dad generally preferred my company, Mom's or his own, over small talk with others. Lillian was still outgoing and enjoyed getting dressed and sitting around talking to others. Perhaps she even sought out other people more since her husband was becoming quieter. At the same time Mom felt pressure at these meet-and-greet dinners because she had difficulty remembering the names of their mealtime companions and what had been said.

Processing new information about the AL's physical layout, schedules, people and procedures would have been taxing for people with far younger brains. I recall feeling grateful that this would be my parents' last move and their final time to learn lots of names of new fellow residents and staff. I saw that doing simple things was becoming harder for my parents.

We're going to fast-forward this story a couple of years. During those years, my Mom and Dad settled themselves into their new life and learned what they needed to know to live comfortably in the AL. I never again saw them make any new friends but we all developed a comfortable rhythm over time. Mom attended her stretching and yoga classes or bingo activities while Dad did his reading. I visited on certain days during the week and longer on weekends. We all would go together to their many doctor appointments and enjoyed sharing a good medical result, when there was one.

The three of us continued to go out for a meal now and again. We'd come back and watch their favorite television shows together or listen to the old oldies on the radio. We reveled in southern California's sunny winter months. I would chauffeur my parents in my convertible, setting a baseball cap atop my Dad's nearly baldhead so he wouldn't get sunburned. We'd cruise down to the beaches of Malibu and Oxnard or up the amazingly breathtaking canyons to lookouts where we'd stop and admire the vistas. I'd bring along blankets for Mom who got cool on the afternoon drives. Mom's face beamed with her love of the beauty and Dad smiled contentedly. I remember feeling grateful just to see their faces all shiny and lit up, content knowing I'd done something that brought them such joy.

Some days when we were all together, time almost seemed to slow down, maybe to give us a bit more of itself. It even felt gentle and natural to be with them. During those couple of years when I saw them frequently, my parents' declines almost seemed to slow down. It had even stopped feeling different to have them live close by. In fact I loved being able to see them casually for lunch or visit them even for a half an hour after they'd eaten dinner.

Eventually my parents did need additional help with their Activities of Daily Living ("ADL's") and I added extra hours of AL care. The AL staff did things like helping my Mom bathe, pick out her clothing and get dressed, take all her medications correctly and Dad too needed some help, too, as time wore on. I must have lulled myself into believing that things would continue on without incident indefinitely but, of course, that didn't last.

Before long I found myself again dealing with the "unexpected." Mom's fall had proven a life-changing event for all three of us. When she'd been unsuccessful in re-learning to walk, the only affordable solution had been for Lillian to move to a skilled nursing facility ("SNF") that could accommodate her current level of attention. Dad had stayed behind at the AL, not needing skilled nursing and liking it where he knew his way around.

I was devastated for my Mom that her cognitive and physical limitations required her to adjust yet another time to another new place. Locating a satisfactory Skilled Nursing Facility ("SNF") that would accept Lillian had been challenging. After the hospital and the rehab SNF had sent her away for refusing to take water, meds and food, my Mom became categorized as "difficult." This severely limited my choices and the only SNF I liked that was willing to admit her was far from my Dad and in the next county.

At the SNF, Mom discovered that her new life "without mobility" would require her to live at the "mercy" of the attendants. Since Mom could no longer come and go of her own volition unless she was in a wheelchair, she needed the staff's help to her get to a meal, an activity or even to bed. Like Blanche du Bois of literary fame, Lillian found herself depending on "the kindness of strangers."

Perhaps she would learn more patience? Unlike other elders who quietly disappear into the background at such times, Mom was determined to stay active and engaged. She tried hard to bend her mind and spirit to that positiveness on the days she could. And on those occasions, I worked with her to encourage her.

I hated watching my parents live apart. A married couple for more than six decades, their distance felt unnatural to me. I also felt the gravity of what a wrenching trauma it must have been for them but I was helpless to prevent all the changes and upheaval.

My parents' separation stirred in me the sense that all stable things were beginning to fall apart and I feared my life would never again feel normal. During the first 25 years of their marriage, my parents had never spent as much as a night apart. That had seemed "normal" to me then. Now, after sixty-something years of togetherness, my Mom's conditions and "being difficult" had necessitated her moving away far from my Dad. To me, it felt like Jack was being left behind.

Neither of my parents talked about these "personal" matters with me. I suspect that his perspective was far less ominous than mine. He didn't seem to feel abandoned and he acted as if he were enjoying his newly found quiet. Dad loved having the individual time he now was able to have with me, he said. But I noticed that he also seemed quite content to have me leave when my visit was done.

But it was on one of those quiet nights when my Dad and I missed Lillian's presence more than we knew. Had she been with him that evening, perhaps she'd have reminded

Jack to put the necessary thickener into his water as he sat watching "Jeopardy." But Mom didn't live there any longer and Dad didn't remember by himself.

Seniors' lungs are extraordinarily vulnerable to a variety of respiratory conditions, including pneumonia, and my parents were no exception. Long after they'd left behind their snowy Northeast winters, my parents continued to suffer from respiratory illnesses and serial hospitalizations. Finally their doctor suggested they add a thickening powder to their liquids as a precautionary measure. A few tablespoons of this thickener which is fibrous in nature, converts liquids like coffee, water or juice into a honey-like substance, prevents the aspirating of liquid into the lungs.

Like many remedies and medicines, thickeners have their "downside." I was really touched when Dad revealed: "It's so unsatisfying. I don't ever get to have the refreshing feeling of drinking a glass of water or orange juice. I miss the taste of a real cup of coffee. Mine gets all gooey from thickener."

Between its unattractiveness and Dad's short-term memory loss, it made sense he might forget his thickener without extra prompting from the staff or me. To mitigate his forgetfulness, I'd previously asked the AL staff to remind Dad to add thickener to his water when they brought him his nightly medications. I'd also asked his waitresses to prompt Dad to add thickener during meals in the dining room. When I'd eat with him at home or take him out, as the "good POParent" I'd bring along Dad's thickener – like my good parents used to bring along Cheerios to a restaurant for me, so very long ago.

It wasn't clear what actually happened that fateful night. Maybe because he hated it, he forgot to put thickener in his water. Maybe he was 91, tired and forgetful. And maybe some AL aide forgot to prompt him. The bottom line was this: my Dad drank enough non-thickened liquid to become ill, require an ambulance and was taken off to the hospital for yet another battle with pneumonia.

A large corporation had recently purchased Dad's AL and the cause of his misfortune was unimportant in relation to the larger corporate interests. They "solved" the problem by promulgating a New Rule: any resident in any facility we own who uses thickeners must leave voluntarily and immediately or face immediate eviction! As we've been warned in song and in life: in a New York minute, everything can change...

The solution seems to have been invented to prevent future litigation so families could no longer sue the corporation for not more carefully monitoring residents using thickeners. The New Rule decimated the AL's previous promises that, once admitted, my parents need never move again. Hadn't they promised me that my parents need never worry about moving again – that they could always be accommodated in the AL?

194

I tried to review the conversations in my mind that I'd had nearly three years previously with the AL's administrator, before I'd brought my folks to California. Could I have misheard or misunderstood our agreement about this key point of consistent living for my parents? I even asked myself if I'd heard what I wanted and disregarded the rest? Maybe I'd so hoped this would be their last home that I'd chosen to believe it without thinking through the possible limitations or changes, should the AL gain new ownership? Hadn't the administrator said there'd be no more new people, places and things for my parents to have to strain to learn? Apparently those promises were not as solid as they had appeared. I reminded myself once again to be more wary of my POP expectations!

I was in Dad's hospital room when the call came in from the AL. I mistakenly fantasized that the heads of this AL chain had changed their minds; maybe they were offering Dad an apology. At the minimum perhaps they were calling to recommend another facility where Jack's conditions might be better served. Perhaps they were letting him return from the hospital and stay until I could locate a more suitable facility.

Not really. Jack would never be welcome back at his AL and the purpose of the call was to have me accept (telephonic) service of process for Dad's eviction notice. If I didn't, the former administrator, now-corporate employee, warned me: a process server would come to Dad's hospital bedside to serve him his eviction papers. The unbelievable truly had occurred! This all made no sense. Like his wife, Dad also would have to leave his home yet another time and learn a whole new facility, set of aides, a new set of rules and residents – and all because of thickener.

The lawyer in me understood that corporations create these kinds of protocols to protect themselves against future liability but she didn't like it. The daughter in me felt sad and "rejected" for my Daddy. The POParent in me was absolutely incensed. My Dad had always been a kind man who said "thank you" three times to everyone for everything. After successfully recovering from brain surgery at 89 and all the work that entailed, now the poor man would have to re-adjust again to new surroundings – and at 91!

I was now informed that Jack couldn't return home. Of course I'd done no research to locate him a new facility because, until the phone call, I hadn't known he'd ever need one. Next I was notified that the hospital planned to discharge him within 48 hours. Discharge him to what facility? Release him! Why? Had Dad recovered from the pneumonia? The hospital was forcing Dad's discharge but not because he was healthy, had fully recovered or had any appropriate facility to go to.

No, the hospital insisted on Dad's discharge because of Medicare's payment rules. These are known as Diagnosis-Related Groups[60] ("DRG's") to some "the dreaded DRG's" and they regulate how many days of hospitalization Medicare will pay the hospital for an illness, like pneumonia. Looking for a solution, I wondered if our family could pay privately, outside of Medicare, for Dad to stay on a few additional days while I sorted this all out. But hospitals rarely permit this and, even had they agreed, his bill would have been astronomical and provided only a temporary fix.

When I'd moved Mom and Dad from New York, I'd spent weeks researching different facilities. When I moved Mom to her SNF, I'd been more pressed but still took the time I needed to find the right place. With Dad, I was given no lead-time at all. I found myself becoming outraged. This whole situation felt wrong to me – me: the lawyer, the daughter and the POParent. It felt way wrong!

What happened to the promises before the corporate purchase, the guarantees my parents could "always" stay at the facility they'd learned to call home? What happened to the notion that sick patients weren't supposed to be dumped out of hospitals without placement in adequate facilities? What happened to the idea that a husband and wife would live together until death did do them part? What happened to our institutions treating elders with respect as the heads of our families? What the hell was going on in this world? Didn't my Mom, Dad and I have any right to expect anything to go as planned?

I finally calmed down, telling myself that being upset wasn't helping my Dad find a decent place to go. I was living under the dreaded DRG's time clock and, no matter what else I had planned for those days, I had to focus on finding Dad's next home. I neglected taking care of my car, my home, my loved ones and myself. I catapulted into high-speed solution mode, locating a place he'd like. I was clearer this time about his requirements than when I'd originally searched for the AL. He liked a facility to be peaceful and quiet, clean and safe, flexible enough to permit "thickener-needy" residents and local enough to allow his doctors to visit him there. If he could also have a window to look through and a view of trees, he would be content.

When Lillian had moved to the distant SNF, I hired a young woman to drive Dad to visit Mom on a regular basis. The visits took up a good portion of the day: the drive took about two and a half hours round trip and their time together could be another two, three or four hours. But even with the help of someone to drive my Dad to Mom and occasionally pick up his cleaning or do some chores for my parents, POParenting two parents in different locations was becoming a full-time job for me.

---

[60] See Glossary.

I was tired a lot and began to notice a disturbing theme emerging: I never had enough time or resources for everything and everyone. I wasn't twenty years old either, I had to remind myself. I accepted that, for a while, I'd have to curtail time with my friends, limit the number of hours I worked and be willing to leave anywhere at a moment's notice for a POParental crisis. I wondered how long I'd be able to manage this multi-shift life.

As my parents' disabilities were increasing, my POP responsibilities were expanding. POParenting two advanced seniors who now had two different sets of doctors, facilities, caregivers and needs was beginning to exhaust me. Since Dad needed more care than he had in the past, I hoped I might be able to reunite my parents in a single facility, an SNF that could accommodate both their current needs.

I was frustrated by the constant changes and allowed a cloud of depression to briefly descend over me. In that moment I became filled with my own helplessness and hopelessness. I also foolishly told myself I should be better at predicting these changes. Where would I turn for more help? I began to fear that nothing I'd anticipated would ever come to pass – except, of course, the certainty of death.

Your Story

There are stages in most POPcycles when it seems that all you can to do is enjoy your parents as much as you can while you observe them and their worlds contract. Some of the POP challenge at this time is that there's often little you can actually do to change it.

If you've proceeded this far, you've already chosen this journey, found out what you needed to know to do POP, put various helpful people, things and legal documents in place for your folks and gotten to know their doctors, neighbors and caregivers. You've seen to it that your parents are being well fed, clothed and sheltered in homes with as much security built in as you and they can collectively tolerate and afford. Since you've already done all that, most of your current POP tasks involve "maintenance." You go see your parents, you check on people and things that are supposed to be helping them and change anything, if that's necessary.

But with little to actually do, if you're like many POParents, you may begin to worry. You may even obsess on what you've done or not done for your parents by asking yourself: do I have enough precautionary measures in place? Can't I do more? There are limits on how much you can do to protect another human being, especially another adult.

Many of your folks, despite having some POP needs, may still be functioning quite well at this maintenance point of the POPcycle. They may be able to do much for themselves and "know a lot," even if all the information isn't readily available to them. Never disrespect your parents by underestimating them.

Even those diagnosed with dementia may have many parts of their brain still working. Particularly with dementia, you may find yourself confused by the extent of your parents' abilities one day followed by the depth of their disabilities that same evening. It's eerie to see your parent forget your name one day and recall in detail the most embarrassing story from your childhood the next. That same adult you've been tenderly protecting may also turn around and push your emotional buttons and remind you of how your family "used to be." They may be old but your parents can still trigger feelings you thought you no longer had.

As you've been observing, aging is idiosyncratic. Each individual declines at a different rate. Moreover, when one of your parent's physical, cognitive and other limitations far exceeds the other's, it can be disarming for everyone involved. The transition to caregiving a partner, living apart or being taken care by your spouse will surely alter the dynamics of a couple. After a long marriage – happy or not so happy – this can be devastating. Even if your parents have a large age difference, it may still feel shocking. Just because it was predictable that one of your parents might age first, when it actually occurs it may be wrenching for all of you.

Even when your family is still intact, you may find yourself "prematurely grieving" the loss of your parents or your family as you used to know it. You may be feeling guilty that you haven't done more when you've really worked hard to be a good POParent. You may be agitated and impatient with many things that ordinarily wouldn't bother you or feel depressed.

Although premature grieving is quite common, it can be very troubling. You might not understand some of the intensity of your melancholy especially since your parents are still very much alive. If any of these are happening to you, it might be particularly helpful at this point to seek out a therapist, spiritual counselor or a POP Family Coach, someone experienced in these types of matters. Give yourself the gift of a few supportive sessions. Remember if you're captaining the POP boat, you've got to stay awake and focused but even the best and strongest captains need a hand.

Some of the times you don't know what to do and feel frustrated, you may decide to do something POP, anything. We've looked at this phenomenon before. Your frustration may result in your "making up" things to do for your parents. Some of those may be useful. You may ask to have your Mom's swallowing re-tested to see if she can have more fun by being allowed to eat more interesting foods than previously. I did that. Or you might bring in a physical therapist or take your Dad to a swimming pool to see if you can lighten his depression with some exercise. I did that too.

Your activities may be fruitful or not, in terms of accomplishing something that your parents truly need. But doing these things may help you as long as you don't "undo" things that are working. Feeling you're doing something useful may be better than sitting around and worrying about your parents but, as you've seen, it may have its down side. At other times you may be feeling very sad as your parents are failing in front of you and becoming less and less "themselves." Your desperation to regain a sense of balance may lead you to fix what *is* working, micromanaging the services and people who are working well.

That is not useful, as we learned earlier in POPlan #11 so, what else might you do that could be? Couldn't you just sit down and listen to what's going on for your Mom and Dad? As with parenting your children, sometimes the most valuable thing you can do when you're POParenting is simply be there with your folks. Listen to them. Pay attention to what they may feel, want and need. When you can become quiet within yourself, you will become clearer what isn't wanted or needed and you can distinguish whether it's more useful to do another POP action or give your parents the gift of your attention and interest.

No matter how sad it is, unless they die at a young age, your beloved parents *will* get frailer, smaller and weaker. And there isn't a lot you can do sometimes but watch. Sure, you can go to hospitals and doctors, recreation centers and church with your folks. But if you are looking and listening, you'll see the people you love and looked up to when you were a child are now getting frailer, weaker and smaller. Often it just plain hurts. It is also part of the Circle of Life.

POPlan #14: Discovering How To "Just Be There" With Your Parents

It might be that one of the hardest POP challenges you'll face will be to sit with your parents and seemingly "do nothing." Of course you're never actually doing nothing as various systems within your body are constantly working on your behalf, however quietly. Similarly your mind is busily creating those thousands of thoughts we humans produce every hour.

When you first try to consciously cease all your doing and just be there with your beloved seniors, it may feel like you're doing nothing even "slacking off." Much of your "doing" as a POParent has involved actively warding off harm to your parents, developing new POPlans and making those into reality. Instead what you'll be "doing" here is giving your folks another part of POParenting: being with them. Fully listening to your parents, sharing yourself with them and just being there is a different sort of POParenting than doing things for them. And you may not yet be able to "just be there" with them for very long since it may be a skill you haven't yet acquired. But, stay with it and you'll find you get better at it. "Just being there" might be your best POP work yet.

I've spoken about the gifts of "attention and interest" you can offer your parents and noted how complicated that seemingly simple thing may be for POParents to effectuate. But how worthwhile it is to give your Mom and Dad the very thing most of us wanted from them, when they parented us? We craved their uninterrupted time, curiosity and concentrated focus. Why does something so straightforward seem that difficult? Answering these questions may help you understand the reasons.

IF YOU FIND YOURSELF DOING "BUSY WORK" AND NOT REALLY BEING THERE WITH YOUR PARENTS, ask yourself:

When I visit my parents, am I often busy, doing tasks rather than spending time with them?

Do I do that because I have too many tasks and/or in part, because I'm (unconsciously) avoiding having painful feelings I don't want to have?

Do I do that because I get upset/depressed/sad/resentful/angry/bored (fill in the blank of your emotions) if I simply sit and talk with my parents?

Do I stay busy when I visit my parents because they are upset/depressed/sad/resentful/angry/bored … and it hurts me to just be with them?

Do I avoid being with them because we haven't really talked for a long time and aren't sure we know how to do that? Would I like to try?

Am I afraid to listen to my parent, perhaps scared to hear what they really want to say to me?

Do I leave them during visits to do POP tasks because I'm more comfortable accomplishing things for my parents than being with them? Couldn't the POP tasks be done later so I could visit with my parents?

Couldn't I learn to just sit quietly and be there for my Mom and Dad, really listening and hearing what they have to say, as I'd wanted from them? Couldn't I learn to share myself with my folks in a way that lets them know who I've become and that I appreciate who they are?

Wouldn't having that between us be wonderful?

"Being There" With Your Aging Parents:

"Being there" with your parents isn't doing nothing. It actually consists of a series of steps. First, you must create the intention to "be with" with your parents in a different way than you may have been recently, a mode that lends itself to openness, candor and caring.

Next, you will need to follow through on your newly formed intention by taking action to ensure that the environment you've chosen to be with them supports that, both physically and emotionally. To do that, you may need to eliminate those things that are likely to divert your parents and you from being peaceful together. That could involve limiting the diversions associated with noise, people coming in and out and your electronic devices.

You may even take steps to minimize whatever interferes with your parents' physical comfort by closing windows, getting blankets or other such steps. All of these are preparing the way for improving the quality of your familial communications so you might also need to remind your parents to put in their hearing aids.

Since you've decided you want to "be with" them, there may be other, more emotional, barriers to intimately communicating with your parents that you'll need to address. The fact that talking about personal things or life and death hasn't been your family's "ordinary way" might be one such barrier you'll need to tackle. Your own discomfort sitting still with them may be another. You or they may be apprehensive about the content of what might arise, were you to talk candidly. It's probably going to be helpful if you start the ball rolling by talking about your desires to connect with them and perhaps your own hesitations.

Even if you've gone this far, you or your parents may still find yourselves feeling a bit awkward since it's easier for most people to have an agenda to accomplish than to just sit and be together, listening and sharing yourselves. Although you all may not feel immediately comfortable with this, you'll find you all get better at it with some practice and, eventually, you will be glad for the effort.

However what I saw myself and heard from other POParents is that some of their best memories are of the times they were just were there with their aging Mom and Dad. Hopefully you will discover that too. It's worth your effort!

POP Music

Country singer Kenny Chesney released an evocative song entitled, "While He Still Knows Who I Am"[61] about a man's feelings upon learning that his father had been diagnosed with Alzheimer's. The lyrics to the tune remind you and me to seek a deeper bond to our roots while there's still time. How much there is to learn from this song and to discover through POP Music!

---

[61] Written by Dave Berg, Tom Douglas and Georgia Middleman and published by Blue Chair Records LLC Columbia Nashville.

Chapter 15

Doing The Only Thing Left: Comfort-Filling Your Parents

My Story:

Despite bringing my parents to a warmer climate, hoping to decrease the number of serious medical events they would have to endure, those situations actually increased in frequency after they became Californians. Their hospitalizations were beginning to occur so often that they felt commonplace but ironically, hardly ordinary.

Going to the hospital often had proven debilitating for all concerned. Relentlessly they battled pneumonias and underwent serious surgeries with the even more difficult anesthesia and requisite physical and occupation therapies. It drained my elderly, fragile Mom and Dad. Being in the hospital with sick people often made them sicker, exposing Lillian to MRSA and other complications. I, too, became exhausted as I tried to balance my life while driving incredible distances between home, work and my parents' respective ALs, SNFs and hospitals.

Aside from something extraordinary – like my birth, Dad's hernia operation when I was sixteen or an infamous hurricane in the early 1950's – my parents had been together without interruption. Until Mom moved away permanently to the SNF, each of these hospitalizations and rehabs had required my folks to manage the additional adjustment of living apart from each other. These events emerged as a major life disruption since, during their six decades of marriage, my parents had arranged it so they spent their days and nights together.

During their early years together, Dad's skin disorder lupus had made him ineligible for the draft. The resulting alternate service he did was local, allowing him to live at home with Mom. Even when he had his office in midtown, Dad would often write songs and conduct his music business from home. After I went off to school, Jack gave up his office and shared all his days and nights in the two-bedroom apartment with his wife.

Their hospitalizations demanded other changes from my Mom and Dad as well. They had to wrap their minds and aging bodies around spending their days apart, sleeping alone and in beds that were different from those they were used to. It was easy to see how they could have become sleepless or paranoid in the middle of a dark night in a strange bed, drugged, disoriented, not knowing who was coming to "help" them. This often led to sleep disruptions and/or to extra medications to calm their disorientation.

Being in the hospital also meant being in a whole new environment and relating to the constantly changing staff there. That became increasingly challenging and each hospitalization added more to their stress. Jack and Lillian weren't only challenged by their cognitive limitations but also by their vision and hearing which were no longer all that sharp. Similarly, their post-operative rehabilitation process also required spending additional time away from each other in specialized facilities with their own new staffs to deal with, uncomfortable beds and novel environments.

All this visibly drained my parents' energies and would have been tough on people years younger and healthier. Their hospitalizations also unsettled my parents' "regular" routine back at their facilities. Each time it was more difficult to readjust to life back at home. Now that they were in their 90's, even small changes were getting harder for my Mom and Dad to accommodate. I wasn't exactly getting younger or healthier myself and, at that point in our POPcycle, I was too often ignoring the advice I gave others about self-care.

It was becoming clear to me just how exhausted Jack had become when I was figuring out where to place him after his last bout with pneumonia. My father was tired of being sick, sick of hospitals, rehab centers and the revolving-door ritual these institutionalizations had become. Lying in his last hospital bed, my Dad's body looked emaciated. Oddly, being so thin made him look almost like a young boy rather than old man.

Had I not felt unbearably sad seeing him so vulnerable there, maybe I'd have better appreciated the humor in his point of view.

"Look at these people, Jane. They're unhealthy. They're fat and I don't mean a few pounds overweight but horribly, morbidly obese. Not only that but they have cigarettes falling out of their pockets. They should know better than to smoke! I'm talking about the doctors here honey, not the patients. How can we trust these people to take care of me when they treat themselves so badly? Get me out of here."

I knew he was right. I'd forgotten that this now-shrunken old man had once been an outspoken health enthusiast, a daily exerciser and a state champion athlete in "an earlier life." Early on when lots of people smoked, Jack proudly told me that he'd never smoked a single cigarette, hoping to discourage my acquiring an unhealthy practice. I smiled, remembering my Dad's vision for vibrant health back in "the day."

When I went away to college and was no longer under his watchful eye, his contribution to my healthy habits was a weekly delivery of a basket of fruit, arriving fresh every Monday. As a youngster, I'd watched Jack's discipline as he worked out in his bedroom every single morning. No fancy gym, no trainer to keep him on target, Jack just used his good common sense. Now that same man was begging me: "get me outta here, Jane. I hate the hypocrisy of obesity and smoking by doctors. I'm tired of being here. Plus it's always freezing in these hospitals. No amount of blankets ever makes me warm enough. Honey, take me home and please never bring me back!"

Notwithstanding the neurosurgeon's earlier disparagement of Jack's brain, Dad revealed he could still articulate his wishes with crystalline clarity. I knew that I should heed his requests. He wanted to be warmer than he'd been in the hospital. Dad understood that he'd been evicted from his original AL due to their changing rules and could not return there. He also knew that moving would require his once again adjusting to a new facility, its staff with different residents and rules.

My Dad did not want to be placed with Mom in her SNF. Jack explained his one contingency in terms of his medical needs, stating that he didn't need the same level of care Lillian did in the skilled nursing home. That was accurate, although less true at that point than it had been previously since he was weaker than ever. I considered that what he really meant by his comment was far different than what he was saying: my now fatigued father didn't want to live with Lillian.

It seemed wiser and kinder to comply with his infrequent request rather than to convince him of something he clearly didn't want in order to simplify my life by having two parents at a single facility as well as the same county. I could see that Dad felt relieved after we'd talked about his not joining Mom at the SNF. He seemed particularly comforted because I'd listened to his hospital-bed requests.

So out I went and found my Dad another AL that seemed to provide more supervision than the first, had an opening now for a male resident and was located near Dad's doctors. If this new AL fit my POParenting standards for him, Dad could be living there within days and within the deadline that Medicare's DRG's had imposed.

I immediately toured the facility and talked with the proprietors, staff and with their residents at some length. It seemed "doable." The AL passed my "smell test," that is: it didn't smell at all bad and the food smelled good. They'd installed cameras at key locations to keep track of their residents and the attendants. I liked the notion of additional equipment to provide "extra eyes" on Dad and was pleased to learn that the owners of the facility could watch out for Dad from their homes.

After conducting as thorough a "due diligence" as I had time for, I employed my best intuitive skills to conclude the staff at this AL would (hopefully) be more careful and attentive to Dad than they'd been at his previous facility. I prayed that the people at the new AL would monitor him better since I hated the idea that Jack might forget to put thickener into his coffee and contract another aspiration pneumonia. I was especially fearful of that happening after Dad had been so outspoken about never returning to another hospital.

At this point in the POPcycle, when my parents were able to do few things for themselves and were feeling somewhat "impotent," it seemed crucial that, at least in their interchanges with me, they feel as respected, heard and as "powerful" as possible. Knowing that I was getting their concerns and heeding their wishes, when I could, seemed more important than ever before.

Dad got into my car at the hospital for this unplanned move with characteristic cool. Early on in his life, he'd decided to be a non-complainer, teaching it to me this way: "Keep your complaints to yourself, honey. Pay attention and you'll see that nobody really wants to hear them anyway." As he'd aged, Jack had become a "triple thank-you" giver, repetitively expressing his appreciation for almost anything done on his behalf. Dad's quiet, easygoing nature and these frequent expressions of gratitude made him relatively simple to place this time, which contrasted with my Mom who often was accompanied by her challenging attitude and her "record."

Driving him to his new AL, I sensed I was bringing my father to his last home, quite literally. The man who had picked out my first home was now graciously allowing me to choose his final one. The new facility was clean, warm – Dad was happy about that – and attractive. Most of the residents displayed more severe aging symptoms and disabilities than their counterparts at Dad's former AL had. The cameras in the halls, common areas and at the nursing stations did provide me an odd sense of security and I gave no real concern to intruding on Dad's privacy since he was, after all, my responsibility.

They gave him a large single room rather than the two-room apartment he and Mom had occupied at their original AL. I'd negotiated with the owners and gotten Dad more caregiver attention in exchange for less living space. Sunlight filled Dad's room most of his days at his new facility. I arranged his furniture so that he had a separate sitting area, near the entryway, although his guests were few in number. I placed his single bed, where he would spend most of the remaining days, at the far end of the large room, facing outward onto the courtyard.

From his bed Jack could look through his large window out onto a beautiful courtyard filled with fruit trees that seemed to be in constant stages of blooming. I loved to watch my father as he warmed his body with the sun streaming through the window and warmed his spirit with the beauty of the trees and the serenity in his surroundings.

Life went on uneventfully for a while for Dad. I watched him getting used to his new home and he seemed quietly content. When I'd come to visit, he'd be relishing his peaceful view, reading a newspaper, watching some nighttime television or resting comfortably. I didn't otherwise know how Dad was reacting to all the changes because, like so many men of his generation, he'd never been one to say a lot about his feelings. Nonetheless, when Jack wanted to make his views known – about not returning to the hospital and not moving into Mom's SNF – he'd made the point loudly enough.

Although he was outgoing and often talkative in the day, he'd gotten a bit quieter over time. But around this time Dad's started to become quite "internal" and withdrawn. He was even less forthcoming about himself or his opinions than previously. When he was in the mood for visiting with me, Jack appeared to love talking with but, increasingly, it was he, not busy me, who would be the one to end our visits, claiming fatigue.

Jack was uninterested in a social life with the other people at this latest home and had no need to be entertained by them or the staff. He found no one in the new AL whom he wished to befriend or particularly even converse with. But that wasn't so very different from his first California residence. Aside from family, Jack preferred to spend his days and nights in a more solitary fashion, a place that he termed "peaceful."

Despite being in a resting mode most of the time and in bed a lot, fatigue seemed to have affected his body, energy, strength and even his motivation to move. It felt like his spirit had even become tired but not necessarily yet peaceful. Dad seemed to lack purpose for the first time I could remember. It felt like he was "off balance," and not at all himself.

I watched as life weariness overtook Jack's mental functioning. As with many writers, my Dad had always been fascinated with life's details. As he settled into his final home on earth, I witnessed him losing interest in many things. I knew he was slowing down when Dad stopped reading. Books had been a great love for my Dad, a quiet spot in a demanding marriage. Initially he'd seemed to forget he was re-reading some books he borrowed from the AL's library and then he limited his sights to shorter pieces, like magazine or newspaper articles. Finally he stopped reading altogether.

Soon watching the news and his favorite television shows lost their appeal and even "Jeopardy's" mental challenges no longer held his attention. Sometimes I thought he was even losing interest in me and when that happened, I tried to not take it personally. Mostly Dad spoke of wanting to "rest," even as he was already lying in his bed.

Even observing all those changes hadn't fully prepared me for the "Talk." One afternoon he called me to his room and spoke without hesitation, saying things that I had difficulty comprehending so I just listened. "Jane, you seem to be doing well and you don't really need me anymore." I resisted telling him I did need him. I wanted my Father to feel vital and strong and for me to be able to lean on him, as I'd done in my youth. The truth was that he seemed tired all the time and no longer available for me to lean on. I tried telling myself I shouldn't need to lean on my father anymore, that I was the grown-up now. But a part of me wasn't 100% sure about that, the part that still wanted her Daddy.

"You know, honey, I'm not going back to the hospital again. Hospitals are cold places with sick people and I don't see any reason to return there. I'm done with hospitals. And truthfully Jane, I feel kind of done with living. I'm always exhausted. I'm tired of fighting this chronic pneumonia and I can't remember the last time I felt well or had any energy. I don't want any more medication with their gruesome side effects."

He took a long pause and continued on. "I can see that you're doing fine, honey. More than fine. You're a good girl and you'll be all right. You've been taking such good care of your Mom as well as me. I can rest well knowing you'll continue to look out for your mother. As for me, I'm ready to go. I apologize to you for not having more energy or sticking around longer. I'm sorry. But can it be all right if I'm done fighting and allow whatever happens to me to happen? And if so, what do we do about it?"

I began to breathe again. I had stopped breathing when he was talking. My Father wanted me to understand in "full color and HD" that he felt complete with living, was tired of fighting his illnesses and, should something lead to his death, he was ready to go that would be acceptable.

Dad wasn't hopeless. He wasn't depressed. He wasn't suicidal as he'd once been back in New York. He wasn't simply insulted with the hypocritical doctors who didn't live the healthy lives they espoused nor merely irritated with being forever cold in hospital beds. He wasn't ashamed that he could no longer do his work or support others. Jack didn't seem to mind the thought that neither his daughter nor his wife needed him any longer; if anything, that seemed a relief to him as he faced his current limitations.

My Dad was tired enough to let go of the struggle, willing to release himself. Characteristically, he considered his death and the process of dying to be his choice. I'd just spent the last seven, eight years of my life focused on creating a better life for my folks. I'd tried so hard to make my parents' world, what? "Safe" from death? And now, one of them wanted to walk right into that abyss and give up fighting the illnesses. A part of me was momentarily confused, I'd say even incensed. I tried reminding myself that Jack's decision wasn't about me. But even though I understood that, I felt profoundly sorry for myself and my "abandonment."

Dad had apologized to that abandoned part of me, the one not yet ready to fully accept what he was going through. Of course he had no reason to apologize for being worn out at nearly 92, not to me or anyone else. But I'd needed some time to allow the full implications of his decision into my comprehension. I needed to figure out how to manage my emotions and then how to "make it happen" for my Dad with comfort and grace. It seemed so ironic that, just when I was finally become a bit adept at being his POParent, I might not be able to do that much longer.

I reminded myself that this was his life. My Dad owed me nothing more. He had given me life, his love, an extraordinary education and the very best of himself. He'd even left me and the world his legacy of music. My more rational self said: there's no more that he needs to do for me, not even staying alive.

I breathed in deeply to access my inner calmness. In my most grown-up voice ever, I heard myself saying: "It isn't your job, Dad, to stay alive in order to amuse or please me. I can't imagine how much I will miss you but, if you feel ready to go, I will honor that. I'll speak with your doctors and see if you can be put on hospice. And after that, I'll do all I can so that your remaining days and nights are as pain-free and peace-filled as possible." Somehow I'd been able to give my Dad the mature and enlightened response I wanted to offer him.

I drove home, read up about hospice and saw how the requirements of getting Dad into Medicare's hospice program. I learned that Dad would be eligible for hospice services after his physician certified that he was suffering from a terminal condition and unlikely to live longer than six months. Hospice services could be given him in a separate hospice residential or in his AL at home. Finally, Jack would not need to return to those cold hospitals nor move again. No, he was home for good.

My next steps involved requesting Dad's doctor to certify him for hospice, which he did, and then choosing one agency from among many that contracted with Medicare to provide him the services allowed under federal regulation. Hospice's palliative care involved rest, water treatments, pain relief for the coughing or discomfort if he wished it and counseling for any emotional and spiritual concerns.

Once on hospice, Dad would no longer be given treatments to "cure" any illnesses that might become opportunistic, just treatments that "comforted" him. Should he get another case of pneumonia, for example, he would not be prescribed antibiotics or other medications to fight it. If Jack wanted to taste his favorite coffee without thickener or eat rich foods again, he could now indulge those cravings.

I was referred to a few good hospices in Dad's neighborhood from other POParents and from my geriatric colleagues. I contacted them, checked out what I could about them online and then went to "interview" the hospice providers in person, just as I'd earlier done with Mom and Dad's residential facilities.

Hospice workers are generally known in the medical and geriatric communities as unusually kind and caring people. I particularly liked the compassion I saw and heard from the staff at one agency and opted for them. Their people came out to meet with Dad and assess his needs and desires. They offered him warm baths, nutritional services, visits from social workers, conversation with spiritual people and lots of information. I stepped back to watch how they would do their work – I knew a lot about aging but little about the process of dying.

After that, I went online and ordered every book I could find on "death and ... HUMOR" and asked that they be shipped ASAP. I wanted to find a way to laugh when life was at its most challenging. I wanted to or I needed to but, either way, my instincts said: "this is part of life, too. You might as well enjoy the ride and see the humor." That perspective was something I'd learned from my Daddy. I could now honor my "mentor" by finding and utilizing the funny side of dying.

One evening during hospice when I went by to visit him, I saw a business card on Dad's nightstand. It belonged to the hospice minister who, I learned, had been by to see Dad several times, as it turned out. My Dad's parents had not been believers in a religion and my Dad had been given no formal religious education. We'd never talked much about his point of view regarding an after-life. But months before "meeting his Maker," apparently Jack was seeking a spiritual perspective from this hospice minister.

I asked Dad if I might talk to the minister although I'm unsure exactly why I did that. I think I'd hoped to somehow reassure myself that Dad was resolving any remaining questions he had, in preparation for his demise. I was pleased when the minister told me they'd talked extensively. It seemed that Jack's comfort was arriving in a variety of palliative packages. I felt very grateful my father had found someone to talk to, maybe as part of his final healing.

My Dad had been kind as usual when we talked after he was put on hospice. He wanted to clarify that his decision to go on hospice didn't mean he was "tired of me." Even before moving to his move to California, he'd told me of his excitement to spend more time than we'd had all those years when I'd only visited.

When he became a Californian, Dad delighted in discovering "the little things" that he felt he could only learn by our spending time together. He'd ask all about me, my work, my ways of being in the world and how I thought about things. I loved hearing how proud he was of my accomplishments and more importantly, of how I treated people. Both Dad and I treasured those times together. Now that he was on hospice and our days together were numbered, I tried to make sure to remember it all. I still think about those loving conversations periodically. I bring them out to savor them and they still make my heart sing. But I'm getting ahead of myself.

During hospice Dad seemed to particularly enjoy our just being together quietly until he faded, which was sooner and sooner. It didn't matter whether we talked about anything or not. Sometimes we just held hands as we watched television. I'd already begun working on this book and showed Jack my earliest drafts. As with my Mom, I had a hint of trepidation, wondering how he'd respond to the book, to the "intrusion" it might be on his privacy and also to the notion that I was POParenting him.

I should have known him better and had more faith in him. My Dad grinned with fully relished pleasure. Not only did he love the concept of POP but he also got how much help my work could be. He was joyous about what POP could do for other families. Moreover, he was proud of my blossoming third career. "Imagine, Jane, you're a writer, too! Finally you're joining the Wolf family business!! Your grandmother would have loved your having that potential to influence the world for good, honey!"

Long ago Jack had figured out how to earn his livelihood as had other Wolf family members doing work he loved, writing. Several years after Dad left the planet, I got to experience some of the power of being a writer. It was the morning after Obama was elected president and I was reading his autobiography, "Dreams of My Father."[62] At that point in the story our new President was chronicling some of the disheartening days he'd had doing community organizing. Barack had resorted to listening to music for encouragement and there, on page 91, were the lyrics of Dad's song, "I'm A Fool to Want You..." which, sung by Billie Holiday, had comforted the future leader of the free world. I swelled with pride.[63]

Like Jack's influence on the young American president, others in our family had been gifted with being able to make a difference in the world through their words. My paternal grandmother had been only a teenage girl living in Eastern Europe when she'd helped many families escape to the US from oppressive conditions there. Later, after giving birth to my Dad and his siblings, she'd written a daily column for a political newspaper, advocating for better conditions for workers and the poor. It was virtually unheard of at that time for a woman to be a writer, have her opinions published and actively discussed in the community!

Dad's younger brother George had gone in a different writing direction, creating advertising copy and minting phrases that would become America's "household names," like the characters in "MAD MEN." My first cousin Dick Wolf, George's son, created, wrote and produced all the "Law and Order" series. He has emerged as a world-renowned writing icon and almost anyone with a TV can attest to the sway of his written words.

Now, I too might be joining the family business and it felt "right" and very good to have my Dad welcome me so warmly into it. He called the family's ethos "writing with the intent to make a difference." Up until then, I hadn't seen myself as any part of that or any other tradition. Starting this book had seemed like adding to

---

[62] Dreams of My Father was published by Crown, 2007.

[63] For more information about Jack Wolf's music, go to http://mpcamusicpublishing.com/catalog/artists-songwriters/jack-wolf-integrity-music.

my psychotherapy and POP Family Coaching practices, not embarking on a third career with ancestral roots. But Dad was right, as usual: it was my intention then and has remained my goal to have this book be of service to the world, to make a difference.

Dad and I decided not to tell Mom that he'd gone on hospice. Attempting to explain the concept of hospice to Lillian would have been wasted on her by that time. Nor did we share with her how soon he might pass. Dad and I agreed there'd be no benefit to that, especially since there was no "time certain." Having vague and incomprehensible information would likely have caused Mom unnecessary distress and there seemed little "upside," since there was no way she was equipped to understand or prepare herself.

When Lillian's conditions had required her placement in a different geriatric setting from Dad's, many things changed in the dynamic of our threesome. For a couple that had previously spent so little time apart, this separation dramatically altered their relationship. Mom was unable to operate a cell phone and the SNF didn't encourage phoning on their line unless there was an emergency. Hearing on the phone was also a problem for Mom. As a result, in-person visits became my parents' way of communicating with each other and I was responsible for making the arrangements.

Once they began living separately, my parents needed me to be the connection between them. Mom got carsick on the mountain roads and had greater disabilities, both physically and mentally, so Dad became the logical candidate to be the traveling spouse. That was always the way, except for once at the very end of his life, when I brought Mom to tell him "goodbye."

The frequency and length of their visits together was determined by how much time I could stay and eventually that didn't seem fair to them. I decided to hire someone to drive him for these visits, which then allowed Jack to dictate how long he'd stay with her. The time they spent together became shorter and shorter, and although Dad would "blame" his short visits on his driver to Mom, I felt he was purposefully disconnecting from her.

Another consequence of my parents' living apart was that I got to have time with each of them separately. That had rarely occurred since I'd left high school. Back then Mom had been a bit proprietary, some might say controlling, in insisting that all three of us share as much time together as possible. Even talking on the phone together long distance, Mom aimed for three-way conversations. I missed the intimacy of one-on-one talks with each parent but these "conference calls" made her less anxious, so Dad and I accommodated her wishes.

My father and I had gotten into a new routine of talking every day by phone. Now there was no Lillian to tell us she wanted to be included, there were just the two of us. We would catch up on our respective days. Our end-of-life conversations were filled with sweet words and abundant affection. I'd tell him I loved him. Dad would insist that he loved me more. I would tell him I doubted that possibility. He'd persist, offering proof of his greater love: "after all, I'm older and wiser." It was hard to rebut that evidence.

Until you've actually been through it, it's hard to fathom how debilitating it can be to watch your loved one, especially a parent, become weaker, thinner and increasingly removed from everything around him. In those concluding months Dad became painfully thin, skinnier every day or so it seemed. It hurt me to look at his shoulder bones sticking out through his pajama tops. It's still hard to erase the memory of Dad's head sitting on top of a body as thin as any concentration camp survivor.

On some visits I'd bring along my dog to cheer everyone up. I knew from my residency work at the Veterans' Administration how healing a domesticated animal can be, especially for elderly folks. My 14-pound rescue dog had a magnetic personality and I watched how the residents at Dad's facility would perk up when he came on the scene. Although the dog and Jack hadn't developed a significant bond earlier, as Dad's days were dwindling down, my puppy would nuzzle him sweetly with unconditional affection. I'd found another way to provide the comfort care of hospice to my Dad.

By the end I was making nearly daily visits to my Dad just to be around him. I would go by before work to check up on him or, after work to feed him, although I wasn't really needed for either. Dad seemed to be eating the AL's food and reported that he even liked it but he was still somehow losing weight rapidly.

In spite of his cheerful demeanor and peacefulness, something about his physical essence reminded me of something I'd seen before – in deprived infants. In those cases it was clinically referred to as a "failure to thrive." I sometimes wondered if Jack had "willed" himself into that condition after making his hospice decision. Earlier in life he'd seemed capable of creating whatever he'd wanted: a wife he adored; a daughter he was proud of (thanks, Dad!); work he loved and a dream home that "Jack built." If that man put his intention into leaving, maybe he was now ready to die by "failing to thrive?"

I tried to let that be okay with me, if that were what he wanted but it was hard nonetheless. I kept my focus on Jack and making sure his remaining time on earth would be special by being as loving as I could and doing things that was full of comfort. I even tried to add some pounds onto him. I'd buy the largest box of Dad's favorite snack, Nilla Wafers and warm them in water until they reached pudding consistency. Gently I would feed him on a spoon simultaneously setting my intention to remain calm. Feeding my Dad, as he'd once fed me, was eerie.

Watching Jack's life clock run down, I wished I could hold back the hands of time. But that wasn't in my power and never would be. I was beginning to see that such a desire might be rooted in my own selfishness. Was it I who wasn't ready, maybe? Despite my own pain and grieving the impending loss, I aimed to be unconditionally loving. Sometimes it felt good to know I'd done so much for him and that the rest was out of my hands. At other times I felt horribly frustrated by my lack of control as I watched my childhood hero fade away. I wondered repeatedly whether there wasn't something more I could do but there was really nothing more. The only thing left was to make my father as comfortable as possible and then let him feel peace on his path towards whatever might await him on "the other side."

I waited for some sign to tell me what, if anything, I was to do next. Would my Dad develop another case of pneumonia, this time fatal? Would I be strong enough to withhold his medication? As it turns out, I didn't need a sign.

In the very room where he'd told me he was ready to leave and within six months of The Talk, Jack's request was "fulfilled." There would be no more cold hospital beds, no more adjusting to new facilities with new rules, no more "forgotten" thickener and no more struggling for Jack Wolf.

Their Story – Dad

I was always very honest with Jane. I thought that was important as a Father. But I'd never told her all my thoughts and feelings. Heck, I hadn't even done that with my wife, my brothers or anyone else. Men of my generation were never all that comfortable doing that "sharing" women seem to thrive on. But not me, I'd kept my own counsel quite a bit. That meant I left some things unexpressed and kept a lot to myself. At 91, I wasn't about to start changing that all just because I was living alone or getting old.

Nonetheless, after she'd begun doing all that caring for Lillian and me, I'd really noticed how well Jane was able to listen to me and get what I was saying and feeling and I appreciated it no end. I noticed that, whenever she could, Jane produced whatever I asked her for. When I was in the hospital that last time, I was miserable. I was tired of the doctors and endless medication that didn't seem to do any good. I wanted to be warm, get out of there and go home. Jane listened and responded to my requests.

I knew I didn't need to have one or two aides carrying me around from the bed to a chair to the toilet and back, as Lillian did. And I didn't want to go to a nursing home, like she had to. What I wanted was to stay in my home where I could rest and have some peace. I know it would have been easier on her to not have the two of us living so far apart since Jane had taken on the responsibility of visiting and monitoring the care for both of us. Jane seemed to notice that I was no longer keen to live with Lillian and even our visits together had become pretty short. It was hard because we couldn't really talk anymore, my wife and I. There was so little left we could talk about, most of the time, although occasionally she rallied and I could see the woman I'd married and loved my whole life. She was becoming less and less "present." It was as if she wasn't quite there anymore.

Sometimes Lillian was even confused about who I was or why we didn't just go home together. It hurt me to watch her become a shadow of the vibrant woman I'd known. I finally did talk to Jane about some of my feelings and she was more understanding than I'd expected. I knew if I moved in just to be with Lillian at the SNF, which I didn't need medically, I'd be sad all the time, upset at seeing her as she was but unable to do anything about it.

I was already continually frustrated when I saw Lillian with how little I could help the woman I loved and had promised to be with 'til death did us part. Her state caused me to hurry off nearly each time I saw her and I found myself making up excuses to get out of there as soon as I could. All the while I felt guilty and decidedly unhusbandlike. Again, I tried talking with Jane and, surprisingly, felt freer for having told her. She listened mostly and offered a few reassuring remarks, inviting me to assuage my guilt.

As a result of all of this, I decided not to spend much time with Lillian in that hospital-like place she lived and Jane did not fight me at all. My visits became shorter and shorter as I knew I couldn't peaceably watch the woman I'd so cherished "disappear" in front of my eyes. I needed to get away and live apart to protect myself from the pain.

Eventually there came a time when I felt I needed to "let her go." She was still alive but only recognizable on the outside. I was still alive but always tired. I wasn't interested in finding another woman or another anything. What I was interested in was finding a way to detach emotionally from Lillian and maybe more. I put up those mental barriers we men do – those compartments – and began thinking of myself as a widower, not a husband. I continued to visit Lillian and stayed as long as I could but my sweetheart had already gone. And I was allowing that to be all right. I let these changes process its way through my system and then I looked around me. My daughter was doing fine. My wife was beyond my grasp and effectively "gone." I was tired. Maybe I wasn't much needed here anymore.

Your Story

Hospice is an alternative type of health care offered in the United States under the Medicare program to eligible people, including perhaps your parents. The requirements include having a diagnosis of a terminal illness with an expectation of no more than six months to live. Hospice care focuses on the palliation or relief of the person's symptoms rather than on curing any underlying disease.

Some think of hospice as being limited to pain relief or that it has to be provided in an institution, but neither of those is true. Since the symptoms your parents may be experiencing during this time in their POPcycle might be physical, emotional, spiritual and even social in nature, hospice offers relief from all of these. The services provided by hospice agencies can be given in your parents' own home, their residential facility or in a specially designated hospice facility.

Hospice care has been around for many centuries, long before there was Medicare or a United States of America but, to be relevant to you, hospice care in 21st century America is designed to permit patients like your Mom and Dad to be kept as comfortable as possible without having to undergo more rigorous treatments aimed at curing their illnesses.

Once your parents request to be put on hospice, meet the qualifications and get certified by a physician, you and your parents can choose a particular hospice agency from a list of such agencies that have a contractual relationship with Medicare. The agency will provide your parents the following services and Medicare will pay the costs in all or nearly all the following categories[64]:

- Doctor services
- Nursing care
- Medical equipment (such as wheelchairs or walkers)
- Medical supplies (such as bandages and catheters)
- Drugs for symptom control and pain relief
- Short-term care in a hospital
- Home health aide and homemaker services including respite care for caregivers
- Physical and occupational therapy

---

[64] You will want to check that regulations and offerings have not changed in the interim since the book's publication. You can contact Medicare directly or go online to: www.medicare.gov/Publications/Pubs/pdf/11386.pdf

- Speech therapy

- Social worker services

- Dietary counseling

- Spiritual and other counseling for your parents and family

Your parents' out-of-pocket charges will be very limited, if any. While on hospice, your parents are entitled to have a person help care for them. That person can be a family member. Medicare even offers respite care to your parents' designated helper and, during that time, a supplemental caregiver is provided to them.

The decision to go on hospice will be made by your POP family and your parents, if they are competent to do so, in conjunction with your parents' physician. You needn't be concerned that being on hospice means your parents will be medically neglected or overlooked. Quite the opposite, the hospice staff will provide medical and non-medical services for your parents, just different types of services than traditional western medicine. They will receive comfort care without the expectation of recovery. It may be very calming, relieving your parents of burdens you didn't even know or imagine they were bearing.

Hospice care is provided in increments of time. Your parents can receive it for as long as the doctor certifies that less than six months probably remain. If your Mom and Dad live longer than six months, they can continue to get hospice care provided the doctor recertifies them. Under current Medicare regulations, your parents are eligible to get hospice care for two 90-day periods followed by an unlimited number of 60-day periods. Hospice certification is not an irreversible one-way street. That is, should your parents unexpectedly recover from whatever illness their doctor had thought "terminal," they're free to go off hospice at any time and they can fight that illness.

After counseling families who'd embraced hospice when the time was right, I came to truly appreciate the many benefits POP families can derive from making that decision. In addition to granting your folks some physical and spiritual comfort, this choice can help you and them psychologically as well. Making the hospice decision has restored a sense of control to many a senior parent, newly confident because they feel more "in charge" of their treatment and their remaining time. That may be particularly true for seniors if they've felt at all "disempowered" by your POParenting them or if their dealings with Medicare, the health system or insurance sectors have left them feeling somewhat impotent.

Your parents may be oddly relieved that they'll no longer have to "perform" medically. Surviving difficult chemotherapy treatments or putting up with painful procedures may just require more of your aging relatives than they feel they have, at their advanced age. If your parents tell you "we've had enough" or "we want to be at peace: let us talk to the priest," you need to get that.

Perhaps you too will need to acknowledge your own mixed feelings and complicated beliefs about putting your parents on hospice. Although your having done so should promote healing and good relations between you and them, the decision to go on hospice can trigger many different emotional reactions. You may feel frustrated, relieved or even disappointed since you worked so hard POParenting them for years and now they're just "giving up." If you listen carefully, you may also discover that what your parents want most is what they'd get form hospice care – peacefulness, comfort, eating what they want and resting. Letting your parents know you hear them is wise POParenting, here as elsewhere.

Sometimes your parents' physician may initiate the conversation about hospice with you, your siblings or with your parents directly. Or you might ask the doctor to raise the issue with your parents, should it be on your mind. Had it been left up to me, I probably would have continued along as we'd been doing, with Dad going in and out of cold hospital rooms more and more often until his eventual demise. By his raising the topic of hospice, my Dad actually made it easier for me to listen to him and then think empathically about what his life had become.

When your parents' discomfort or prognosis warrants it, you may be the one who needs the courage to bring up going on hospice, especially if your Mom and Dad can't. If that falls to you, try talking to them about what you'd want, if these were your sunset days and you were in your Mom or Dad's shoes. Probably that will open up useful communication about their range of current choices, including hospice.

When conversations about hospice are going on, some of you may find you're feeling increasingly anxious. You may be concerned about how little time is left in your parents' lives. You may be worried for yourself – about how little time you have left with them or how to fully process their upcoming departures. You may even be dismayed by your parents' end of life choices. If that's the case for you, try to keep in mind that it's YOU who has this problem – they're fine with their choices. As a loving POParent, it's unnecessary and unkind to lay your problems on your parents, especially at this time.

Perhaps you still have unresolved issues with your parents and doubt those can be "fixed" in only six months. Consulting a qualified professional therapist or POP Family Coach, even for a few sessions at this particular time, has helped many and it's likely to help you. You will want to release the feelings that seem to result in negativity or conflict and doing some work on yourself can provide renewed energy and better ways to help you complete the POPcycle with grace. Giving yourself some short-term help during challenging points in your POPcycle, like this one, often produces unexpectedly useful and profound results. On the other hand, not resolving your concerns may further stretch already-strained relations between you and your parents.

Please note that I didn't say anything you needed to involve your aging parents in your resolution process. If you still feel the need to resolve your issues directly with your parents, before "confronting" them, ask yourself this: "do my Mom and Dad really *need* to know now how I feel about something that may have happened 50 years ago?" They may not. "Is there anything my parents could do that would change the past?" If answering those doesn't dissuade you from raising unnecessary historical material with people who may not recall breakfast, ask yourself: "how would discussing my issues help my parents?"

Frankly, your parents have bigger things to deal with at this time than your difficulties with the long ago past. You would be wise to find a different venue to air your old hurts or missed opportunities than your Mom and Dad. Given the limited time you have left with them, wouldn't the time be better spent focusing on joy that is currently available than sadness from the past?

If you or your siblings are upset with your parents' imminent death or other end-of-life choices, that lack of "acceptance" may engender a problem of its own. During hospice what your parents need most is comfort in its various physical, psychological and spiritual forms. That means being as stress-free as they possibly can be. Conflicts between you, your siblings and others on your TEAM POP may also source much stress to your parents and surely you can see that family dissent would add to their stress. You must be wary to see that this doesn't happen in your family and do your best to get along.

For example, if your parents choose hospice, your POP job is to acquiesce and align those on TEAM POP to be on the same page, aiding your beloved, ailing parents towards their serene transitions. As you become more comfortable with their choices and more accepting your parents' decision, they *will* be able to rest better. If going on hospice or working with a particular hospice agency feels right to your Mom and Dad, it could be right for you, too. After all, it is their life.

In a very helpful book called "Companioning the Dying: A Soulful Guide for Counselors and Caregivers"[65] the authors report that the dying are most often and best comforted by those unafraid to stand with them and their decisions without judgment, advice or expectation. As they move through this extraordinary passage, your parents want your companionship in this courageous way. Even in their final journey, it seems your parents still long to be connected to you and derive comfort from that connection. It may be a small consolation to you that the only thing left to do is to become as calm and compassionate as you can, but that may be the best way to support your parents at this time.

Then again, maybe not. There may still be some important interventions you can try in your parents' situations that I was unable to do in mine. My instincts about my Dad's "failure to thrive" led me to further research what was then a relatively new syndrome. Adult failure to thrive ("AFTT")[66] may be caused by multiple chronic conditions and/or the losses associated with limited and decreased functioning. Your Mom and Dad may be experiencing one or all

---

[65] Greg Yoder, Alan D. Wolfelt, Companion Press, 2005.

[66] See Glossary.

four AFTT syndromes that are predictors of adverse outcomes: impaired physical functioning; malnutrition; depression and cognitive impairment. If your senior parents show significant decline and weight loss and their physicians are unable to attribute it to any medical condition, ask them to check for AFTT. Many interventions by the medical and hospice communities have resulted in positive changes and a lifting of the AFTT symptoms. It's certainly worth your inquiring!

POPlan #15: Getting Comfortable With Our Parents' Decision To "Go On Hospice"

As hard as it was doing POP up until now – making all the arrangements for moving your folks from their homes, reordering your own priorities and schedules, effectuating the numerous choices and POPlans you've made for your parents – your hardest emotional work may lie ahead of you. Doing those things was finite, task-oriented and, happily, brought you its own form of competence and self-confidence as a POParent. You were able to accomplish things and check them off your list, even while you could emotionally detach sufficiently to ignore that your "to do" list contained items such as pre-paying your parents' funeral expenses or selling the home you grew up in.

The hardest part may well be getting yourself to "grow up" enough to see your parents as the individuals they've become today and respect them as such. This actually will take you beyond forgiveness and into a realm of true compassion. If they say they wish to let go of their "earthly struggles," hear them and honor their expressed desires even if, in your opinion, they're not "ready." If they can't form the words or the thoughts to tell you their intentions, check for written instructions (such as Health Care Proxies they may have signed when they were legally competent) or review previous conversations you've had with them. Apply your most loving POParent training to listen to your parents' final requests and carry them out in the most affectionate way you can.

Your most awesome challenges, like mine, lie in the quiet, internal work you're doing within yourself. Teach yourself to respond with love and without judgment even if your parents sound like they're "giving up" on you or life. Hear their pleas whether they are for no more hospitalizations, painful treatments and debilitating medicines or anything else. Become sufficiently "detached" in a healthy way so you don't make their choices be about you. Re-organize your thinking so you can and do react more compassionately to your folks in the present you have left. You'll avoid feeling regret in the future.

Try out these POP tools to help you get more comfortable with your parents' hospice decisions and the likelihood of their imminent deaths:

<u>*TOOL #1: EXPANDING YOUR COMPASSION AS A POParent*</u> involves finding tools to open your heart to the experiences of another person, in this case your aging parents.

Any steps you take to expand your compassion, even reading this, will add to your ability to relate to your parents in the present and with their existing conditions. For example, looking down at the frail short people in front of you, can you visualize them as defenseless young children? Can you see them as vulnerable to their own challenges and parents, to the things and people who helped form them? Or, quite the opposite, within those "vestiges" of your Mom and Dad, the short people you see before you, can you make out the big, powerful parents you once looked up to, quite literally?

The more you can do this type of "mental mending," the more easily you'll be able to grow your compassion, allowing you to not only tolerate the changes in your parents but also to better understand what and how will please them now. So often in the Circle of Life, we "come back" to ourselves – something you see physically as your elders shrink down, sit and lie down more often and then eat from our spoons and wear diapers.

- *Aim to see your parents exactly as they are now. They may be weak, disabled, sensory-deprived versions of their earlier robust selves or not. Having lived long lives, your folks have undoubtedly lost loved ones to death, divorce, war, poverty, racism or hatred and, as a result, they may seem overwhelmed with sadness or angry at the world or upset that life will soon pass them by too. Or they may be filled with gratitude for a loving and protective family, relieved that you're help-ing with important financial decisions or ecstatic with childlike abandon about the holidays. Maybe they have bucket lists of unfulfilled dreams for themselves and perhaps for you too? Or perhaps they are content in spite of some obvious aging.*

- *See them as they are – still growing even as they complete their final weeks or months. Maybe they're seeking to make sense of their experiences and make peace with all that's happened to them and what never happened. Hopefully your parents have found a place of no regrets and no resentments. Knowing that, can't you?*

- *As best you know how and even if you believe you've done it before, forgive your parents. Forgive them for what? They became who they are, as you did, in part because of who parented them and how. Didn't they have their own life chal-lenges? Can you forgive them for drawing the conclusions, right or wrong in your book, which they drew from their life experiences? Maybe you can "free" them for* not living up to your pictures of how parents should be? Can you possibly forgive them for their abuse or neglect, if your parents did that to you and/or your siblings?

- And now, the hard part. Forgive yourself. Maybe that's whom you need to forgive rather than your parents? And what "sins" have you committed? You moved away from your parents and their home: was that a sin? Isn't that what you were supposed to do? You rebelled against your parents' religion, political beliefs or life-style? Probably you did and probably the positions you took were heartfelt. Can you forgive yourself for growing apart from your Mom and Dad when, perhaps what you really wanted, was to feel more connected and unconditionally loved? Can you forgive yourself for the things you wanted to do for them but never got around to?

- Visualize the "ideal" parents you wanted as a child. Then incorporate those same parenting qualities the ideal parents had into your model for POParenting your aging loved ones. Especially after forgiving them and yourself, this will allow you to treat your aging parents with more acceptance, kindness, compassion, interest and maybe even the kind of loving you craved from them.

- Imagine yourself "time-traveling" into the future where you are the old person, the age your parents have now become. How is it that you might like to be treated by your children as you're setting out to meet your "Maker?"

TOOL#2: POP LETTER WRITING allows you to express things to yourself and/or to the addressee and, in the process, you uncover what you "need" or don't need to say to your parents. These letters can be stored or sent to the intended recipient.

After you've engaged in the POP visioning process above might prove a good time to sit down and express yourself. Some POParents find it very liberating to get in touch with feelings and then write a personal letter to their Moms or Dads. Even an unsent letter can be very therapeutic, since it allows you to clarify and write down things you may not even know you're feeling.

If you want to communicate something emotional or spiritual in nature to your dying parents, like reading them or mailing them the unsent letters or revealing a long-untold "confession," hold on a minute! First, answer this set of questions and, after that, if you still feel it's beneficial to POParenting, go ahead and share it.

- Am I saying/writing this to benefit my parents (or me)?

- Will my parents knowing this help our shared hospice goal of comfortable-filling them?

- *If I'm clear it won't really benefit my parents, do I really need to share this? Is that kind or necessary? How do I expect to feel afterwards if I tell this to my parents?*

If your response to any of these is "NO!" then keep your communication to yourself.

This is your time to be the thoughtful POParent. If sharing or confessing certain things is bound to upset your parents or they can't do anything now to change things, then don't confront them. When it's timely, share those thoughts and feelings with your partner, POP Family Coach, therapist or your best friend instead of your parents. Be gentle with them at this point in life.

POP Music

Listen with your now-experienced and compassionate POParent ears (and opened heart) to Harry Chapin's song, "Cat's In the Cradle."[67] As a young father, the singer had been too busy to find time for his young son. Later in life, when he did find the time, he found his son had become "just like me."

You can stop this cycle of regrets! You can show your parents that, no matter what they gave you all those years ago – or didn't give you – you have become their loving POParent now. You can learn through POP how to love better and more unconditionally and be more present than you've been before. You can be proud if your children turn out "just like you."

---

[67] The song was written by Harry Chapin and his wife, Sandra Campbell Chapin and published by Story Songs, Ltd. c/o WB Music Corp.

Chapter 16

Letting Go Of The Beloved
Parents We've Parented

My Story

I put off this chapter until I'd written all the others. It was simply too tough to have to relive my last goodbyes, first to Dad and then to Mom. When people live as long and fulfilled lives as my parents had lived, for the most part, it's not necessarily sadness those of us left behind feel.

For me, it was different than sadness. It was as if I became very conscious of their "non-presence" on the planet. Even today I sometimes find myself saying: "If he were here, my Dad might say..." And just talking about them and remembering them out loud eases the residual eeriness of my parents' "non-presence."

I remember when I first heard about death. My folks had a family friend who was a legendary film actor named John Garfield. His kids and I used to play together. I was about to turn five and he was barely 39. One day he had a heart attack and the next he was gone. I would later learn that the man whose death I pondered for months would have a funeral that was mobbed by thousands of fans in the largest funeral attendance for any actor since Rudolph Valentino had passed.

I recall thinking: "how odd is that? Our friend Julie (his real name, not the screen name given him by Warner Bros.) woke up dead on Wednesday. I hope it didn't hurt him." I wondered how David and Julie were bearing up without their Dad and what being dead felt like?"

As I took in the larger meaning of this one man's death and saw how it affected his family and mine too, I slowly recognized that, someday, all of us would die. My parents would die and leave me too, just as Julie and David's Dad had left them. Even I wouldn't get to "escape" alive. For many years thereafter, a part of me lived disquieted by the inevitability of that fact. I believe I have made some peace with it, thanks to POP.

Starting with my college years, when I moved away from my folks, each time I'd part from them after a visit, I'd think that this might be the last time we'd all be together and continue "obsessing" about it. In this context, I define obsessing as re-thinking the same thought without resolution as if I were on a continuous mental treadmill. Reminding myself of the fragility of my family by replaying that dreaded thought sapped me of energy and generated depressing feelings. I was putting myself through a lot of unnecessary angst and it did absolutely no good for anyone.

So I worked long and hard to devise tools – which I've been sharing with you – to help me interrupt the anxiety I was generating with such fear-filled thinking. I taught myself to avoid obsessing over these thoughts by creating a series of steps I could take to prevent myself from staying caught in that one destructive thought. After figuring out this technique, I still needed to practice it by engaging with the process over and again. And as a result of doing that, I was freed up to feel calmer and calmer. Eventually, when and if that thought showed up at our departures, I let its recurrence not trouble me much, if at all.

My little four-stepped process began with simply allowing myself to notice myself having that thought again, the one about "our last time," without any judgment about its happening, almost like I was watching the thought go by. Next I saw that thought as merely one among tens of thousands I knew myself to be having every day, subtly diminishing this particular thought's significance. Third, I interpreted the thought for what it was – a mere symbol of my feeling alone or abandoned, not the reality of that happening to me, again minimizing its impact. Last, I interrupted that isolative, sad interpretation with a more positive one, by reminding myself: my fears – symbolic or not – were ideas I'd made up. My old idea had no basis in reality as neither Jack, Lillian nor I had any plans on dying and their love for me could never be lost.

During that final step another useful place to put my thoughts was on gratitude. What could I be grateful for in this moment rather than what could I fear? The answers my mind found to that inquiry were numerous and included my gratitude for the time I had left with my parents. By replacing my worry and other upsetting thoughts with thankfulness, I watched as my apprehensions about the future begin to fade. It felt as if I were refreshing myself with the flow of gratitude, like the cool spray of a sea breeze on a relentlessly humid day.

When I remembered to do that four-stepped process, it became much harder to be "bullied" by my own nagging, "negative" thoughts. To be fair, though, however predictable it was, I found it hardest to remember in the days immediately preceding my parents' ends. Like most people, I'd often "forget" my tried and true tools when stressed and of course, could have used them most.

I thought I would more often "remember" to get relief, if I could narrow it down to three simple steps: breathe in and out a few times; come completely into the present; feel gratitude! Couldn't be easier. Nevertheless, some days even doing that was "hard work." That seemed particularly true when I was feeling sorry for myself, so I'd "try harder" to locate the wellspring of gratitude I knew I had down in me somewhere.

But how to find it? I occasionally resorted to gratitude lists, mentally checking off everything for which I felt grateful. I'd start with myself. I was alive and breathing; I could see, feel, smell, touch and taste (on my own and without machinery). My mind was still sharp. I had the capacity to create this list and even remember what I was grateful for. I was healthy (knock on wood!) and had a great support system of people who wanted to share themselves and loved me. And, most of all, I was thankful I could be there for my Mom and Dad in their final days.

As I got on a roll inventorying my gratitude, a shift would occur inside me. I'd begin to warm to how much goodness there was around me and even feel more protected. I could sense my gratitude expanding into peacefulness. These tools absolutely resulted in my becoming a much more appreciative daughter and, in turn, a happier woman.

Another way I learned to "comfort myself" was by finding a spiritual philosophy that offered me the optimism I wanted to embrace. Through that, I was able to see our human form as one part of a larger and ongoing divine experience and to realize that we might lose our physical connections but never our attachment through love. I'd also been educated to the remarkable powers of the human brain and body to send and receive communications of love, even at great distances. Intervening in my Dad's suicide attempt years before was one of many such times I'd witnessed that "miraculous" kind of knowing at a distance about people I loved.

So, at this juncture of our POPcycle, when the time came for the three of us to have our last time all together, I'd done enough work on myself to be able to be less concerned with my own loss to concentrate more fully on my parents and their losses. Through practicing these techniques of detaching from fearful thoughts, invoking gratitude and through my years of POParenting, I could see I'd expanded my compassion and even lost some of my self-centeredness.

Dad was far more cogent and also verbal about it than Mom, but I was interested and pleased to note that they both perceived their imminent demises to be less about tragedy or loss than about relief from some of the burdens of being mortal. Shakespeare's Hamlet spoke of it in his famous "To be or Not to be" soliloquy as follows: "... to die, to sleep no more; and by a sleep, to say we end the heartache and the thousand natural shocks the flesh is heir to..."

In the western world, we have an almost knee-jerk reaction to hearing of someone's death. Even without knowing any details, we call it a "tragedy!" But maybe that's not so. Perhaps if your highest goals involve living a full life, contributing what you have to give, being a loving human and feel loved, once you've accomplished these, your death need not be considered "tragic." Perhaps a better description would be "fulfilled." I prefer to consider that the death of such a person is an opportunity for a glorious tribute, an outpouring of expressed appreciation and positive reflections. It seemed my parents did, too.

After months of obvious decline, Dad truly appeared to have little time remaining and little energy left. When I talked with the hospice staff, they agreed his energy was at an all-time low and his attention span was similarly waning. The number of hours he was sleeping had been growing markedly. They said that was another clue that, soon, he'd be at his end. His waning interest in food, other people, activities or television was extending to everything else. I watched my Daddy as he was taking the final exit ramp from life's highway.

I felt strongly that my Mom and Dad should be given an opportunity to say their goodbyes to each other. We'd never explained Dad's being on hospice or the severity of his current condition to Mom. Nonetheless I felt I owed it to them, as individuals and as a couple, to share some last private moments together. It no longer mattered, as it had earlier, how much each of them would exactly understand about what was occurring. I didn't concern myself that Mom might be confused or Dad might want peace and quiet. I just went on instinct that they were entitled to a fond and formal farewell.

I picked my Mom up early in the morning from her SNF. During the long drive to Ventura County, I tried to prepare her by explaining that Dad might seem very poorly to her, much weakened from how he'd been when he'd last visited. It was her first visit to Dad in this AL and Lillian was curious about where he was living. When we entered his room, Mom was clearly delighted to see her husband again, as she always was cheered by his presence in these years. But she was clearly confused and distressed by Dad's weakness, skinny body and low energy.

I respectfully left the lovers who'd created me to savor their final embraces and private words. I'll never know what they said there that day or how much either was able to understand about the implications of the visit. While they were having their private time in Dad's room, I sat in the corridor and tried to envision what this moment might feel like for each of my parents.

Did Mom really get that she was going to outlive the man she had loved for as long as she could recall? Did she fear she couldn't manage without him? Was she angry with Dad for "leaving" her by dying or "abandoning" her by not moving into her SNF?

How about Dad, did he still feel that choosing hospice was best for him and them? Did he feel guilty for "abandoning" the woman he'd pledged to take care of? Was Jack relieved to be free from the challenges of Mom, her illnesses and his inability to fix these as well as free from the burdens of a physical body? Had they each been preparing themselves for this goodbye for decades?

I started imagining what this moment would have been like, had it been I, instead of my Mom, saying goodbye to the man who'd been my family and partner for over six decades... I'd be huddled under a cozy blanket in a wheelchair; he'd be seated next to me, his hand in mine. Whereas once we'd been new to each other, now I'd be gazing at a face more familiar than my own.

As I contemplated having being about to have our final embrace for all of eternity, I saw memories come flooding back: when we'd wed, raised our child, run our music business and built our home. Together we'd have journeyed thousands of days and nights together to where we'd now be sitting, having left behind the places and people where we'd grown up, our parents and siblings all buried back there. We'd have come this far to where we were being cared for by the daughter we'd made and loved together since her birth.

It's likely I'd be thinking about my own future, comparing those times with him with my days ahead, knowing that I'd be alone. I visualized holding my gaze on the face of my beloved, a face I'd wiped tears from when we'd shared family losses, a face I'd seen laughter and wisdom etch into lines over the course of a lifetime together. I would kiss those lines around my lover's lips and eyes for the last time and try to hold them in my memory bank for all the times ahead when I'd need to remember those golden days.

I'd catch a glimpse of my husband's tired, now skinny arms. These were same arms I'd felt safe and loved in for so long. His were the arms I'd reached out to, held onto and known peace in. Soon I'd need to release those precious arms forever. To have only one last hug, an eternal good night kiss, perhaps a parting laugh or a shared song together.

I had to stop my fantasizing there; my tears were welling up and flowing down my face. To me, my parents' finally separating was incomprehensible in its sadness. It was more than I wanted to grasp. And, if all that weren't challenging enough, my thought then went to me. How would the imminent end of our little family alter my life? The Wolf threesome we'd been in many ways, since my childhood, was coming to a close. Soon we'd be a trio no more.

Most of my thoughts that day were over-the-top but I gave myself permission to go there. The day I'd "dreaded" for so many years, the day my family was altogether for its last time, was a good enough excuse for some melancholic musings. So I let myself get into the feelings deeply and let them touch my soul.

Then came that fateful Monday in November. Before going to my office in the early morning, I drove over to check on Dad. As I entered the building, several hospice staffers approached me. "It's likely that today's the day," they stated quietly. For a minute I was confused, stopped in my tracks. What did that mean? How did they know? What was I supposed to do next? How was I to react to such information? I took some very deep, remarkably cleansing POParental breath. And then I knew that I already understood whatever I'd need to know at that moment. I had long awaited it and, now, it was here. I was oddly clear.

My first step was to call my nearest and dearest and let them know the information I'd just gotten about Dad's status. I asked them to come and support me and my Dad, as well as bear witness to his imminent passage. I wanted him to have only a beautiful, serene gathering of four loved ones, none of whom would bring in drama and turn Dad's event into being "all about them."

Then I saw to it that all my patients and other appointments for the day were cancelled. Having done that, I was now clear of other obligations and free to concentrate on what would be needed of me over at Dad's, whatever that might be, one final time.

Next I decided I'd feel most comfortable, in this totally uncomfortable situation, were I to return home and change from my professional attire into more "comfortable" clothes. While there, I could pick up whatever "supplies" might feel appropriate for the occasion of my Dad's passing. At home I looked for a loose-fitting outfit and specifically wanted to put on a fabric that felt good next to my skin. I chose nothing black – too negatively mournful. I looked around for what else might provide me comfort of any kind and grabbed my worn copy of Ernest Holmes' "Science of Mind."[68] This wonderful book had served me well as a source of exquisite enrichment for decades. Finally, looking around, I scooped up my dog and brought him along for the emotional comfort he would hopefully provide Dad and me, as well.

It was with a very full heart that I drove back to Dad's AL for a second time that morning. This time I knew I was going to say goodbye to my Father. Walking into his room, I knew immediately I should move with almost reverential grace and peacefulness. It was eerily still, almost as if his bedroom had transmuted into a sacred space where silence and order were natural and fitting. Dad was pretty much as he'd been earlier, resting fairly peacefully, almost without consciousness. He never became more alert or active in any way.

I opened the blinds, letting in the day's last sunlight for Jack to see or, at least feel, the late autumn warmth. I checked to see if his eyes strained or even moved with the brightness of this new light but they did not. All was still. I paced a bit around his room, straightening out a few things to create more order. I thought of how odd but intuitively fitting it was to want to impose external order at precisely the moment I felt so internally disoriented. I tried to stay busy, occupied and useful in some way. Whether or not any of that was constructive, at least I was doing no harm.

Staying busy felt somehow more purposeful than standing still. It was old programming but productivity felt comforting and anything comforting just then was okay with me. I considered new ways I might bring my Dad the "palliative care" he'd requested when he originally asked to go on hospice as I placed the little dog I loved gently next to the father I loved. My hope was that, as his soft canine fur pressed up next to my Father, his rhythmic breathing would provide Dad ease in its regularity. I even wondered if, as Dad was exiting the planet, this contact would remind him of when he'd entered it, breathing right up next to another body.

Another palliative effort I tried was tuning Dad's radio to the station that played the "The Music of Your Life" format. For a moment, Rosemary Clooney was alive again, singing her hits and working with my Dad in their early days. I hoped that a disk jockey might have chosen to spin a Jack Wolf song as his last sun began to settle in the west. I didn't hear any of Dad's compositions that afternoon.

---

[68] The Science of Mind by Ernest Holmes, published by G. P, Putnam's Sons, NY, 1926.

But listening to their selections as the day slowly faded into evening reminded me of the music of my childhood, when my Daddy had been my all-time favorite song-writer. He'd come home from Tin Pan Alley and the Brill Building brimming with tales of "peddling his songs," as he called it. These were the same songs I'd been asked to write down when he'd originally thought them up at his favorite muse-site, the bathtub. He'd call out from behind the shower curtain: "Lillian or Jane! Come here! Bring a pen and pad!" I'd scurry in, trying to be there first to write down the lyrics.

Later on, after the lyric writing/bath stage, Jack would choose the best composer from among his favorites to work on a particular piece. Thereafter he might contact his early partner Burt Bacharach, who primarily wrote with Hal David or Joe Darion the composer of the beautiful "Man of La Mancha," Bugs Bower who also wrote "Itsy Bitsy Teeny Weeny Yellow Polka Dot Bikini" or Joel Herron, with whom Jack wrote his hauntingly beautiful standard "I'm A Fool to Want to Want You." Then he and the other writer would collaborate and make their respective parts into a song.

Next my Dad would go into the studio to create a demo record with simple vocal and instruments to play for prospective record companies, recording artists and others showing how the song would ultimately sound. Then he'd "shop the demo" and "miraculously" out would come – fabulous 45 RPM's (funny-looking records with little holes in the middle) and 33 1/3 LP's (larger, long-play) vinyl records)!

The sound of the familiar old tunes on the radio felt reassuring to me. Thanks to him, I knew almost all of them. And though I'll never know this, I believed the old favorites comforted Jack as well. After listening for a while, I joined in to sing along. It just seemed like the right thing to do. I sang with all my soul to my departing Dad, trying to reach into his heart with the love in my voice. Despite my renowned off-key vocalizing, neither that nor anything disturbed Jack's reverie that day.

He was in his own world. I like to believe he heard the music and knew my loving intentions but, had Frank Sinatra himself come back to croon for Dad, I'm not sure he'd have noticed. Hours passed as the November dusk turned to evening. But in Dad's room, a part of me wanted time to stand still. My breathing seemed to have slowed down to a pace similar to his. I walked outside for a few minutes for a breath of new air. That was actually helpful though a part of me didn't want to leave his side for even a moment.

Then I remembered I'd brought along The Science of Mind. When I picked up the large book and let it fall open at random, I not so secretly intended it to open up on some unexpected spiritual support. When I read the passage I'd "accidentally" opened to, I almost fell off my chair. I smiled, believing that the universe was, even this afternoon, on my side. It seemed like Dr. Holmes had written this for me and for this very occasion.

What about Death?   The Science of Mind teaches the eternality of life. It accepts that our physical bodies operate within a natural cycle of birth and death. However, even though we may have a body, we are not just our body. What we really are is the Life that animates our body, and that Life is infinite and immortal. As we become increasing identified with our divine and eternal nature, our underlying fear of death begins to dissolve and our experience of life become more joyous.[69]

At a point of such sadness and despair this random reading arrived like amazing grace, redefining death as I had been thinking about it. My faith was reaffirmed as a warm blanket symbolically wrapped itself around the parts of me that had been cold.

The "invitees" I'd asked to my Dad's room included my adopted brother, Rick - the person on the planet who'd known me the longest aside from my parents - and his girlfriend at that time. She was a talented and respected healing professional whose powerful work included "helping people ease their path off the planet." I remarked at the synchronicity of events for, although they lived up the coast, she and Rick "just happened" to be staying with me in southern California on that day. She generously offered to help my Dad and, although I had no idea what her work really entailed, I anticipated no harm and gratefully consented.

I watched as she prayed and made various gestures over parts of Dad's body. She occasionally asked me questions to assist her mysterious process. Beginning at his feet and moving upwards I saw Jack's body noticeably soften beneath the motions she was making. She was working over Dad's chest and heart region for a while and finally asked: "how long has Jack been apart from his wife?" Although she knew nothing of my parents' history, she stated matter-of-factly that Dad was still "working through that separation." I was awed by her suggestion that Dad might still be resolving his issues as close to his earthly transition as this was.

I have no proof that her healing movements, words or prayers helped my Dad in any way. Nonetheless I choose to believe that her appearing on my doorstep on the day of Dad's transition was a remarkable gift for Jack as well as for me.

I've been fortunate enough never to have been at war, in a fire, earthquake or other disaster where someone died right next to me. Until that day I'd never seen the passage of a human life, someone taking in and exhaling his last breaths. It felt like an honor to be permitted to attend such a special moment in the life of any other

---

[69] www.scienceofminduk.org/believe_faq.html#15.

person, especially in the sacred space of your beloved parent's last breath. As sad as I'd felt previously, I was very conscious of feeling fortunate to be present. I took a deep breath to center myself and then a few more breaths as I aimed to become fully present to what was about to occur.

I found a place to sit on the narrow bed where his emaciated body lay peacefully. I reached out and held his hand in mine. I lifted it to my lips and smelled my Father's skin as I kissed his frail hand. I hoped the warmth of my touch would please him and that my affection would reassure him. I watched the rising and falling of my Dad's chest, his breathing had become nearly imperceptible now. It contrasted with my dog's strong, regular breathing alongside of him. Imperceptibly, my Dad's breathing quietly stopped. I wasn't sure when it happened. There was no obvious body wriggling, no sign of pain and no evidence of a struggle! Dad had been released from his body's constrictions and limitations.

Afterwards, Rick's girlfriend related that what she'd seen: Dad's spirit lifted up from where his body was still lying on the bed and, just before it ascended towards the sky, it came from behind and wrapped itself around me in a hug. I took delight in that possibility, one of those ideas we're offered that can give us joy, should we choose to accept it. And in the dark of that unforgettable November night, I believed her. What I'd seen and what was clear to me was that my Dad, as I knew him, was gone. There was now only a body that remained behind with us in the room and this felt noticeably different than earlier in the day when Dad lay there nearly comatose. Now, his essence was gone. Jack Wolf belonged to the ages and thereafter I had only my memories of him.

The next morning when I drove down to tell Mom about Dad's transition, I was clearly withdrawn and sad. She sensed immediately something was wrong. When I explained the reason for my melancholic state, she became something akin to giddy, seemingly intent on amusing me out of my sadness. Maybe it was Mom's way of comforting me or her grief or just someone at her stage of cognitive decline reacting what we'd say was "inappropriately."

In the midst of all this, Mom showed me a new white-haired resident at her facility that she found attractive. With an uncanny use of her verbal skills, she told me: "What a great haircut that handsome man has! I'm sure he also uses expensive hair products. He must be well-heeled." What?? I was dismayed at Mom's apparent detachment from what had just happened to us all – to her husband, her, our threesome and yes, to me. Even understanding her conditions, I momentarily allowed myself hurt feelings.

Although Lillian seemed unable to fully comprehend that her husband had passed away, it occurred to me later that maybe I'd been wrong about that. I considered how Lillian's "pre-women's liberation" mind might be interpreting the events from within her world. Maybe she did understand that her husband was gone and that his passing affected her status: moving from "married" to "widowed" at age 92. Mom's generation, as those before her, was taught a woman needed a man to take care of her. Maybe her survival skills had kicked in and Lillian was already "moving along" to scout for decent candidates as her next husband? It seemed so out of place as I was just beginning to mourn the loss of her last one.

I was always intrigued when "my old Mom," would peak out through the veil of her dementia and other illnesses to have a more lucid awareness of herself and others around her, however temporary that was. Mom's medical situation was complicated. During her advanced years, her body that had so resiliently withstood diseases earlier, developed a series of debilitating pneumonias and a deep disturbing recurring cough.

When the cough reappeared, it would inevitably lead to another course of antibiotics. Antibiotics are "wonder" drugs in many instances but their usage is controversial because they can severely weaken some patients, including many elderly patients. I hated that she was prescribed these powerful medications so readily since they killed off not only the bad bacteria but also her good ones. However I also understood that, unless they treated her with these drugs, she probably would not survive.

Every few months usually late into the night, it seemed, I would get a call from her SNF. "Lillian had been feeling poorly..." or "Lillian was running a fever" and most often: "Lillian's cough has just gotten too intense ..." California law requires facilities to contact the next of kin to advise them when a resident is taken to the Emergency Room. Almost always the hospital would admit Mom. I'd go over and usually leave her as I found her, sleeping soundly and connected up to a series of monitoring machines. When she was awakened, Mom would often be confused but, seeing me whether in those foreign settings or at her home, always brought a smile to her face.

Periodically when the dementia overcame her more deeply, Lillian would cry out for her own mother and be distressed that her Mother wasn't visiting her. Like many in her condition, she'd retreat into her childhood memories and think I was her sister or her favorite niece, Harriet. Mom's early life had been riddled with abandonment and I wondered if she were also reliving her father's dying when she was only seven or the loneliness she'd felt when her siblings left home, leaving her alone with a now busy, hard-working widowed Mom.

This pattern of early "abandonments" had made it difficult for my Mom to trust people or develop much self-confidence. But, by the time she'd gotten used to being POParented, Lillian had come to understand that she'd never again be abandoned: I would be with her to the very end! Even without her husband, siblings or her own

Mom, I felt she knew that I would be there for her through the remaining years. I so hoped she was able to internalize my love and devotion and finally rest more peacefully.

During her last few years most of Mom's hospital stays were 3-5 days' long, though occasionally they'd last longer. It felt like a revolving door of admissions and discharges. I wondered how much more her poor body could stand of the routine of coughs, drugs and hospitals. I appreciated my role as her caring POParent was somewhat limited since, once that plastic bracelet was attached to Lillian's wrist, the hospital ran the show. Nonetheless I'd learned – as we all eventually find out – that the presence of a family member at an aging person's hospital bedside helps nurses and aides, even doctors, come more quickly and attend more responsively to our loved ones.

So I would show up, ask my questions, intervene if I could but, mostly, I was there for her, to hold her hand. Very recently I was listening to Judy Collins sing[70] about her own Mother's siege with Alzheimer's in an homage that brought streams of tears down my face. Hearing "In the Twilight" reminded me of those moments, when waking to see me sitting on her hospital bed, my beautiful Mom's whole face would light up. "How did you know where to find me?" she'd ask over and again.

Disoriented in a new setting and confused until she saw me, I watched Lillian grow in her gratitude and her happiness in those last years. Now something as everyday as finding herself being attended by the daughter who loved her could bring my Mother joy. Since my being there for her seemed to make Mom happy, I wished – fruitlessly – that just showing up was all it would take to keep her healthy, too.

During one of the apparent lulls in hospitalizations, I felt it'd be okay to make a short, much-needed trip out of town for business. No sooner had my plane landed in New York than I got a call from her SNF. Mom was moved back to the hospital. I spoke with her physician who reassured me. This pneumonia looked like Mom's other ones, he said, and didn't appear to be life threatening. But I was reminded that these bouts were never easy for Lillian who was just about to turn 95. From his report, I determined to stay the few more days until my planned return.

Fortunately my Mom's condition had stabilized or so I thought. The afternoon of my return, just as I was about to head over to the hospital, I got a call that my Mom's situation had changed dramatically and for the worse. I was told that it looked as if Mom wouldn't make it through the night.

Sighing heavily, I gathered my dearest and he and I headed north in rush hour traffic to the hospital. I remember the crawl of the cars on the 405 Freeway and

---

[70] Judy Collins wrote and released this song on Wildflower Records in 1911.

wondering if we'd arrive there "soon enough." What I saw in front of us was a long string of brake lights that seemed interminable, unconcerned with my need for speed.

I tried employing my time-tested tools to get calmer. Breathing deeply, keeping focused, staying in the present and not anticipating what hadn't yet happened were tough going for me during that timeless drive to say goodbye to my Mother.

"Tough" was also a good word to describe much of my experience of POParenting Lillian. She'd never been as easy as my Dad for me, not since I was a kid. And, from the beginning, she had resisted me in everything POP. She hadn't initially wanted to be POParented, to come to California or, as she'd said at the time, to "submit to my will."

When she finally did come out and found I didn't run her life, Mom soon warmed to POP, adapting happily to my caring for her. By the time Mom moved to her SNF and away from Dad in the AL, his health was waning and Jack had begun withdrawing from her emotionally. He was always fatigued and seemed relieved to transfer to me most of the physical and emotional caregiving he'd been giving her for their many decades. I did fill in for him in caring for her and, after his demise, I was "it."

Then, for these last two and a half years, Lillian and I "toughed" it out together. I had a particularly difficult time because Mom didn't remember me or was behaving oddly, I'd stop by for a visit with my friend Sue for some support. Sometimes, when it was hard to face what she and her life had become, I'd even ask Sue to accompany me there. Everybody doing POParenting should be lucky enough to have a great support person like Sue live geographically so well suited to their aging parents. Now, in Mom's apparently final hours, it was Sue I phoned, requesting that she join in, one last time as we waited for the end that was becoming more and more certain.[71]

Despite the many ways my Mom had tried to find happiness, which had included good psychotherapy, medication, taking courses, immersing herself in her husband and then her daughter's lives or volunteering her time in service to things she believed in, little seemed to result in her true serenity. Still, over our POP time, I'd seen my Mom grow to be genuinely appreciative and more confident with the knowledge I was POParenting her.

Funny the thoughts that come to us at a moment like this. Driving to the hospital I considered: now that Mom's life was ebbing, there'd be no more time for her to become any happier. By the time we arrived at the hospital and located her in the ER, my Mom was already comatose. She lay quietly throughout that evening, never rousing again.

---

[71] By the time I was writing this chapter, Sue had unfortunately joined Mom and Dad in their post-mortem existence. She was two months younger than I and, she still "tells" me to not waste our time on the planet.

Her delicate, remarkably unlined skin was now pasty white and she was cold to my touch. Electronic buzzers continually interrupted anything resembling reverential reverie. Unlike Dad's peaceful room at home, the hospital setting offered coldness and confusion. Her environment was bustling with medical staff in their colorful uniforms and the noises of machinery that seemed to be doing little good for her.

People prodded her, poked her, took readings and made copious notes. More people walked into and out of her area. They looked at my Mom, adjusted her machines, said nothing and left. I asked all the questions I could think of but still knew little of what to expect or when.

After a few hours, which felt like weeks, two orderlies wheeled Mom into a more private room. There for the first time all night we were allowed to stand close to her, hold her hand and mop her brow but the setting was unbearably cold and antiseptic.

Lillian was quietly but definitely failing. I lacked the skill to read the stages her body was going through but all the trained medical eyes were darting back and forth between Mom's face and the monitoring machines. She looked unbearably fragile and small and particularly unprotected in spite of all the people and monitors. I wondered how long she could hold on.

I tried to imagine what my Mother would be thinking or if she were able to compose thoughts at all at this point. I wondered if she were still working on her "unresolved issues" right before her earthly end, as I'd been advised by Rick's girlfriend that Dad did. At one point a nurse came by to give Mom her late nightly medication and I sent her away. "Please leave her in peace," I said quietly.

Lillian Wolf would no longer need her medications, not tonight and not any other night ever again. "Are you willing to sign for that?" the nurse wanted to know. Of course, the hospital needed to protect itself legally. I understood. "I will authorize you to stop medicating my Mom. She has so little time left, please just let her be in peace, please," I now said with more force. The last hour or two of my Mom's life passed uneventfully. It felt unnatural to demonstrate much emotion in that sterile hospital setting. Perhaps that was a good thing, making the next moments less filled with public grieving?

I caressed her hands and her face. I hoped she could still hear the words of sweet serenity and love I whispered in her ears. Knowing it was our last time, I sat on the crisp white bed with the woman who'd raised me, sacrificed for me and loved me every day of my life. She'd been with me at my opening breath and here I was with her at her closing one. And then I "willed" my Mom to let go of her body and release herself into the peace. I wondered again: could she hear me? Did she have thoughts or feelings at that last moment? Was she finally at peace? I would never know.

Then the noises and the little electronic lights commanded our attention to the machines Mom was attached to and we were made aware she'd stopped breathing. I observed not only that Lillian's body lost its vitality but also that her spirit appeared to have simultaneously disappeared. Like with my Dad's passing, it was clear she was there no more. Her transition was otherwise a remarkably quiet event and, much like my Dad's, hardly visible to the inexperienced eye.

Getting back into the car to drive home in the opposite direction on the now empty freeway was eerie, almost existential. I felt as if time had stopped. Almost immediately my thoughts turned to me: the POP role I'd signed up for ten years ago had come to an end and I'd just become an orphan! My second parent's departing had left me without anyone to POParent, no matter how challenging that had been on occasion. I also wouldn't have a parent around to be proud of me or smile up at me like I'd just invented ice cream. And, without Mom, there was no older "generation" left to buffer the ever-narrowing distance between "My Maker" and myself.

There was an unexpected moment of amazing relief, even exhilaration. My job was done! It almost felt like the day I'd graduated from college or graduate school, having completed a long sought after goal! In its way, POP was a project I'd undertaken that had required years of loving, focused attention and hard work. Now that it was about to be done, I allowed myself to feel good about having been consistent, trustworthy and resourceful.

I'd also begun to recognize that doing POP had allowed me to give Jack and Lillian an unexpected gift of great value: they developed renewed pride in themselves! Part of the way my parents interpreted POP and my way of POParenting them was they must have done a really good job instilling family values in me. Hence they felt satisfaction in having parented me well. Because the very thing parents cherish the most is being able to be proud of their offspring, my unplanned-for gift, when their "pride and joy" lovingly POParented them, was they got to feel good about themselves.

It wasn't long before I realized that, even after my parents were done living, my POP job was still not totally over. Part of what was left was dealing with a lot of paperwork, legal matters, funeral arrangements and more. There was closing their bank account(s); informing Social Security, IRS, Medicare and ASCAP; terminating the agreement with the SNF and calling the Neptune Society to make arrangements for Mom and more.

Another part of my remaining POP tasks involved their "stuff." I still had many items of clothing, memorabilia, furniture and business records to sort out, give away or keep. When the dust settled on all their belongings, legal formalities and my immediate emotions, what was left to plow through was my grieving and adjusting to a "new" life, *without parents to parent and, eventually, after some time, discovering the next trajectory for my own life. Now I'd have the time to apply what I'd learned and become a better "parent" to my loved ones, my community and myself! Maybe I'd write a book ...*

During the ten years of POP my parents weren't the only ones to have aged. I, too, had grown – older and hopefully wiser, truly enriched from what my parents and I had shared. I was certainly not the same woman I'd been before POP.

Your Story

If you've chosen to do POP, it's likely you'll have to face the death of at least one aging loved one you've been POParenting. It is a deeply profound experience to attend the passage of your own parents from this planet, whether you're single or married, come from one cultural background or another, are an only child or someone with siblings. And as a result, this is the time you'll need to take special care with your parents and yourself.

As your final tribute to your Moms and Dads, you'll want to handle the "details" around their deaths with grace and thoughtfulness. Maybe you can discover some "little" things you can do that will actually make a huge difference to your parents' final days and also to the memories that others will hold of your parents as well. For example, I've seen POParents gather the people who'd want a last visit with their parents for a "going-away" celebration. Other aging parents might want to reconcile with an estranged sibling. More simply you can arrange, as I did, to reunite couples who've been separated (due to differing levels of aging, illness or other reasons) for their last moments of togetherness.

Arranging these types of get-togethers can be very meaningful, both for your parents and for those who've loved. Saying their "proper" farewells will allow some of your parents to go more peaceably. Your thoughtfulness in these areas can tap into the remarkable healing power in forgiveness and be transformative experiences for all concerned.

If you get the opportunity to be present when the parents you've POParented make their passage, it's likely you will wish to do so. Why? No matter how sad or difficult your parent's death might be for you, it can still be a blessing to attend such a remarkable life passage for someone who conceived and birthed you and is now leaving behind offspring and terra firma. You may have sufficient time and resources to gather family members from the four corners and organize a lovely tribute for their concluding days but such a plan requires you to know when and where their deaths will occur and that's not ordinarily possible.

If you've been given yourself the chance to be their POParents, to comfort their final emotional and physical concerns, by attending your parents' transitions, you also get to observe the profound separation between life and death. It is a remarkable experience. What you'd considered your parents' "essence" seems to depart on their deathbeds, leaving behind a physical body – an unanimated, cold cadaver.

Having talked with people unable to be present at the end, many carry around guilt and other painful thoughts for years. Although it may be optimal to be there when your parents are taking their last breaths, sometimes that will be impossible. Your parents may leave their bodies in ambulances on the freeway or at other times and places when you simply can't get there. If that is you, I discourage your holding onto such feelings any longer.

You can only be where you are and you can only give what you've got available to give. Even when you want to act "perfectly" – like when you're parenting your children or your parents – you're still human. Sometimes you will disappoint yourself and others. But you do the best you can and carrying around baggage about this doesn't seem to help anyone.

I felt very fortunate to be able to bring my Mom to say goodbye to my Dad and then to be present when each of them departed this mortal coil. What you should *not* do is to hold onto POParental regrets or resentments, especially if you enriched your parents' lives by doing POP. Regrets and resentments are two of the most effective ways to program yourself for unhappiness. At this uniquely vulnerable time, it's best to avoid these and all other self-destructive sentiments.

You might personalize or "customize" other fitting tributes for your parents. This might take the form of honors, awards, plaques or other memorial statements that reflect your parents' contributions to the communities in which they lived, loved and served. Since your parents gave of themselves to their work, clubs, families, charitable organizations, religious organizations and the like, you may wish to have them take note of your parents' lives (or deaths) and honor them in some special way. You may particularly want the younger generations who never knew your parents that wello learn more about their "ancestors," your parents.

When it was "Jack's turn" to be honored, I waited until we held our memorial celebration event to give him an on air tribute. I called the Los Angeles radio station that plays "The Music Of Your Life" format and requested they say some "nice words" about his songs and play of the songs my parents used to dance to and that Dad had written. I still remember it. In retrospect, I wish I'd done that when he was still alive.

You can use this opportunity for ritual, to post the POP music you've come to love to the website's blog at www.ParentingOurParents.org and for other symbolic statements that express the ways your parents distinguished themselves. If you and your siblings are still engaging in "contests" at this point in your POPcycle, this could be your time to get better aligned by putting the unpleasant past behind all of you. Some POParents find it healing and unifying to sit with family and share stories as they compose an obituary or other appropriate means of honoring their parents. Other siblings, far-flung from each other, may collectively create such eulogies on email. You can use this meaningful time in life and these types of experiences to heal your old wounds.

If it makes sense to you, I encourage you to do this: celebrate your parents while they can still understand and appreciate your accolades and acknowledgements. Honor that they've lived full lives and concentrate on the good feelings that evokes. It is important to remind yourself to have a good time while you're doing POP: just like raising kids, POParenting will be over sooner than you think. And if possible, rejoice even at its conclusion.

Most of us in the Western world have similar reactions to hearing about death: it's horrible, to be feared and avoided at all costs. Your experience, like mine, may well be to the contrary. Death is often a welcome relief for those who've lived well and then spent a lengthy time in a deteriorating physical body. We POParents aren't always willing or able to hear that. When Jack chose to be put on hospice, I had to face that issue, whether or not I liked it. Doing so helped me to understand what he and so many other seniors were saying to their loving POParents: you don't need to mourn for the conclusion of my long and happy life.

Instead of traditional grieving, you might substitute basking in the recognition of how much you've helped your parents feel and function as well as they did during their sunset days. By choosing to POParent them as you did, you supplied your folks with additional reasons to feel satisfied with their lives and accomplishments, including being caring parents to you. They may even see your POParenting as the crowning achievement of their own parenting.

Rather than focusing on your losses, you might gain more serenity by deciding your parents are finally peaceful. After all, the fullness of a life well lived needn't bring you tears but could leave you enriched. Poets offer us this insight:

> Though nothing can bring back the hour
> Of splendour in the grass,
> Of glory in the flower,
> We will grieve not, rather find
> Strength in what remains behind.[72]

You need not limit celebrating your parents to a single time or method. Perhaps you'll even choose to do things "backwards," like eating dessert first. For example, during the earlier stages of your POPcycle when everyone can actively participate, you could arrange a wonderful POP party to honor your parents, show them your gratitude and make sure your grandchildren get to know your parents better. After their deaths you can host another event, a memorial or a funeral as fits your beliefs, to show your respects.

---

[72] William Wordsworth, "Splendour in the Grass."

POPlan #16: Caregiving Yourself

Since most of your parents had qualified medical personnel, hospice people and, hopefully, you and your POP family attending to them in their final hours, it's crucial thereafter that you take steps to get some caring attention pointed in your own direction. As a devoted POParent witnessing your parents' transitions, you may have strong reactions. In the immediate time afterwards, it's often the surviving POParents, left behind, who are the most defenseless.

But you and I have been through a lot and know the truth about your POParenting: you've done the best you could. Your POPlans, like mine, may have been interrupted, ignored by the universe and even, on occasion, fulfilled. If you hadn't been able to do all you'd wished in your POP life, start forgiving yourself now. Remember, you want to treat yourself as kindly as you tried to treat your parents.

Pause now to appreciate yourself and all you've been able to do and give your family. However flawed, overwhelmed or inadequate you may have felt during your POPcycle, you've generously shared a huge amount of yourself – your time, thoughtfulness, money, energy and resources –- during your parents' end of life. Even if you feel horrible that you "made them move out of their home" or didn't get them to the right doctor or can't afford the plane ticket to your Mom's funeral, you can still remind yourself kindly that: you've done what you can. Even your aging parents would have understood that. And you can, too. There's no need to lug around harsh judgments about yourself because you may have chosen incorrectly, not had more to give or based your decisions upon misinformation. These feelings serve no one well unless you use them to grow "next time."

By applying the "reframing," compassion and forgiveness tools you've practiced throughout these chapters, you know how to extract "the upside" from your experiences, reduce your unhappiness and undermine your self-blame. Remember to refresh yourself under "showers of gratitude" – both on a regular and "as needed" basis. By using these and the other POP tools you've been working with – like breathing deeply and consciously into the moment – you will be more fully present to take on whatever new or old challenges you're facing at this critical time.

You will want to take action to set up a buffer against the harshness of your own predictable POP losses. The utility in your having stockpiled these techniques in your arsenal against the pain of grief and related stressors is that now you have them to bring out and use. Doing so should result in your making better choices and will make it harder for you to be bullied by any of your own "negative" thoughts.

What additional steps might you take at the time your parents are leaving to maximize good self-care? If you know in advance that this will be your Dad's last day, as I was advised, "caregive" yourself by bringing along your own "comfort" items – your comfortable clothes, reassuring dog, inspirational writings and evocative music. You can also request, as I did, loved ones, partners and maybe some trusted friends to be present at your parents' transitions to help *you*. If so, choose your invitees wisely with an eye to having everyone emotionally aligned with you. In the empty quietness of the aftermath, these intimates can remind you, even without words, that your parents are relieved of their pain and bodily demands and that you're responsible, in a good way, for their peacefulness.

If your siblings have a long tradition of arguing, this would be a good time to try getting better agreement especially amongst the "worst offenders." Now that your parents are gone, it's just you guys left here now. You might as well try to get on better. Your parents would have appreciated it too.

If you find that time is passing after your parents' transitions and you're not recovering from that to your own satisfaction or if your loved ones feel you're not "healing," you may consult the POP Family Coach you've been working with or another professional who has experience with grief. Support groups can also give you an excellent sense of perspective and practical advice.

I have a banner that hangs in my office quoting Buddha. It states: "You yourself as much as anybody in the entire universe, deserve your love and affection." I leave it up as a reminder to myself as well as my patients of how differently we can view life's bountiful opportunities. Without true compassion and love for ourselves, suffering will inevitably follow.

In your final moments as the POParent, promise yourself a practice you will follow for the rest of your life: care for yourself as kindly and lovingly as you cared for your parents.

Chapter 17

Facing Pop Is Over And We Need
To Launch Our New Lives

My Story:

The ultimate objective of POP was to get my parents safely across their earthly "finish lines" with minimal discomfort and maximum serenity. Much time has now passed, it seems, since my Dad and then my Mom made their earthly departures. Some days I can see them and even hear their voices as clearly as a recording. My life is very different, post-POP, without them here. In fact, I was changed forever when I chose to parent my parents. I'm so grateful I did.

When I'd cared for them, although the three of us lived in expectation of it, death was never really discussed, like the proverbial elephant in the room. How differently my generation interacted with our kids and our friends! Maybe we went too far in the other direction, sharing too much and "over-talking" our feelings with our children? We thought we were applying the notions we'd learned in our physics classes, that nothing disappears: matter turns into energy. For many Baby Boomers and others, when important words or feelings are left unexpressed, they only go "underground" and, if unresolved, return later in unexpected formats and time frames.

But in our parents' generation, much was left unsaid. Dad and I had spoken, of course, about my arranging for hospice but never really of his passing or his view of an afterlife. Sometimes not talking about hard topics, like their dying, was simpler for me as well as them, apparently, but this absence of our discussion left a void.

Mostly in the book I've used the word "transition," which I prefer to "death" because it's better aligned with my faith. I believe that our souls are on a journey without end and continue on after our mortal bodies have turned to dust. From my spiritual perspective, it was as if our little family had been running some long distance marathon together for my whole life. Our pace slowed during the last phase, the POPcycle, as my Mom and Dad headed towards the completion of their earthly time. And so, Jack and then Lillian's final breaths were contemporaneous with their souls' successfully crossing the finish line. The next step of their voyages would be taken alone since, as far as I knew, no life partner or POParent could accompany them any further. I could no longer protect them from whatever they might encounter nor share in the joy and peace I hoped they'd now found.

Like so many POParents while they were still alive, I'd spent time prematurely grieving for Lillian and Jack. I'd even anticipated how my life might change after they'd moved on. To their credit and reflecting their wisdom, they'd discouraged my fears about the future, reminding me to stay in the present. "We're not dead yet, Jane," they'd commented one day when I was particularly "pre-nostalgic" and a bit weepy.

In the aftermath of their transitions, of course, I was left with an immediate void in my life. But unlike many who'd given up careers, jobs and homes to attend to their aging parents, much of my pre-POP life seemed to be still intact. I felt fortunate about that, expecting I could "pick up" where I'd left off before that Christmas a decade ago had changed everything. Surely I'd now have more time to be with my patients and family, more energy for me.

I told myself it was just as natural to launch our children towards college, marriage or their first home, as it was to send off our aged parents to their hereafters.

However no matter how normal, predictable or expected this was supposed to be in theory, when it was my parents departing, nothing felt normal or comfortable. It felt more like there was a hole in my heart that might never be filled again. Throughout history, sages have consistently offered one adage about grief: time heals. I clearly would need some time.

Immediately after my parents' transitions, there was another flurry of POP activity. There were things to do. I had legal work, banking, Social Security and Medicare – POP paperwork galore. I had to go through their possessions in their residences and decide what to keep and what to give away. Although I did these final jobs with care, it was more like I was going through the motions since my heart just wasn't in it. Without Mom or Dad around, doing these tasks felt very different than when they were here, less relevant or important.

Soon I was POP-free. With no parents to care for, I could continue keeping busy and a part of me definitely wanted to do that. But since those goodbyes at college I'd been "ruminating" about the time our family would "end" and, now that the time had come, I needed to stop doing and spend some time just being with my feelings and myself. I wanted to give myself all the time I needed to salve my wounded parts.

Even with my grieving, I had a way I wished to conduct myself. I'd seen some people lose themselves in their grieving and I didn't wish to wander aimlessly and endlessly through sad thoughts. My end goal was to live in the present fully. In order to do that, I knew I couldn't go into denial but would need to feel my emotions as deeply as possible and do so when they were still freshest. And yes, I even allowed myself some "self-pity." Later, when I felt complete about my losses and, hopefully, appreciated some of my "gains" from POP, I wanted to allow the feelings to depart or, at least, find a useful place to reside inside me.

After my both of their transitions, my immediate and predominant feelings had been fatigue, relief, numbness and, in spite of knowing they had lived full lives, gnawing grief. A part of me felt abandoned, in spite of knowing my parents had no intention of deserting me and their passing wasn't "about me." Although I was already a mature woman and my folks were very old, that didn't matter in that moment.

My grief seemed to be triggered by a thought, a smell and, very often, by the sound of a song. It had no regard for whatever I was otherwise doing at the time, sometimes even interrupting me when I was at work. My reactions seemed to rise and fall in waves, rushing over me unexpectedly and I told myself, rather dramatically, that my life would never be the same. POP seemed to have become a metaphor for life's only constancy, change. When I'd tell myself, as a comforting thought, that nothing alive ever stays the same, my mind wanted to answer: what will remain the same hereafter is that I'd never be anyone's daughter again. In those self-pitying moments I found that anything could generate my feeling sorry for my parentless state.

My beloved would respond to that by calling me "the Orphan." It was his way of offering me a hand up and out from this sorrow and these unwarranted conclusions by means of our shared sense of humor. I didn't need to be called "the Orphan" too many times to get the point. I was neither a sad dejected child stranded without her parents nor a soul bereft without a loving connection to the universe. That just wasn't the "real me."

In those moments, my mate understood me better than I did. He understood that, when I was thinking more clearly and not overwhelmed with grieving, I'd think it was silly, too and maybe even damaging to view myself in that way. When I wasn't temporarily blinded with feeling sorry for myself, I was better able to feel the love I had from so many people, both related and unrelated to me – dead and alive. His faith in me inspired me to come back to myself: I could never be an "orphan," an unloved and abandoned person, not unless I chose to put that label on myself.

When, from time to time I'd still felt lonely for Jack and Lillian, maybe a bit like an orphan, I was usually able to remind myself fairly quickly by focusing on his love and employing my rational, re-framed thinking: I was neither a child nor in need of protection. In truth, Lillian hadn't functioned as my Mother for many years but I who had acted as hers.

When I separated myself from these false conclusions, I was careful to not disavow my authentic feelings of mourning and loss since I realized they were necessary and appropriate. I also found anger and disappointment interspersed among my other emotions. These were occasionally confusing. Although I knew from clinical research that such feelings often emerge, I'd asked myself: anger, what's that about? What am I angry about? Then I would comfort myself by with its "normality:" anyone who'd just loved and lost might feel angry, confused and disturbed.

During this process, I did my best to allow myself to feel it all but only to react to a few of them. When I focused on the loneliness and abandonment, inevitably I became unhappy because I'd go back into feeling sorry for myself. This actually deepened my sense of isolation. And when I remembered to breathe into the moment and bring myself back into the present, I always functioned and felt better. I wanted to be experiencing my life through a healthy balance of owning my emotions but not wallowing in them so I breathed a lot more.

As the realization that the weight of doing POP and its responsibilities were lifting, I also had an unexpected sense of relief, something akin to freedom. For so many years, it had felt oddly normal to be constantly concerned about my parents' wellbeing. With their transitions, I'd gotten a reprieve from that worry and releasing it altogether would help me take the first steps in the direction of my "new life."

No longer on call 24/7, 365 days a year for Jack and Lillian, I could now let my phone go unanswered until I felt "available" to be interrupted. As a mental health professional, I'd always been "reachable" but now knowing I wouldn't be missing a time-critical POP message, I could check later. Right after savoring that exhilaration, I thought I heard Janis Joplin croon: "Freedom's just another word for nothing left to lose."[73] How complicated grief really is!

Since my birth I'd been part of the Wolf triangle with each "leg" needed to complete the whole. After Mom's dementia set in and her hip condition required my parents to live separately, I'd experienced the loss of their "coupleness" as weakening our triangle. When I drove Dad to spend time with Mother, the three of us would sit together in her room or go out to the SNF's garden. Then I'd momentarily recapture a childhood fantasy – that our family was invincible and timeless – only to come back sharply into the present day. Like the wounded soldier who "feels" his now-absent limb, a part of me longed for the phantom triad of a strong, vibrant "Mommy, Daddy and their little girl."

Instead I had now become the sole historian of Wolf family lore as well as keeper of all its possessions. I felt inexplicably dislocated. I'd assumed, as an only child, that one and then my other parent would leave me here "alone." However becoming the last runner of our "marathon team" left standing, I was again learning the tolls of being an only child. From that time forward, only I would laugh at the inside jokes we'd enjoyed together and only I would understand the familiar references we'd spent our lifetime together creating.

On some occasions I saw my grief resulting in questioning my POP performance, evaluating the choices I'd made and those I'd declined. Fortunately my spiritual tradition invited me to more neutrally observe that thinking rather than judge or blame myself for things I could no longer change. I also comforted myself with the thought that I'd done my best at POParenting, the best I knew how – given who I was and what I had to work with at the time.

Facing my parents' mortality required me to face my own as well. In turn, thinking about my own death led me to examine my life and contributions. What had my

---

[73] This line is from the song, "Me and Bobby McGee," written by Kris Kristofferson and Fred Foster, published by EMI Music.

life, up until this time, been all about? What were my core values and was I living by them? When I left the planet, how would I wish to be remembered?

Throughout our POPcycle, I'd periodically wondered: where will I be spending my senior years? Would I "inherit" my Mom's dementia? Would I request to be put on hospice like Jack had done? Might I spend my final days in a facility staring off into space? Or would I be like my Aunt Frieda who played her last round of golf at 88, walked off the fairway and immediately expired? Would I be the healthy senior enjoying life, loved ones and contributing right up to the end, as I hoped and dreamed?

Seeing it from this vantage point, POP seemed to involve a lot of consideration about my own aging and me. It was almost as if my involvement with POP was a "rehearsal" for my own old age. When I'd gone to look at senior residential facilities for my folks, I'd often pictured the scene, years ahead, when I'd be the prospective resident. Without even being conscious of it, entering a facility's front door, I'd be asking myself: if it were me, would I want to live here? Years from now, who would scout facilities for me?

With their passing I saw my parents' absence from the planet and my life in yet another context. It was now my generation who'd become the heads of our families. Gone was the "buffer layer" between my Maker and me: we were "next up." I even wondered if my parents were continuing to "watch over me" now that they'd crossed over to some other plane?

As time wore on and the last time I'd seen either of them grew longer, my memories of Lillian and Jack grew a bit dimmer. Even my vision of them as old people was fading and, in my mind's eye, sometimes they were young again. It seemed I was less sad when I remembered them as vibrant. As the days continued, when I thought about my Mom and Dad, a smile would light up my face more often than a tear descend on it.

I longed to hold on to those smile-making memories and the sweet recollection of things I'd experienced doing POP and there were many. Another offering from Buddha helped me remember how much control lay in how I thought about my experiences. "Your worst enemy cannot harm you as much as your own thoughts unguarded. But once mastered, no one can help you as much, not even your Father or your Mother." I practiced this advice, guarding against "engaging with" disturbing thoughts as I did when I meditated. Instead I'd practice the technique of noticing they'd gone by, evaluating them for their irrationality and letting them go.

As I drew farther away in time, the challenging feelings became less intense. Gradually, as I began to feel in greater control, I wondered: what would my post-POP healing look like? Even if it occasionally upset me to remember my parents, I didn't want to banish my memories of them. Of course not and, thinking about them or their absence, could trigger my feeling badly, but it could also, more often now, trigger my smile.

I tried permitting myself to bask in the warmth of my happy remembrances. "Recovering" from the loss of POP could look differently than I'd expected – more like permitting the memories to come up naturally – and knowing some might trigger pride and joy, while others might bring on my nostalgia. I sought to pro-actively evoke comforting thoughts, insights and recollections because those lead me to feel lighter emotionally. On occasion I'd aim to recall something specific and positive, like my parents' satisfaction when I was graduated from college or the way my Mom's face would beam, when I'd done some POP kindness for her. As time went on, even childhood memories - like Dad teaching me lyrics to his latest song - could source my smiles.

I came to see my parents' transitions as part of a larger irony in the human condition: we live and die in our solitariness as well as in our connectedness. We come onto the planet apparently alone, hopefully make deep human connections which we'll eventually need to leave and pass off the planet, apparently alone again. My spiritual perspective refuted the notion that the appearance of aloneness was reality, offering me the view that we are always with God.

It also suggested that there was a major difference between "losing" my parents because they'd left the planet and they're being "lost" to me. I still retain my memories of Jack and Lillian and their vast influence on my life. Since that was so, I reasoned I could "find" my parents whenever I wished. They weren't lost – they'd simply moved on.

Time continued to pass and, of course, my life went on. My emotions kept coming and going in waves but for the most part, these seemed diminished in size and potency. Then, out of the blue, some powerful memory would wash over me and I'd be overwhelmed with tears, loss or even, sometimes, laughter. In an instant I could be that child again, back with my parents when we'd all been younger together.

Driving one day, an Elton John song about his father came on the radio. In a New York minute I was my Daddy's little girl all over again. I'm dancing awkwardly, trying to look grown up, totally embraced by my Father's love. My small arms are reaching up towards his faraway shoulders and my feet are planted on top of his adding at least two inches to my short frame. That vision seemed to stop my heart in its tracks; I pulled off the road to sit and weep.

Even though Mom and Dad are now long gone, there are still times when I find myself musing, "wouldn't Mom love this beautiful museum exhibit? I want to bring her here …" Or I think, "I can't wait to tell Dad about that…" Entering an overpriced Beverly Hills boutique, leaving a funny film or randomly, I find myself quoting one of Jack's many witticisms. Other times, I catch a glimpse of myself in the mirror, see my resemblance to Lillian and think: I am my Mother's daughter.

Today these recollections almost always make me smile. Some days I get the notion to carry around a little "piece" of Lillian or Jack with me for support, comfort or good luck. I'll put on a special pin Mom bought me, a piece of clothing that belonged to her or one she knit for me back in the day. Or I'll be driving and decide to play a song of Jack's and sing along with the words he taught me. I recognize these gestures as symbols of my ongoing life healing process. They are small sacred steps, refilling the emptier parts remaining in my heart and it feels like I'm honoring my parents' memories as I savor the special influence each of my parents had on me.

I admit to sometimes feeling envious of people who still have living parents. Fathers' and Mothers' Days are predictably challenging for me. Even seeing an adult woman strolling arm in arm down the street with her Mom occasionally triggers reactions similar to those I had in my more immediate post-POP days.

As my little rescued "puppy" become increasingly older and frailer I noticed I'd started associating my dog's last days with my parents' final exit and became a bit concerned. The pet I'd brought over to be with my Dad on his last day was himself becoming too weak to reach down to eat food or drink water. I feared that my 18 year-old dog's imminent demise could stimulate another wave of grieving. Instead of going to that place, I tried to examine my thoughts with a clearer lens and distinguish my feelings about him from those about my parents. I had to literally say to myself: "This is your dog, Jane, not your Dad or Mom" and I needed to remind myself of that reality more than once.

I also reminded myself how long and wonderful the dog's life had been. This mode of thinking brought me into a different quality of "mourning" about him, one similar to thinking about our parents having lived lengthy and robust lives, where I wasn't so much saddened as tearful with appreciation, honoring a life well and fully lived. This helped and, afterwards, I was better able to hold onto that more rational reframe. Doing so added to my strength, making it easier to appropriately end my dog's suffering. At his end, he too left the planet, serene in my arms.

It took me yet another year after Mom's departure to put together the POP-concluding celebration of my parents' lives I wanted to hold. I invited those people who were closest to me to my near-oceanfront home and decorated the library with my parents' "accomplishments." I displayed Jack's statewide athletic trophies, some unique objects of art Lillian designed and put out lots of their memorabilia. Nowhere in my home could there have been sufficient space to display the hundreds of poems, cards and letters Dad had composed and Mom had saved over their years together. Nor would such an exposure have been "proper," given how private and modest my parents truly were.

For the gathering I enlarged a photo of the three of us to poster size. In it my parents are sitting around their little girl and they are vibrantly, beautifully youthful! The man who now owned my Dad's music publishing made a special CD of his songs for the celebration, so my favorite Jack Wolf songs provided the background music as conversation focused on my days of doing POP. In the foreground Benny Mardones, a singer friend with an amazing voice, crooned Dad's tunes for us. Even though some people there had never met my parents, few eyes remained dry that afternoon.

The final step I'd planned was to release a portion of their ashes into the welcoming waters of the Pacific after my beloved minister friend Sue offered us powerful words of spiritual inspiration. I asked everyone to grab a balloon and a marker, write a special message on it to Jack and Lillian and carry it to the ocean where we'd let the messaged balloons ascend into the heavens.

Meanwhile I'd brought along two beautiful champagne flutes that I'd filled with some ashes from each of their urns on this walk. When the processional arrived at the water and the words were said, I emptied the flutes and watched the contents mix together as I invited the sea to "have its way" with their remains. I wondered but never knew whether the waves kept their ashes together or sent them out to sea apart. Like so many POPlans, this last one – to release the balloons overhead – met with some unexpected resistance. One of my guests was the Los Angeles Police Chief who said that our balloons couldn't be let go safely as they posed a hazard to LA Airport's congested airspace. The irony of seeing a part of my final POPlan dissolve in front of my eyes was hardly lost on me.

And afterwards POP was, undoubtedly, over.

It hit home more poignantly than ever that everyone I love comes into and out of my life so quickly. Therefore the most important POP "lesson" is to live joyously with those we cherish during the time we have with them. That core realization continues to guide me as I help my patients, loved ones and those I POP Family Coach live their POPcycle and the remainder of their lives with more joy.

Recently I was sitting with a patient. She is a 44 year-old woman who has unexpectedly been called upon to care for her 73 year-old Father with advanced Parkinson's. Their history together had been occasionally stormy but she's working with me, in part, to become a more patient POParent. On this day she was furious with her father over some incident she's unlikely to recall for long. I asked her a question and later I realized that it had emerged from my current view of POP. " If you were told your Dad had only six months to live, how might knowing that alter your anger today?" She stopped and thought about it. "What I'm so mad about probably wouldn't matter at all to me, then."

She paused and I saw a light of recognition appear from deep within this woman's eyes. Then we both heard her enlightened response. "What would really matter would be to best love the man my Dad is today and forgive the man he is no longer. I suppose I can let go of the anger I'm feeling today too, since it's not rage but love I wish to grow between him and me." I could see that, for her like for me, POParenting often resulted in healing.

Thinking about my aging and my own future, I found myself posing Oprah's great question. "What is it, Jane, that you know for sure?" My answer is: I know that I don't need to plague myself with scary thoughts of being homeless, impoverished, unloved or disabled in my senior years. These are not what I want, foresee for myself or intend to ever let happen.

And still, I can never know what's ahead. But I needn't add worrying to my not knowing; I can just admit that tsunamis, companies not paying pensions, Ponzi schemes and unknowable unknowns can change everything. Probably we're not meant to know the future fully until we get there. I also don't know for sure that I'd ever wish the younger generations – stepchildren or grandchildren – to bear the awesome responsibilities my parents entrusted to me. But I do wonder what lessons and conclusions the people in those generations are reaching, having witnessed their parents doing POP.

For myself, it's more likely I'll want to find –– or maybe create – an intentional community where I'd age alongside my beloved and other "like-minded" friends who've essentially become a second family. Maybe I'll want to "age in place" in my own home? Maybe something completely unexpected will occur? Once I decide which direction I can go, I'll need to consider what steps I should be taking financially, legally, emotionally and spiritually in order to ensure that my choices will eventually occur.

As I look back over my life thus far, little helped me to grow up faster than parenting. Learning how to "be the grownup," first in my 20's with my stepchildren and later, in midlife with my own parents, brought out the most adult and, at other times, the most childish parts in me. Both parenting opportunities advanced me "giant steps" towards becoming more nurturing, compassionate and patient and, I can only hope, my clients, loved ones and I will be ongoing beneficiaries of that. I expect that you're noticing, too, you're expanding your compassion and other qualities you need the most as you're moving through your POPcycle.

What I've aimed to do in this book is to empower you to create your own "best" version of a good POPcycle by sharing my own, however "flawed" and however "different" from yours it may appear to be. I stated, in the beginning, that such private revelations have challenged me but it was well worth it, if MY STORY helps you develop more competence and confidence in constructing your best version of POP.

Early on I also noted you're likely to discover how alike we all are, when we're doing POP, how much YOUR STORY and MY STORY have in common. Just stand in line at your grocery store with a package of adult diapers and see how quickly another POParent will engage you in conversation about your POP story and theirs. It's likely you're making many different POP choices for your parents than I made for mine or than the person at the market has made. And that's how it should be, since this book has never been about your following the same options I chose for Lillian and Jack or that any one path is the right one.

We in the POP generation are each part of a bigger community, we're all in the Family of Man. Our numerous opportunities for loving, healing and giving span across nations, cultures and families. You and I are among tens of millions of POParents who now spend time with our parents, seek forgiveness, get "do-over's," invoke gratitude, savor today's goodness and reverse the roles from our childhood with our parents.

I began to notice how "universal" POP was when total strangers, people whose names I never learned, shot me what I came to call the "POP look." I'd be doing something small for Mom and Dad, like patiently getting them in or out of my car or adjusting a scarf for one of them against the cold, when I'd be flashed this warm sign of recognition, even faint approval. I got the "POP look" more often as Jack and Lillian "advanced" from walking upright to needing canes, then walkers to lean on and, finally, to being pushed in their wheelchairs as they'd pushed me in my stroller.

Most often this "POP look" came to me from my peers, middle-aged men and women, but not always. They seemed to be offering me a silent blessing in their "POP look." It was a powerful connection because it meant that another person, perhaps a POParent, got what POP was and what we were doing here together. The "POP look" startled me with its unexpected depth of camaraderie and, each time, I experienced emotional warmth, a connection, I'll never forget. Now that my POP days are over, I miss receiving it but I still give the "POP look" to other POParents repeatedly every day!

When I did pursue talking to such a stranger, most of the time, they now were or had been POParents themselves, had lived their POPcycle struggles and joys and understood mine without knowing "anything" about me. In its way, it was the universality I felt, getting the "POP look," that helped me birth the idea of the global POP community you and I are currently constructing together here, online at the POP website and wherever else we are traveling.

To answer Oprah's fascinating question with regard to my POP journey: I know this, for sure. I received far more by doing POP than I ever gave. Together my parents and I shared the opening and closing of the Circle of Life and somehow we created a beautiful love story.

It is because I parented Lillian and Jack that I also know this for sure: I don't want any of you to go through more of your POPcycle without the community you need to help you do it well. Read on in the book's final chapter to see where we go from here and what's next. What we need to accomplish this demanding work in a satisfying and loving way is here. Parenting Our Parents is growing exponentially, one family at a time with every family and every POP story welcome!

Their Story – Dad

Jane honey, I want you to have the benefit of everything I've come to understand during my lifetime. Gosh, can you believe it? I've had 92 years of so much richness and so much living?

First, Jane, you've got to know how very proud I am of you! Your Mom and I both were for years. I told you that many times and I hope I've told you often enough. I'll happily tell you again now: you were a wonderfully devoted daughter. When we got old and needed you to help us, you took consistently good care of your Mom and me. And, if anyone knows, I do – we weren't always easy.

Second, I'm okay with everything. Specifically, I'm just fine with your writing a book that we're all in to help other families do even better, after they read what our family went through.

Privacy can be greatly overrated, especially after you've gotten old. I'm better than "just fine" with your writing this book. I highly approve of the project because so many people desperately need help parenting their parents.

They need your help. You've had so many relevant life experiences, studied law and psychology, physiology and philosophy and integrated it all to become who you are now: a source of comfort and "normality" for people parenting their parents! So anything you deem relevant to include in the book about us, that's all right by me. After all, we writers have got to share what we've learned. And, by the way, my dear daughter, congratulations on becoming a writer – your grandmother, Uncle George and I will all want to take credit for your choice, I'm sure.

Third, you'll remember my always telling you that living well came down to a few basics. Turns out that your old Dad was smarter than either of us knew or, at least about that, honey. Human life is simple. Ultimately it's about love, joy and contribution.   As I have been closer to leaving my body, I've developed an appreciation for how hard it is to be in a human body while it ages. Although our senses are gifts to enjoy the human experience, once they start to go, it becomes challenging to live as fully. It became hard not to focus on the changes I was seeing in Lillian and me too.   Frankly, the planet on the whole seems very different to me now than when I was younger. Damned shame, so many people I've loved are already gone and then there's your Mom. She's almost worse than dead – looking and sounding like herself but not really my Lillian any more.

Aging felt like a long string of losses. For the first time in my life, an overwhelming sadness descended over me. My God, I even tried to end my life three times. And Jane, I am so sorry for those attempts and how my forgetting the joy of living may have hurt you. Thank you for saving me from myself! From my current vantage point, I see again that life is grand but not unless I actually enjoy it. So my darling daughter, it's time for us both to become peaceful, give up any struggles we may carry and enjoy what shows up.

I expect there may be pain during this upcoming passage. Hopefully I won't feel it except maybe the sorrow of watching your face as my body leaves Earth and you for the last time. But do not grieve because that will be my last moment ever of human sadness. Thereafter, I'll be free of all the body's pains and aging. In my next life, I will be new again.

I want you to always feel the love I have for you, no matter my form or yours. Those of us for whom you sacrificed when doing POP thank you for our sunset years! We will love you forever and we hope that you healed yourself as much as you helped us to heal. As far as I know, you're right in thinking that your mother and I will never be "lost" to you nor you to us, not even after we leave this planet. But, after all, you did inherit my intelligence. Soon you'll also be inheriting my membership in ASCAP, the songwriters' and publishers' association, and

I love that you'll receive my love "reminders" ongoingly in the form of royalties from the music I wrote.

Speaking of music, I hear it's gloriously musical on the other side, Jane! Maybe there's an ongoing vibration that's harmonic and magnificently peaceful ... Life after the life I gave you may be even better than life on earth. Death seems to be its own beginning rather than a final ending. Not only that but, where I'm going, I won't need those damned thickeners and can finally get a decent cup of Joe. I'm thinking it will be sweet there, hopefully with other spirits I've loved, throughout eternity.

And Jane, one last time my dear daughter, thank you for being in my life! I love you!

Your Story

With the passing of a parent, each of you will be required to make changes, one last time. Every POParent grieves in a unique and special way. There is no right or wrong to it. Bereavement experts report there are many different types of losses, everything from the loss of faith to the loss of limb. You can lose your parents, children, pets, health, friends and your money. You can lose your way, your sense of values, misplace your things and even the companionship of other people. People process their losses and specifically their "goodbyes" in a wide variety of ways. Some deny, some regret, some pine away. The loss of an aging parent may be predictable but does that mean it isn't painful or hurts you any less than if your parents had died when you were younger?

After your POPcycle is completed and while you're contemplating what you've lost, you can also discover who you've become, as a result of participating in this extraordinary and transforming experience with your aging loved ones. Soon you may be asking yourself: since I've fulfilled my POP mission, what do I want next? But that time is not quite upon you yet. First you must take a bunch of deep and cleansing breaths, discover where you're at now, rest up for a while and regroup. All of this may take some time. If you give yourselves sufficient therapeutic time now, it's likely you'll complete your healing more thoroughly and you won't need to deal with it again later.

The end of a POPcycle represents many different things depending, of course, on how you choose to look at it. If you're like most people, you'll soon be focusing a lot of attention on how much you've lost. Your friends may see it as their "new job" to listen empathically as you recount what you no longer have. For those of you who substantially rearranged your lives to accommodate POParenting, your losses may now include the POP life you've created, its accompanying life-style and maybe even your recent self-identification.

Not only have you been deprived of your parents' companionship – and the various consequences that may have – but you've also been left without your recent central responsibility and, perhaps, your reason for getting up in the morning for some years.   Certainly you've lost the satisfaction gained from performing helpful POP tasks, watching your folks enjoy your giving to them and a myriad of other good things that joined your life with theirs. Some of you may find yourself grieving, as I did, for the loss of your original nuclear family and the absence of your parents' "coupleness."   You may be feeling emotional losses reflecting your sense of abandonment at being left behind as the sole family historian or with siblings you never liked that much.

Can you interpret your "losses" in an empowering way, rather than being overwhelmingly sad over loved ones no longer here? Yes, you can try to place your attention on being grateful for all your positive POP times and rewarding opportunities. Think about all you've gained from the last years or months you had with them. Concentrate on your having been there for them at the end or resolving your differences and finally knowing they were proud of you. You could even be thankful that you've "lost" some things you're happy to be rid of, like dealing with their Social Security and Medicare problems, accommodating your schedules to your parents' needs or worrying about them.

Certainly the parents who saw you attend to them so lovingly wouldn't want you to suffer for long after they'd gone. Instead of struggle and strife, you can adopt a more uplifting point of view. For example, remind yourself that since completing POP, you have more space and time opened up to explore new things, that all endings can be seen as beginnings for other things. By making that type of mental "fix," it will become easier to gain your desired closure on POP.

When you stopped taking care of your children, you found more time for your hobbies or to return to school. Similarly when you complete your POParenting, you'll have more resources to put into expanding your world in other ways. Perhaps what will unfold ahead will turn out to be your best time yet the occasion to take up a long-awaited pursuit worthy of your now more available time and energy. Maybe you'll want to become a POP Family Coach and help guide other families from what you've learned?

So how do you move on and let go? What does it mean to "move on?" Let go … of what? Since you're not letting go of loving your parents nor moving on from your tender memories of POParenting, how can you let go of your sadness, regrets, resentments, losses and angers? How do you move on to your next project or even discover what it is? You've been developing useful tools throughout your work with this book. It's time to apply them so you can better manage your feelings of loss and vulnerability and become more resilient and creative again.

Those tools have included: re-framing your POP experience to extract the valuable lessons for yourself; forgiving your siblings, your parents, yourself and whomever else for the "small things" you've done or omitted to do (and that is, most things); practicing the "habit" of gratitude; remembering there are always things about POP for which you can find some appreciation; savoring your good memories of times long ago and more recently. Working these practices is the road to helping yourself feel more enlivened and energized not only in your POP life but now in your post-POP days as well.

Another "secret" tool is this: LEARN TO MAKE FRIENDS WITH CHANGE!!! Put differently: by accepting the "now" that you have, you can – and will – complete your grieving sooner and more completely than if you persist in fighting what's so!

By engaging with these tools that utilize your intelligence, you can "re-organize" some reactions into more useful perspectives. You have been expecting your parents' inevitable departures, even if you haven't admitted it, felt okay about it or known the exact day or cause in advance. You were realistic enough to acknowledge that the time would come when your aged parents would surrender to fatigue, a chronic illness or some "bug" making its way around their SNF.

Sooner or later, everyone you love will disappear from the planet, as will you and I. Since longevity is certainly a goal for many, the longer you live the more losses you will predictably need to face. You have a lot more choice now, because of these tools you've learned from POP, to either "suffer through" your losses or "get through to the other side" of grief, with grace and gratitude.

By practicing your POP techniques, hopefully you can avoid repeated "wreckage" when you encounter predictable and inevitable losses. By doing so, you can preserve some of your energy and be less susceptible, emotionally and physically, when such losses occur. You can program yourself to appreciate that, although nature didn't give humans a body that would last forever, you needn't be overly dramatic about it.

Simply because mortality is a fact doesn't require you to fear the imminent deaths of everyone you love on a daily basis. Nor do you need to evoke the kind of apprehension I did, when your parents leave you "alone" at college. How much better to choose fully enjoying the experiences afforded by your bodies, friends and relatives when you're all still alive and have each other to enjoy. What a way to live that would be!

Many of you have noticed some very favorable changes in your relationships with your parents since you started doing POP. You may have observed a mellowing in long-held withdrawn emotions or felt a sense of relief and gratitude from your parents that feels boundless. Others may have been disappointed that POP didn't do all you wanted to minimize your differences with your parents and/or your siblings. But your life with them is not over just because POParenting is done.

If you never developed the relationship you wanted with one or both of your parents, their deaths may have made that seem impossible to rectify. I do not agree. Just because you never created the perfect parent-child relationship or didn't achieve all you wanted from doing POP doesn't mean you're without options. I've worked with people to heal their relationships with alienated, neglectful and even abused parents after the parents were no longer alive. Award-winning novelist Tom Robbins put a different slant on it when he suggested: "It's never too late to have a happy childhood!"[74] Even after your parents have gone, you can forgive them and see how that changes you.

What's it like for those left behind after someone you've parented leaves home? If you ask that question to parents who've recently launched their youngster off to college, the armed forces, marriage or even to an apartment down the street, you're likely get one consistent answer: life is very different! Much the same can be said here. Each POParent is likely to feel their parents' absences differently depending on a whole variety of factors, such as: how much you disrupted your former life for POP, whether your post-POP life is fulfilling and what expectations of POP were never met.

After POP is through, your life *will* be different. Each POParent is likely to feel their parents' absences differently depending on a whole variety of factors, such as: how much you disrupted your former life for POP, whether your post-POP life is fulfilling and what expectations of POP were never met. If you brought your parents to live with you, you may have needed to reorganize your home, built some space for them and even revamped your life altogether. It's hard to know anyone who's been employed during POP whose work life hasn't been affected by that.

In order to do POP, many of you had to postpone doing things in your careers and jobs that might have influenced your pay, advancement, early retirement or other benefits. You may or may not be able to jump back into those endeavors or the other plans you'd hoped for and put off – like traveling or going back to school. To pick them back up, you'll need to be able to afford to develop those interests as well as have the stamina to do them now.

Sadly some of you have carried around unconscious fears of abandonment and neglect from your earliest moments. Others actually were left behind, abused or uncared for during childhood. Some adults retain residual effects of early childhood fears and trauma for their whole lives, creating a mental template where loss seems ever present and even a small loss feels like a major rejection. Graduations, weddings or other occasions marking the passage of time, which are joyous for many, can be sad for them. Funerals may be unbearable for people with seriously unresolved issues of abandonment.

---

[74] Tom Robbins, Still Life with Woodpecker, Bantam Press, 1980.

Even for those of you without such challenging histories, recent losses can re-trigger the suffering of your earliest and usually most painful losses, whether remembered by you or not. Part of the reason you may cry when you see others experiencing loss is you're "reliving" similar feelings, even if they're below the level of consciousness. During your most vulnerable times, as when you're grieving, it's easy to pull up "the string" that binds painful losses together.

Since any hurtful loss can potentially "tug" on your string, "unrelated" events in your life seem to look alike and a small loss can feel like an old, deep one. You'll want to be on the alert to these new waves of "old grief" since they may feel inexplicably strong. When you've undergone a recent loss, make sure you separate it out from your former losses. For example, it's easy to reach false generalizations that are destructive to you and are usually unwarranted, such as "it's hopeless. I'll always be alone. People have been leaving me since I was born" or "I'd be better off never loving again because (wo)men always abandon me sooner or later."

Discipline your thinking! Now it's your time to apply the many POP tools you've learned and practiced to fight the seemingly magnetic pull to feel sorry for yourself. For example, when my dog lay in my arms dying, it was very hugely sad for me, of course. Momentarily I evoked the memory of being with each of my parents during their transitions but I was much better off when I could detach the "string" of losses, separate the animal from my parents, and then focus on my gratitude for all the years we'd had together. I was much calmer when I stopped concentrating on the loss and instead savored the memory of his rascal-like behavior and how many times I'd had to reign in his playful ways.

You need to experience and express the grief you're feeling in a way that's best for you. Some people talk with their intimates; some write in journals; others work out at the gym. It's of little value to compare your way of mourning to others. Disavowing your own pain because someone may have seen greater pain honors no one. You may have lost only a parent and someone else their whole family or a whole village in an earthquake, but one person's sadness can't really be compared to anyone else's.

There are also no time limits on how long it may take you to recover from the demise of someone you've POParented. You can speed up the time you spend living in the sadness however, by working with the tools, insights and other people who've been where you are in the POPcycle. Your family or others may want you to "recover" more quickly than feels right to you. They may not know how to cheer you up and are likely to have good motives for wanting you to feel better. They may even acknowledge that, since POP is over, they'd like you to be more present with them. But they may not be the most objective people to evaluate your course of healing.

Sometimes the people who ordinarily "support" you aren't able to help you much at this time. If your nearest and dearest are concerned you're not "snapping back" quickly enough, take their remarks seriously and respectfully. They may be correct that you're wallowing in your grief or have become somewhat dysfunctional. Just in case they're right, heed their concern and get yourself checked out by professionals. A therapist, pastoral counselor, POP Family Coach or even a short-termed grief group may help you better assess how well you're resolving your emotions.

As you're becoming less overwhelmed with sad feelings and more proficient managing your loss, try experimenting with "bringing out your good memories" in a somewhat controlled manner. Interrupt the automatic "lonely" feeling you get every time you pass the coffee shop you used to take your Dad after his doctor's appointments by trying something different. See if you can recall some happy times with your aging loved ones Instead of feeling melancholic or pining for the good old days. Reach into your bank of positive memories and find one with more enjoyable feelings for you than sadness.

Take a breath and see if you can smile as you fondly recall some sweet moments. Warm yourself with your recollections of how your Dad loved his vanilla lattes, blowing on the foam so he wouldn't burn himself and getting it on his nose. As you get more distance from the intensity of your loss, you can be more pro-active in encouraging your pleasurable POP memories to become a bigger and better part of your everyday life.

It may help you to complete POP by creating a ceremony to recognize your parents' passing or perhaps the beginning of the end to your mourning. You might like to create the type of small "public" event I did or take private time to think, look at photos, read poetry or whatever seems appropriate. Use these events to guide yourself into the present, where you can live in the now of your post-POP era.

Remember this: the people you POParented, your parents, would never want you to live indefinitely with your grief. You can tell you're beginning to move on when your sadness lifts, you spend less time every day thinking about your parents and your losses and/or you actually feel more "like yourself." Another sign may be that you're looking around, seeking to "reinvest" yourself again – wondering whether or not, where and how you'll proffer your unique talents in your world. You won't have to look too far to locate people and places where you can continue the circle of giving and receiving you engaged in during POP. Creating your unique loving post-POP gift can transform yourself and your world.

I know you can also make a meaningful contribution by going to www.ParentingOurParents. org where you can discover how doing POP has resulted in lessons or information you'd like to teach others or learn more about.

POPlan #17: Creating What's Next For You

You've done your POP job well! It is time to stop and congratulate yourself! I hope you see your POP experience as a job well done.   Look at all you've learned.   See your having chosen to do POP and all of your POP tasks as a demonstration of your ability to be of great service to others. Acknowledge yourself and your TEAM POP for all your hard work and loving care.

Now it's time for you. However you're feeling – exhausted, relieved, satisfied or whatever – now you should take seriously your own R & R, resting and relaxing. If possible take time to sleep without alarms to wake you. Be "irresponsible" for a while and go on a much needed "communications holiday" where you neither send nor answer emails, texts or phone calls (if doing so causes no one harm).

As you conclude this unique and finite period in your life you're also likely to find yourself reviewing, recollecting and re-evaluating the experiences you've been through during your POPcycle. Asking yourself some final questions as you've been doing throughout in these POPlans, will help you create "closure," that is, the most satisfying conclusion possible to your POP years.

In this POPlan, I've provided you my list of post-POP inquiry. You may wish to add to or subtract from them to compile your own list and customize it to your POPcycle. If you wish to share the additional questions you found helpful to gaining closure, contact www. ParentingOurParents.org and do so.

As you've done in the past, find a quiet, private time and space to ask yourself these questions.

- *What parts of my POParenting do I feel really good about and why?*

- *What POP actions did I take that brought me particular pride and satisfaction?*

- *Am I still concerned that I left POP things undone or should have done things differently? If so, can I forgive myself or whomever else I'd need to forgive? What is the best lesson for me to learn about this?*

- *What did I learn while doing POP about my partner, siblings, children, extended family, employer and myself that will help me as I go forward and grow older?*

- *In what ways has doing POP influenced my life? Do I feel I've healed and, if so, in what ways? How have I "expanded?" How have my skills and knowledge base grown? Am I more peaceful or more loving now?*

- *How can I avoid lingering for too long in sadness and grief about the end of POP and the death of my parents?*

- *Regarding POP, is there anything I need to forgive myself for? Is there anything standing in the way? If not, when will I do that?*

- *What POP memories do I wish to savor? How can I best do that?*

- *What am I most grateful for about my family's POP?*

- *What rituals or celebrations do I want to create to memorialize the end of my POPcycle and the conclusion of my parents' lives?*

- *Will I ever want my children to POParent me? Can I trust them to do the kind of job I did for my parents? Can I feel good about that? If yes, when do I start talking to my children about their doing POP for me?*

- *If I don't want to be POParented by my kids, how, where and with whom do I plan to grow old? Do I want to age in place at my home and will I be able to do that? Do I want to be living with close friends/family in a communal setting or elsewhere, like a supportive residential setting with other seniors?*

- *Regarding the journey I've been traveled during POP, what do I know for sure? (The Oprah Question).*

Epilogue

Where Do We All Go From Here?

Many of you POParents are already seniors like me or will be, sooner than you'd imagine. It's likely you've long harbored dreams, after decades of working hard and raising your families, of what your life would be like when that was behind you. Perhaps you and your spouse were excited that you'd finally have the time, freedom, health and wherewithal to travel and do other "fun projects" you'd felt you had to postpone earlier. You may have envisioned being able to slow down, having fewer people you needed to answer to, learning to paint and spending more "quality time" with your grandchildren.

If you'd stopped to analyze your expectations – something there probably wasn't much time to do – you might have seen your ideal future involved having fewer responsibilities, financial and personal. "Downsizing," "living a simpler life" and "getting back to the basics" are some of the words you may have used to describe how life could be for you, at this age. But, if you're like most people I know around our age, your real life hasn't yet produced those daydreams.

To the contrary, most Americans are all still very active well into our sixties, seventies and often years beyond than. Many are employed full-time or part-time in order to keep up our "lifestyles" and countless Americans are helping to raise our grandchildren, hardly a life of leisure. You may have also noticed, with some regret, that although you seem busier than ever before, you miss having the energy you used to possess.

Since, as we've seen here, the course of human aging varies substantially from individual to individual, it's hard to know what to reasonably expect from yourself or your parents. When your children were growing up, you had "norms" you could utilize to make decisions, since your five-year old boy's development could be measured and compared to his peers. By contrast, with your own and your parents' aging, there are few significant "norms" of how energetic a 65-year old woman should feel or how hard she "should work," and, even with your two parents, it's likely they declined very differently from each other.

The demands on people who used to consider themselves ready for retirement at 55, 60 or 65 have changed, too. We're all so on the go these days that it seems ludicrous to recall the predictions we heard back in the 1950's that our "modern appliances" would create an excess of leisure time! Ha! The "modern appliances" didn't save us any time; instead, they morphed into computers. And as the electronic age exploded, many of the constructs we'd long operated under were blown away.

For example, Americans' workloads grew when texting, emailing and voice mailing became commonplace and former expectations of availability and accountability expanded dramatically. An unwritten law seems to have been passed, when you and I weren't looking, which first deemed us "accessible" 24/7, far exceeding the "9-5" hours customarily required of your parents' workday and, second, required us to reply to these transmissions "now." As a result, today's employers and others often expect they can intrude in ways no one would have imagined just a few years back.

Much of what used to be called "leisure time" and "good personal boundaries" has fallen by the wayside if you're always available or "on call" to anyone aware of your phone number or email address. Privacy, as we used to know it, has nearly disappeared when cameras are on street corners and anyone with a cell phone or access to a computer can discover personal details about you within several clicks.

Maybe some days you'd like nothing more than to slow down, take some time "off" and turn back the hands of technology. Nonetheless there are untold benefits that the Internet and much of technology offer you and me, especially in our role as POParents. For one thing, being connected is a two-way street, going back and forth. That is to say, if others can get a hold of you at anytime, you too might be able to timely access the people and data you need to best POParent your Mom and Dad. Because of technology, you may be able to get in touch with your parents' doctors, your children or much-needed medical records at any hour of the day or night. This can be very comforting.

Like me and those to the right and left of me, you may be one of the millions of Americans who hasn't yet been able to invest in your own leisure, travel or dreams. Why not? Because you've been busy investing your "self" and many of your most precious resources into parenting your aging parents. All those years ago your parents "sacrificed" for you, committed to you and parented you. And all these years later, when they needed you but may not have been willing to admit it, you stepped up to accept an "invitation from the Circle of Life" – to POParent them!

Each of you made your POP commitment for your own reasons: you wished to avoid future regrets; you felt it was the right thing to do; you adored your parents and cherished every day spent with them; or you felt obligated. But whatever your specific motivations, the bottom line was you wanted to help make those who raised you feel better and live more enjoyably during their sunset years.

Throughout time people have always given attention and care to their older relatives. That's nothing new. Nonetheless here in 21st century America a confluence of extraordinary factors has simultaneously come together that makes parenting your parents totally different than it was ever before. Those of you who've been engaging in POP often live, as I did, with a residual fear of whether your money will hold out and what else might lie ahead that would affect your parents' wellbeing – and your own. You know better than anyone that our nation's families are at a critical moment in so many ways and something has to change in a radical way.

What are these factors that make your being "older" and/or having aging parents so challenging and unlike any other time or place in history? First, there are unprecedented numbers of Americans aging. "Baby Boomers" is the term used to refer to the "crush" of people born in the aftermath of World War II, between 1946 and 1964.[75] The extraordinary birth rate has been attributed to post-war economic prosperity and the returning veterans' interest in and ability to afford large families. Because of their age, Baby Boomers have played a prominent part in the forefront of POParenting. Now they stand poised to join their aging parents by dumping an unparalleled volume of additional seniors into an already-swamped system. As of June of 2012, Health and Human Services Secretary Kathleen Sebelius reported that every single day there are 11,000 Baby Boomers reaching 65 and becoming eligible for Medicare!

The demand may become insatiable as Boomers descend daily on an overburdened Medicare/Medi-caid/Social Security system. Governmental officials, politicians and involved families all recognize the huge implications and hazards ahead. But, at this point, there are few if any viable solutions being offered and much finger pointing. Many public entitlement programs that long served the poorest, oldest and hungriest of our peoples are in disarray, the last remnants of the safety net envisioned by Franklin Roosevelt and expanded during Lyndon Johnson's Great Society initiative. Even private retirement plans and pensions are dissolving under the weight of demands and bad investing; some will never pay out benefits to trusted employees who relied for decades on receiving them. All of this will affect not only you in the POParent generation but potentially will impact your parents, your children and perhaps even your children's children.

A second significant factor adding to the brew is the transiency of Americans: we've moved around a lot! After WW II it was your parents and mine who started the trend; moving away in their new cars on brand-new highways, far from old neighborhoods and family scrutiny.

---

[75] This definition is the one used by the United States Census Bureau.

Frequently that generation escaped from cities to distant verdant suburbs. Before, family members lived right next door to each other, often on the same block or in the same building. They provided not only support for raising kids but also made demands that things be done "the old-fashioned way." That included everyone taking care of older grandparents as well as respecting them.

When your parents moved away, they left behind not only familiar surroundings but also much of their family's everyday influence. Your folks also developed the new habit of doing things "their own way." The lessons they extracted from that, self-sufficiency and independence of spirit, would persist throughout your parents' adult lives. These qualities may have tested you when you became their POParents.

The self-reliance that used to be a "badge of honor" to many in your parents' generation may challenge you as well as them during your POPcycle. But if you think about it, it shouldn't surprise you that these same folks in their older years still "want their independence," "don't want to bother you," would be reticent to give up their car keys and might even say: "you're never telling me what to do!" Back in the day when you were growing your hair long or otherwise expressing your individuality, you might have used the same words on them.

In the beginning of any POPcycle, your aging parents may well see you as interfering. Becoming dependent on their own kids, of all things, must seem bizarre for some of your already-confused senior parents! Hopefully your parents never acted as covertly as mine did that Christmas visit, when they hid the state of their health and home from me. Perhaps you're among the lucky ones whose parents agreed more readily to your initial POP involvements and admitted their growing need for your assistance. But undoubtedly for some of your parents, aspects of POP must seem like "déjà vu all over again" with their family imposing its ways. Only this time, it's you and me playing the role of their POParents, who are "making demands" on them. Perhaps this is where the POP role reversals begin to occur.

Your parents were not the only generation of Americans to leave home and move away. When it was your time and mine to pursue our education, jobs and new families, we usually distanced ourselves too. Back in the 1960's and 70's, our generation often added even more miles than our parents had between ourselves and our families of origin, physically and perhaps emotionally as well. As a result, when the notion of POParenting first appeared on your horizon, you and I were often living a continent or, at least several states, away from Mom and Dad.

When your parents start to need more of your assistance more frequently, the roles begin to shift. You can try doing the difficult dance of "long distance" POParenting. I tried it, as you know. Although it only lasted a couple of years in my family, that approach may work for you throughout your whole POPcycle. However, in my experience, if your parents live long enough and/or they decline far enough, someone(s) may have to move. Either you, your siblings or your reluctant parents may need to "bite the bullet" or risk inadequately POParenting them. The essential point here is that geographic distance within American families is adding substantially to this complicated problem.

Today's longevity is the third factor that explains why caring for your aging loved ones is very different today than ever before. It's likely you've struggled, as did I, watching aging loved ones live longer but, unfortunately, not necessarily healthier lives. This is the key to my desired longevity: living long and healthy with my loved ones close by. But that's not necessarily how it's been during your family's POPcycle and, some days, you may even glimpse how fatigued your parents have become: a random sigh may "cry out" to you or you may hear the words I had to face with Jack: "I think I may lived long enough, honey."

Longevity is currently a "mixed blessing" for many families. What we know now to be true about your parents' longevity and the POPcycle is this: be prepared to parent your parents longer than you parented your kids!! It's entirely likely that your 70 year-old Mom who's beginning to need your POParenting now may live 25-30 years. Your POPcycle with your Mom and Dad may well exceed the eighteen or twenty-one years you spent parenting your children. And how old will that make you!?

Much of the reason for your parents' life cycle increasing over the past years is that they're taking lots of prescription medications. The primary purpose of many of these is to fight off diseases and keep patients alive. One little-discussed concern many POParents are beginning to have is that these drugs pose dual threats.

First, some of your parents' meds will have conflicting interactions with other prescriptions. To avoid that, channel all your parents' prescriptions through a single pharmacy and ask them to check for the correct geriatric dosages as well as warn you before filling prescriptions for meds that pose dangerous drug interactions. Try to be in partnership with your parents' pharmacy.

Second, even the "weakest" of medications may have potent effects on your parents' frail bodies. These reactions are usually referred to as "side effects." But naming them as such doesn't minimize the influence of those hazardous "effects" on some of your aging parents. As careful POParents you'll need to read up on all the drugs your parents are taking – hopefully beforehand – online and/or on the packaging. Read the commentaries from consumers who've taken the drugs, if you have access to those. Then watch your folks carefully to see if any negatively described reactions occur. Try to be in partnership with your parents' doctors: ask a lot of questions, get cell phone numbers, tell them what you're seeing, feeling and fearing.

Another approach some POParents are taking and you may find helpful is to get better acquainted with what's been called "alternative," naturopathic, holistic, complementary medicine. Primarily these branches of medicine differ from more traditional Western medicine in that they attempt to prevent problems before they begin rather than trying to fix them once they've happened. They also works to heal patients' existing problems through educating patients and using herbs, supplements, specific changes in diet and exercise, chiropractic, massage, acupuncture and so on. Many Western-trained physicians learned little in school about alternatives to pharmaceuticals but that too is beginning to change. Younger doctors are emerging with more expanded viewpoints and some well-tested holistic health measures are making their way through previously more conventional medical portals. Most of these medical approaches are not yet covered by either Medicaid or Medicare because the federal government doesn't consider them a part of mainstream medicine in 21st century America. Nonetheless many of you will wish to explore different elements within alternative medicine, as I did, when I took my parents to my longevity doctor. You may find some nutritional supplements improve your parents' memories, see that their acupressure, acupuncture or therapeutic massage is relieving their pain and allowing them to focus.

These measures may be improving the quality and even the length of your parents' lives and, if so, you may decide to pursue such alternative forms of treatment. At this time, it's likely you'll have to pay "privately" from family funds and outside of your parent's Medicare's coverage. But that may not be so as regulations change and it's worthwhile to check since sometimes your parents' particular medical conditions will allow for coverage of unexpected services. If you see good results from these "alternatives," you may be willing and able to pay for them privately.

Dietary, herbal and other supplements remain unregulated by the government, resulting in great variety in their purity and efficacy. If you wish your parents to use these, that will require you to be "accountable," by learning about these products – their beneficial and negative effects, purity, shelf-life – and the best place to make your purchases.

During their younger adulthood your aging parents and mine probably never had the benefits of much planning in the way of preventative medicine, longevity or good nutritional education. Most adults back then drank and smoked cigarettes regularly and exercised little after finishing high school. Courses in anger-management and stress-management were unheard of. Since many of these practices and their underlying philosophy have become a part of our POP generation's healthier "habits," hopefully the long-term result will be that you and I will live both longer and healthier than your parents.

The fourth factor that makes doing POParenting so compelling and unlike other times or places is that here in the United States we lack a strong tradition of revering our elderly. We don't operate like they do in most other countries and cultures where old age is respected and experience valued. More often than not, in America, we prefer and even revere our youth.

If they resided in most other nations, your older parents would have a recognized, secure and respected place in the structure of the family and society as a whole. Because of this difference in values, most other developed parts of the world provide universally for their older citizens' health and welfare. Seniors living in those countries and their not-so-young children mature with far more tranquility and less stress knowing they will be taken care of. Their governments have reassured them: in your later years you won't need to worry about food, clothing, shelter or health care.

Think about how differently you might live and what decisions you might make if you knew that you, your spouse and your parents would have "enough" in years ahead and that your country would take good care of you when/if you couldn't? In this nation, self-reliance and the frontier spirit have been prized. Given what you and I have seen recently with our government, we can't rationally envision that to change– under Democrats or Republicans – sufficiently to offer you, me and our families an uncompromised net of safety and support in the foreseeable future.

For the first time in history, these factors are all dangerously colliding and may ultimately collapse on each other and all of us! You and I must face facts. This nation is laboring under: an unprecedented number of seniors and soon-to-be seniors stretching already overworked resources; a historical penchant for moving away from our roots; pharmacologically-altered longevity and still considerable geriatric disease; a void where other nations possess both reverence and a complete social net for their aged.

If you and I aren't going to be able to rely on governmental programs, training and support, where will the help we need come from? How will you manage these stressful POP demands at 3 AM or even 3 PM, whenever your parents need help? However desperately a majority of Americans may wish for a comprehensive governmental protective net with well-developed infrastructure, it simply does not now exist. Nor does it seem that our political leaders are finding better solutions to the many POP challenges you and I have been bearing alone all these years. Quite the opposite, it looks like there are fewer workable, affordable options than before.

Hopefully this book has been of ongoing assistance, giving you more than just a good beginning but also an understanding of how you want to structure your POPcycle. In the future, it can serve you as a reliable place to turn, over and again, for information and support. Keep it handy so you can grab it easily from the shelf or put it on your tablet to carry with you, when you're on the road. Use it to get informed about the next stage you're facing and to calm yourself as you continue to meet your family's challenges and your desire to grow while doing POP.

Other generations of parents had Dr. Spock's book and the many other volumes that followed his to explain a child's normal development. Pregnant parents similarly had the well received "What to Expect…" series. Until OMG! POParents didn't have much guidance on how to make order out of random geriatric facts, how to characterize the huge life changes the family was going through or how to recognize when to intervene with Mom and Dad. Without any books, our generation was forced to remain, isolated, overwhelmed and confused by shifting family relationships, role reversals and increased parental dependency.

When your kids were young, books and periodicals jumped out at you everywhere from supermarket lines to pediatricians' offices. They offered all kinds of advice to assess whether your children were progressing normally and how to "fix" anything that ailed them. But until now, there's been no book or authority to direct us through the complex developmental stages of the POPcycle when just about everything feels turned "upside down" and one of the biggest variables in life is how people age differently.

This generation also been "blind-sided" without magazines devoted to Parenting Our Parents, courses on POParental education or forums where people can discuss their POP concerns. Until now, you and I have had nowhere to go to even think about this part of our lives with our parents as a journey of love.

Everyone has been acting as if parenting were over when your kids were no longer young. Now you're discovering that parenting may actually begin all over again in its new format: POParenting! And POParenting may "happen to you" when you're 62 and your 83 year-old Mother stops acting normally or your older parents no longer can function on their own. But what is "normal" for an 83-year old and how are you supposed to know what's abnormal?

How are you supposed to know if you're doing POP "right?" What will signal you that there's something wrong or that you should bring your parents to see a doctor? A therapist? The priest? How long is a "normal visit" with your Mom who has dementia and lives in a skilled nursing home and what "should" you do and talk to her about? Are there topics to avoid or activities to embrace? How are you expected to know "good" POParenting from a poor performance?

This book will do much to help you discover that. So will your setting up POParenting Groups at your churches, schools or synagogues where you can be discuss with others how each of you navigates the treacherous POP waters. As a society, we haven't yet begun to have court-ordered POP classes to teach better skills. Nor have we in this country evolved to the point where we seek to prevent POP elder abuse and neglect as we do for child abuse and neglect. I feel confident that, with the growing consciousness of POP and the POP community, these courses will also be offered soon in the future and those of you doing POP in the next several years will have additional supports of all kinds focused in on POParenting.

During your reading of this book, you've likely concluded that, in many ways, your POP story is different from mine and, in fact, uniquely yours. "One size" doesn't fit every family in POP any more than it does in the rest of life. The nature of POP is inherently unique since there's only one Wolf Family and your family is also "one of a kind." Moreover, since every person perceives experiences through a unique or personal "filtering system," no POP story will ever be the same. Even within your family, it may surprise you how differently your sister or brother describes their version of your POPcycle.

In spite of these differences, I'm hoping that you saw much of your own POP story revealed in the pages of MY STORY. If you "plotted out" the stages of your parents' increased dependency, it's likely that they resemble those of my family's growing neediness. If you walked into the type of disaster I did, I hope you grew from reading about my thoughts, feelings and actions. It has been my intention that, by seeing much of yourself, your parents and your own story in MY STORY, you'd experience POParenting more ably and enjoyably.

To get the most value from MY STORY is to appreciate the parallels in all POP stories – yours, mine and others whose stories you know. After all, we all share the same basic tale involving love, caring and figuring out how to apply our family values. You and I chose to parent our elderly parents at this time and in this country and that has made all the difference.

Take a moment to look at your own POP story in this way. You may live in a different part of the country than I did, have been born in a different decade or, unlike me, have many siblings. Perhaps as the eldest daughter in your culture you may've known forever that your parents would end their days in your home because that's how it's "always been." Maybe your family would never have accepted placing your parents in an assisted living facility as I did when I brought mine to California. You may not have had a husband, stepchildren and grandchildren or been running a new small business from several office locations when you were parenting your parents as I did. Your POP story, unlike mine, may have included making sacrifices like giving up a job you loved, selling your home in a bad market or moving back in with your parents when they refused to leave their family home.

In the pages of YOUR STORY, I further expanded out from telling my version of the Wolf POPcycle to exploring yours. To do so, I selected portions of many POP stories I've been privileged to hear over time from my patients, POP Family Coaching clients, colleagues and my friends. I also drew upon academic research, popular literature and even today's blogs.

Because this is a handbook to help you figure out how you want to "be" as a POParent, what you need to "do" and what you'd wish to "have," I also included other sections in the book to help you with those goals. In THEIR STORY you're offered some aging parents' (presumed) points. In POP Music, there are thoughts to inspire you or make you laugh and in the highly detailed POPlans are tools, showing you how to do POParenting more competently and satisfyingly.

But without better assistance from the government, your employer, your family, your pension plan and your faith for starters, you'll need more than this book to really succeed as a POParent. How will you be able to care for yourself and your elderly family members for ten years or twenty years or even longer? Part of the answer is that you'll need to keep on "growing."

You've seen both from your own POPcycle and from reading this book that it will be advantageous to further develop some of your personal qualities and learn some practical skills you never thought you'd need. For example, you've read in the POPlans how to better access more compassion, patience and kindness, the qualities POParenting will increasingly demand from you.   Perhaps, when you determined how your parents could "age in place" safely and happily, you had to learn to become a part-time social engineer. And, if you're like me, you may still need to find out how to use the spreadsheet program on your computer in order to best calculate the affordability of your POP options.

One thing is for sure. You will NOT be able to do it all alone!! Therefore if help isn't going to come from governmental coffers, your siblings aren't going to be any less busy or easy to deal with and your lottery ticket isn't going to "come through," where will the additional assistance you need to POParent (the support, information and everything else you'll need) come from?

Your help will have to come from the millions of other Americans who are also doing POP! After all, ask yourself this: who else is wide-awake at 3 AM when you're feeling totally alone and inadequate to doing POP but nonetheless need to decide what to do about Dad's diabetes and his threatened home foreclosure? The answer is simple: other POParents! When you're lonely and so "fried" from POP responsibilities that you think you can't make one more decision, I recommend the best thing to do for yourself right then and there. Go to www.ParentingOurParents.org and chat with another POParent who "gets" what you're feeling and doing and who can offer you some practical advice as well as genuine understanding.

Sharing your POP problems and, even better, your POP solutions with peers, people who understand you and your challenges without a lot of unnecessary explanation, will get you more than one good night's sleep. There are countless POParents all over the globe at this very moment you have your very same deepest thoughts, worries and feelings. You just don't know them yet. And they may well have good answers for you ...

Incredible though it may still be to imagine, there's a shift is in the wind just now beginning. You're about to be able to find countless other POParents with precisely your same concerns! As soon as you sign up at www.ParentingOurParents.org, the portal for all things POP, you'll become a member of the POP community and receive your personal and complimentary VIP invitation to share your POP journey with others.

Once a member of the POP community, you can write on the blog, meet other POParents who share your particular concerns, learn about others who might provide you much-needed POP services. Your postings might allow you to: reintroduce your parents to other seniors they want to see again; locate fellow POParents who live down the street from your Mom; send a "shout out" by means of a great video of your family reunion; or get a recommendation from your high school friend in Florida for a caregiver to your favorite Uncle, now living alone in Kansas.

At www.ParentingOurParents.org the individuals you'll meet and come to know can probably offer you whatever POP info you're seeking. They *will* be there for you, and if it's not at 3 AM because they're lucky enough to get some sleep, you can communicate with someone else on the website who can assist. In today's global POP community, there will always be POParents awake and ready to help you.

Not only will you be able to get help, but you can be reliable and supportive to other POParents too! You can offer others on the site the benefits of your experiences, insights and POP problem solving. Despite the fact that there are literally tens of millions of Americans already caregiving their elder relatives,[76] we've been living in the old paradigm where each POP family is operating in an isolated "parallel universe." All that isolation is changing with us!

You and I need each other doing POP! We are the builders, constructing whatever resources we require to effectively Parent Our Parents. With this nascent POP community, you and I will finally have each other to learn from and "lean on." With all our collective skills, connections and knowledge we will be able to find whatever we need to Parent Our Parents! You and I will create things that don't yet exist to do POP better!

With the publication of this book and the growth of the community at www. ParentingOurParents.org, you and I officially declare: THE POP COMMUNITY HAS BEGUN!!

This website is the 21st century equivalent of a huge home for our POP community. Go there to find what you need and contribute what you already know. You'll have access to everything POP – geriatric links, reviews of services provided to POParents, videos about POP and a blog with varying points of view. The POP website offers the advantages of social networking but is beyond and different from that. On the POP blog, you'll also have access to ongoing counseling and advice directly from me. Personalize your version of the web page and apply all your social networking interfaces. "Pin" photos of your POP family, post music and videos to inspire your new POP friends and keep up with your old ones. Of particular help to you on this site may be sharing with and "meeting" others on the blog who are POParenting loved ones with similar disorders.

Hopefully being part of this community means that by doing POP we're all part of a bigger whole and you'll never be as alone, scared, uninformed or isolated again! How will you

---

[76] In 2009, nearly 44 million "non-professional" Americans provided unpaid care to one or more family members 50 + years, working on average of more than 20.4 hours, according to Caregiving in the U. S. 2009, p. 13, published by the National Alliance for Caregiving in collaboration with AARP.

participate in the POP community so you can best teach and learn from each other and from me? Go to the site and share your POP lessons, needs and wants and then receive suggestions, solutions and support from others. Show yourself how your participation in the POP community will make a crucial difference in your life and also in the lives of others. Test this out!

Americans have a tendency to view aging in general and seniors in particular in rather unattractive shades of gray and pallid white. We imagine family "caregivers" to be perennially overworked, depleted and sad. While there may be some truth to aspects of these generalizations, the significant question is this: what do you and I want to be, do and have during this amazing POP journey of love? We want a warm, healing and color-filled POP experience – one that's anything but gray, depressed and worn down. After all, you're doing POP and are on a mission of love!!

This mission needs all colors and every hue of humanity to contribute to our vibrant rainbow. It also needs what used to be termed "a good attitude." Whether it's time to review your parents' monthly bills or take them to the dentist, you can bring along your rosy POP outlook. Everyone will benefit. Rather than viewing your POP tasks as obligations and acting like they're a burden, you can brighten everyone's day by making your POP experience really "pop!"

If your personal mission is bringing joy to your family's POPcycle, you will ultimately require three things to succeed: your focused intention; the right "equipment" and a robust interactive POP community to help you update your information, get enough support and share what you have to offer.

Hopefully this book and the accompanying website will get you well on your way to having everything you'll need. However, you may find you still need more focused help for yourself and your family's "bumps" in the journey. If so, try out some POP Family Coaching or seek counsel from an experienced professional who's been down the POPcycle with many other POP families: they can often help by lifting you from feeling "stuck" with problems to functioning smoothly with solutions.

Perhaps my single best piece of advice is this: don't try POParenting alone! You need companions on your trek since you simply cannot do POP as well by yourself as you can with the support of other POParents. You'll ultimately need to depend not only on your family but also on your old friends, your parents' professionals and even on POParents you've never met before.

As demanding as your POP journey may have been, I've never yet met anyone who regrets having made it. When you can convert your remarkable set of POP challenges into a journey of love, Parenting Our Parents will offer you and, in turn, all your relationships, more peacefulness and more joy.

Photographs

From a time when my parents (and I) were all in our younger years …

My folks celebrating my being "sweet sixteen" at a party they gave me during their middle years.

My parents come out to California to visit me during their early senior days.

Just before I moved them to California, as mom and dad were getting old.

Here I am with Dionne Warwick singing Jack's songs, in my post-POP days.

GLOSSARY OF TERMS[77]:

ACTIVITIES OF DAILY LIVING ("ADL'S"): These are the basic activities and functions of daily life that are ordinarily done by adults without assistance. They consist of self-care tasks such as: personal hygiene and grooming; dressing and undressing; functional transfers (moving from bed to commode, wheelchair, etc.); continence of bowel and bladder as well as the ability to feed oneself. When a parent is unable to perform some or all of these tasks independently, this is not only an independent measurement of their functionality but also a sign that someone needs to intervene: they will need caregiver help, perhaps part-time, or to move into a family member's home or a senior facility. Being dysfunctional in several ADL categories is often a threshold that must be met for many Long Term Insurance policies to be activated.

ADULT FAILURE TO THRIVE ("AFTT," sometimes referred to as GERIATRIC FAILURE TO THRIVE): This is a state of decline that may be caused by chronic concurrent geriatric diseases and involves impaired physical functioning as well. You may see seemingly unexplainable weight loss, decreased appetite, poor or malnutrition, depression, cognitive impairment, progressive apathy or inactivity. As a POParent, you will want to get your parents medical attention to rule out that the side effects of medication, drug interactions and/or suicidal thinking aren't contributing to failure to thrive. This diagnosis may represent a key decision point in the care of your parent(s) and might prompt discussion of end-of-life options, including hospice, to prevent needless interventions that may simply prolong their suffering.

ADVANCED HEALTH CARE DIRECTIVE (sometimes referred to as a "LIVING WILL" and other times as a "HEALTH CARE PROXY"): A document in which an individual appoints a proxy to hold certain powers and responsibilities. It includes a list of specific instructions regarding what health care decisions should be taken, in the event the person becomes too ill or incapacitated to do so alone.

AGING SPECIALTIES: The growing fields of geriatrics, aging, longevity and gerontology now includes many subspecialties such as: doctors; lawyers; movers and storage services for seniors; occupational and physical therapists; certified POP Family Coaches; social workers; aging-in-place specialists; GCM's; nutritional consultants and many more.

---

[77] The term is followed by the acronym, if any, that is used in this book.

ASSISTED LIVING FACILITY ("AL"): A type of senior facility where residents live independently in their own apartments. The POP family may add on additional assistance services at a fee.

CAREGIVER: A paid or unpaid job involving observing, monitoring, supervision and care of someone. Tasks often include bathing, dressing, grooming, shaving, personal hygiene, medication dispensing, purchasing and preparing food, cleaning, laundering, transporting the person to doctors and other appointments as well as encouraging appropriate physical and mental exercise. Costs will depend on what services are used. Non-medical workers, like housekeepers, cost less than nurses or physical therapists; similarly, some home care agencies are less expensive than others.

CONTINUING CARE RETIREMENT COMMUNITY ("CCRC"): These facilities offer a long-term continuing care contract that provides for housing, residential services and nursing care as needed throughout the POPcycle. CCRC's offer residents the opportunity for continuity during their entire senior lifetime, usually in a single location.

"DO NOT RESUSCITATE" ORDERS ("DNR"): A legally enforceable order written to respect the wishes of patients to not undergo one or more of these CPR, intubation or other advanced cardiac life support, should their heart stop or they cease breathing. Patients who are "on a DNR" can continue to receive chemotherapy, antibiotics, dialysis and any other appropriate medical treatments, as set forth in the document.

DIAGNOSIS-RELATED GROUPS ("DRG's"): These regulations determine how many days of hospitalization Medicare will pay for a diagnosed illness. In use since 1983, patients with similar clinical diagnoses are "expected" to use the same level of hospital resources as others.

GERIATRIC CARE MANAGER ("GCM"): A health and human services specialist whose services include advocacy, monitoring and resource-providing for families caring for aging and disabled relatives and particularly popular when the seniors live at a distance from POParents. Some have backgrounds and experience in one or more of these fields: nursing, geriatrics, social work and psychology. There are a number of different professional organizations that provide certification and training for GCM's.

GERIATRICIAN: A medical specialist trained in geriatrics, which like pediatrics is a branch of medicine that involves internal medicine and specializes in studying and treating age-related diseases, but for the aged not for children.

GERIATRIC PLACEMENT AGENCY: An organization that provide residential placement services in senior facilities, a service that parallels those offered by employment placement agencies. After a senior is successfully placed at one of the recommended facilities, fees are paid to the agency by the facility rather than by the family.

GERONTOLOGY: This is the study of aging and its various social, psychological and biological aspects. It is distinguished from geriatrics, which involves disease.

INSTRUMENTAL ACTIVITIES OF DAILY LIVING (IADL'S): Unlike the ADL's, IADL's are activities that are not essential to living but may be critical in whether or not an aging person can live independently. IADL's may therefore be delegated to others while an individual still lives independently, depending on finances. Evaluations of a seniors' IADL's tend to be done by occupational therapists. Examples include: shopping, housekeeping, accounting and financial management, food preparation and clean-up, compliance with prescribed meds, ability to use the telephone, health alarms and transportation, care for pets and others (including selecting and supervising caregivers); manage and maintain health directions and respond to emergencies.

LIFE REVIEW: Although some consider this to be the "near-death experience" ("NDE") where one's life flashes before one's eyes, the term encompasses a much larger palette of space and time.   Many in the field of aging see much value when seniors review their life stories verbally, draw out the significant messages and experience closure in the process of sharing those memories with others.

LONG TERM CARE INSURANCE ("LTC"): An insurance product which helps provide for the expenses associated with care for individuals unable to perform some or all of the ADL's. Obtaining coverage under these policies is not determined by age but ability/disability.

MEDICARE: Medicare is a social insurance program administered by the federal government. Since its inception in 1965, Medicare provides health insurance coverage to people aged 65 and older and to others who meet specific criteria. To find out if you and your POP family are eligible for Medicare home health care or other services, go online to http://www.medicare. gov/Publications/Pubs/pdf/10969.pdf or call 1-800-MEDICARE (1-800-633-4227).

MEDICAID: These are state-run programs whose purpose is to provide services for less affluent seniors and disabled adults. Your parents would likely qualify for such benefits if they have a sufficiently low income and few assets. To find out specifically, call your State's Medical Assistance Office. Go to the Contacts Database of the Centers for Medicare & Medicaid Services online at: http://www.cms.hhs.gov/apps/contacts. You can also call 1-800-MEDICARE.

MEDI-MEDI: A designation for patients who are covered by both Medicare (for the elderly) and Medicaid (for low income) programs.   There may be times during your POPcycle, such as when your parents leave the hospital and need admission to an SNF for rehabilitation, when they may qualify for Medi-Medi.   This might entitle them to additional certain services or "extra" funds.

NATIONAL FAMILY CAREGIVER SUPPORT PROGRAM ("NFCSP"): This program is funded by the Federal Older Americans Act and helps states provide services to family caregivers. Although each state offers different amounts of support and types of services, the programs funded by NFCSP share a common goal of relieving the emotional, physical and financial hardships of providing continual care. The program helps POP families access support services, individual counseling and support groups, caregiver training, including respite care. Supplemental services, supplies, and equipment, such as home modifications, emergency response systems, nutritional supplements, and incontinence supplies may also be provided. To determine your parents' eligibility and services, contact your local Area Agency on Aging.

_PARENTING OUR PARENTS ("POP")_ᵀᴹ: Parenting Our Parents consists of many parts. It's a vast global community of people, primarily in their 40's, 50's, 60's and some in their 70's and older, who perform various tasks and roles for their aging parents. These activities may be of many different natures – emotional, practical, spiritual, legal, economic, and psychological. POP is the personal tale of millions of men and women who thought they were finished parenting but were drawn back in to care for one or more aging family members. POP is also a stage of life, the POPcycle, in which a journey of dependency and love unfolds, encompassing a complex, innovative role reversal with the potential of transforming the lives of all involved: those doing POP; those receiving it and the younger generations who are looking on.

PHYSICIAN ORDERS FOR LIFE-SUSTAINING TREATMENT ("POLST"): This is a form which is in effect in many states that specifies what kind of medical treatment patients want towards the end of their lives. Printed on bright pink paper and signed by both the doctor and patient, POLST helps give seriously ill patients substantial control over their end-of-life care. You can go online to http://www.ohsu.edu/polst to discover if POLST forms are used in your parents' state.

_POP FAMILY COACHING_ᵀᴹ: This is a life-coaching program designed to help families navigate their way through all or parts of their POPcycles on an "as needed" basis. Certified POP Family Coaches specialize in customizing POPlans and incorporating workable approaches that will maximize family attendance, involvement, convenience and good results. As a result, sessions are held where it works best: in the coach's office; in the POP family home; and, most often, on Skype (and other teleconferencing means). They are best begun before encountering a traumatic "Christmas visit." Most families continue working with their POP Family Coaches even after the POPcycle is officially over to successfully resolve post-POP issues that sometimes divide families forever. For more information on receiving coaching services or becoming a POP Family Coach, go to www.ParentingOurParents.org.

_POPCYCLE_ᵀᴹ: This term describes the process that unfolds, however gradually, as the younger generation, POParents, take on more and more responsibility for various aspects of life for their aging parents and often for other beloved senior relatives. This cycle reflects a developmental stage of life in which older family members may shift from living as fully independent adults move towards a growing dependency, sometimes even complete reliance, on their adult children or POParents.

POWER OF ATTORNEY ("POA"): A document which appoints one or several individuals of time to make decisions and take specified actions for a specified period and/or if the appointee becomes unable to do so.

REASON TO LIVE ("RTL"): A special gift a POParent can create for a senior loved one to help offset some of the apparent losses associated with aging. Examples are: videotaping your aunt Celia sharing the best memories of her life (a life review) and then showing it to her alongside of her grandchildren; selling your Mom's travel business so (s)he can "consult" and be valuable but not have full responsibility for running the business; giving your 90-year old Father his first Bar Mitzvah or Christening since his parents couldn't afford one when he was a youngster.

SKILLED NURSING FACILITY ("SNF"): Often referred to as a nursing home, convalescent home, rest home or old people's home, this type of facility is for residents who require constant nursing care and have significant limitations in their ADL's. The facilities are certified and patient's fees are reimbursed to them through Medicare. Services SNF's provide their residents may include physical, occupational and other rehabilitative therapies, especially after your parent has had an accident, hospitalization or serious illness.

SOCIAL SECURITY ADMINISTRATION ("SSA"): Social Security refers to the Old-Age, Survivors, and Disability Insurance (OASDI) federal program as well as the agency in the United States federal government that administers the 1935 Social Security Law, its amendments and regulations through its social insurance program. It is the largest such program in the world, consisting of administering benefits to retirees, the disabled and their survivors, and is the most expensive item in the federal budget.

Acknowledgements

Nothing of any importance is created alone. There are always many people who contribute to any project and this book is no exception. My profound appreciation goes out to all those who have invited me to listen to their POP stories, encouraged me to write this book and even demanded that I move along to get it out to ASAP.

I wish to express my profound appreciation of and for my parents, I. Jack and Lillian Geist Wolf – for who they were, what they did and said and also for who they weren't and what they didn't do say or do: it all got me to here! I am forever grateful. A parent's pride in their child's accomplishments is special, no matter our age, and Lillian and Jack gave me that throughout my life with them. But it was during their latter years when they were increasingly vulnerable, that my parents demonstrated their ultimate confidence by allowing me to POParent them. I hope they knew how much that meant to me.

Who I became and what I was able to offer in this book is, to a great extent, a product of my growing-up – physically, intellectually, spiritually, socially, legally and psychologically. Some of the most important people in my maturing in those ways included: Dr. Rick Moss, his parents and others from both the Wolf and Geist families; so many wonderful friends of long-standing and you know who you are; Dr. Ernest Holmes and the teachings of Science of Mind; all my teachers in the law at Boston Legal Assistance Project and my long law practice; all my teachers in psychotherapy, including my patients and those who trained me; Dianne Weinrich, MSW and the terrific "team" in geriatrics at the Veterans' Admininstration; my supportive fellow therapists and teachers Dr. Adele Fry, Dr. Judith Schorre, Dr. Donna Sexsmith, Dr. Evelyn Freeman, Werner Erhard, the "happiness scientists," Richard Bartlett, the "attachment people" and, of course, my mentor, office partner and dear friend, the late Dr. Michael McGrail.

I wish to show my extraordinary appreciation to all the people who helped me POParent my folks, all part of our TEAM POP I spoke about back in chapter one. I am grateful to my parents' lawyers, accountants, dentists, audiologists, doctors and especially to Dr. Daniel Tavari and the late Dr. Barry Fox; their devoted caregivers, most especially the patient and kind Florence Walkes; the caring staffs at Hillcrest Inn, Fireside Convalescent Hospital, Thousand Oaks Royale, Los Robles Regional Medical Center and numerous other facilities.

There have been so many people who were critical in helping get this book to you: my colleagues; my friends who claimed they and their parents were in serious need of guidance; the seniors who claimed their adult children required my help. Certainly I am grateful, too, to the patients and people I coached who have been so generous in sharing their POParental joys, sorrows and progress. My "thank you's" go out to the "friendly" readers who commented on the pre-released version of the book and encouraged me to "hang in." And my deep-felt appreciation to those on the editing, graphics, publishing and printing teams who were so helpful in bringing this book to print.

Perhaps most critically, I've been privileged to be part of several families, each of whom helped me formulate my theories, thoughts and feelings about family and POP as well as profoundly impacting who I've become in this lifetime. The Wolf and Geist families where I started and later the Eldridge clan, the Waterman crew and the Frances family were all major influences on me, significant and special. Most of all, I wish to thank and acknowledge my beloved, my partner and my finest friend, Andrew Frances, for all he's done as well as for all that he is. His consistency, thoroughness, energy and vision have been irreplaceable in my bringing this book to you; his love, generosity and kindness have allowed me to see in new ways how journeying through life with loving family truly transforms us all.

Made in the USA
San Bernardino, CA
22 September 2016